PRIVACY IS HARD
SEVEN OTHER MYTHS

PRIVACY IS HARD AND SEVEN OTHER MYTHS

ACHIEVING PRIVACY THROUGH CAREFUL DESIGN

JAAP-HENK HOEPMAN

THE MIT PRESS CAMBRIDGE, MASSACHUSETTS LONDON, ENGLAND

First MIT Press paperback edition, 2023

This book was set in Stone Serif and Avenir by Westchester Publishing Services. Printed and bound in the United States of America.

Library of Congress Cataloging-in-Publication Data

Names: Hoepman, Jaap-Henk, author.
Title: Privacy is hard and seven other myths : achieving privacy through careful design / Jaap-Henk Hoepman.
Description: Cambridge, Massachusetts : The MIT Press, 2021. | Includes bibliographical references and index.
Identifiers: LCCN 2020036516 | ISBN 9780262045827 (hardcover)—9780262547208 (paperback)
Subjects: LCSH: Computer security. | Data protection. | Privacy.
Classification: LCC QA76.9.A25 H626 2021 | DDC 005.8--dc23
LC record available at https://lccn.loc.gov/2020036516

10 9 8 7 6 5 4 3 2

To all that try, regardless.

CONTENTS

PREFACE

Technology is neither good nor bad; nor is it neutral.
—Melvin Kranzberg, historian, 1985

Architecture is politics.
—Mitch Kapor, founder of the Electronic Frontier Foundation, 1991

We live in an increasingly digital world. We shop online. We share our lives digitally. We are tethered twenty-four hours a day through our smartphones, wearables, and tablets, connected to our family, friends, work, and everything that happens in the world. The 2020 COVID-19 pandemic has spurred this transition from the real to the virtual world.

Governments apply new digital technologies to perform their tasks more efficiently, to increase our safety and security, improve our well-being, and to combat fraud. Businesses similarly embrace these technologies for new systems and services that are more efficient and more personalized, disrupting existing brick-and-mortar businesses in the process.

All these systems collect huge amounts of personal data and use that information to monitor or influence us, without many of us being fully aware of this. Common myths ("You have zero privacy anyway"; "You've got nothing to hide") trouble our vision and lull us into indifference. This book is intended as a wake-up call, to allow people to recognize poorly designed systems and challenge them.

We fail to see that the way systems are designed has a tremendous impact on our privacy—and that we, as a society, actually have a choice here. A guiding principle of this book is that technology does not develop in isolation, does not have an independent, inherent purpose or destiny of its own. Instead, technology is made by people and is shaped according to their agendas and beliefs. These beliefs are embedded in how technology functions and determine what technology affords us to do, what it prevents us from doing, and what it does regardless of our own intents and wishes. Systems can be designed in a privacy-friendly fashion, with respect for our autonomy and human dignity, without a negative impact on their functionality or usability. If we want this to happen, though, we need to get involved and influence these agendas and beliefs.

Privacy is often ignored when designing systems. Sometimes this is out of ignorance. More often, it is on purpose because of the huge economic value of all that personal data. This approach is no longer sustainable. Stricter regulations and growing privacy concerns among the general public call for a different approach. But purely regulatory approaches to protect our privacy are not enough. Privacy-friendly *design* is essential.

A little bit of effort and consideration can prevent a lot of privacy harm. In fact, just as technology can be used to invade our privacy, it can also be used to protect our privacy by applying privacy by design. This book convincingly shows how, thus busting the myth that privacy is hard. It explains existing privacy-friendly technologies and showcases privacy by design approaches, in plain language, addressing a broad audience. These approaches are applicable to many systems we commonly use today.

When preparing the final manuscript of this book, the COVID-19 pandemic broke out, pushing us into endless videoconferencing sessions and forcing us to collaborate online using all kinds of cloud-based tools. Suddenly the whole world depended more than ever on the digital tools offered by a few tech behemoths. These tools are not necessarily designed with our interest, and in particular our privacy, in mind. But we had no choice; there simply were not any viable and usable alternatives. With lockdown measures slowly loosening in certain areas of the world, and the exciting news that an effective vaccine may soon be available, it is time to prepare ourselves for a better future. We should ensure that we do have a choice, that viable, privacy-friendly, and usable alternatives become available soon. Not only for use during an emergency, but to use whenever we want or need them, with the confidence that we can use these tools without fear of risking our privacy.

Privacy is like safety or sustainability. Today we take safe cars, energy-efficient buildings, and environmentally friendly production more or less for granted. Like safety and sustainability, privacy is a reasonable and natural civil demand. A demand that businesses and governments can and should comply with, through careful design. It's not hard.

READING GUIDE

Each chapter in this book busts a common privacy myth. In the process, it shows how technology is currently used to harm our privacy and explains how different technologies and system-design approaches can be used to protect our privacy instead. Chapters open with drawings inspired by Franz Kafka's famous novel *The Trial*, which is often seen as a fitting metaphor for a world without privacy. The chapter openings have been wonderfully drawn and graciously provided by Gea Smidt, linking the topics discussed in the chapter with the vivid images that sprout from Kafka's book, visualizing the absurdity and direness of our predicament (and that of Josef K., the central figure in Kafka's book).

Supplementary materials and possible corrections can be found at https://www.xot.nl/privacy-is-hard/ (including links to all online resources and articles cited). This includes a section with advice on how you can protect your own privacy online.

The author can be contacted at info@xot.nl.

ACKNOWLEDGMENTS

Quite a few years have passed since the seed of this book finally found some fertile ground to grow. During those years, I was fortunate to be able to meet, listen to, and talk with many experts and practitioners in the field. You have all shaped my thinking one way or another. I am also incredibly lucky to be working both at the Interdisciplinary Hub for Security, Privacy and Data Governance of Radboud University and for the IT Law section of the University of Groningen. Working with so many smart and enjoyable colleagues from a wide range of disciplines has proven of paramount importance for writing a book like this.

Several people and organizations deserve a special mention.

First, I would like to thank Djoerd for asking the question that started it all and for commenting on very early rough drafts of the manuscript. Sander Ruys from Maven Publishing deserves credit for suggesting that I structure the book around myths. I am forever grateful to Bert-Jaap Koops for offering me a temporary position at the incredible Tilburg Institute for Law, Technology, and Society, which allowed me to allocate some days per week to continue writing this book while discussing research (and so much more) with the awesome people over there. I would like to thank the Dutch Research Council (NWO) for financially supporting this. I am also incredibly thankful to the Weizenbaum Institute in Berlin for offering me a fellowship that allowed me to visit during the fall of 2019. The relative seclusion of Berlin allowed me to submit the first manuscript for this book on New Year's Eve.

Many people have read earlier partial drafts of this book. I am particularly indebted to Bert-Jaap Koops, Esther Keymolen, and Hans de Zwart for their comments, as well as the anonymous reviewers that offered very valuable suggestions for improvement. I would like to thank the staff at the MIT Press, and Marie Lufkin Lee, Kathleen Caruso, Alex Hoopes, and Melinda Rankin in particular, for their support in publishing this book. Marie for her belief in this project, Kathleen and Alex for answering all my questions, and Melinda for her meticulous editing that uncovered glaring omissions, stupid mistakes, and all the little errors a non-native speaker invariably makes.

Finally, I am eternally grateful to Gea, who, in addition to creating the stunning chapter opening drawings, has stood beside me for every step of the rough and winding road.

1

WE ARE NOT COLLECTING PERSONAL DATA

Last year I visited the local hospital by car. The hospital had a large, modern car park, with a pay-for-parking zone for visitors. When I drove in, I took a paper parking token from the ticket machine at the entrance. This raised the barrier so that I could enter the car park to find a spot to park my car. I put the parking token in my wallet and walked to the hospital.

After my visit, I walked back to the car park and took the parking token out of my wallet at the payment terminal. Only then did I notice something peculiar: my car's license plate number was printed on the token. I had never noticed this before. And I really wondered why it was printed there. There wasn't anyone around to ask, though, so I just paid, walked back to my car, and drove out.

And that's when the penny dropped. I was ready to stick the parking token in the machine to open the exit barrier as usual, but it turned out I no longer had to. The barrier opened automatically as I approached the exit. Beyond the barrier I saw a camera that filmed all cars exiting, apparently scanning and recognizing their license plates.[1] Presumably (because I hadn't noticed at the time), a similar camera had been present at the entry gate when I entered the car park, scanning and recognizing the license plates of all cars entering. This would explain how the license plate of my car got on the parking token I obtained when entering.

So apparently a modern car park works as follows: All cars entering are filmed and their license plates scanned. When you take your parking token at the entrance gate, the license plate number of your car is printed on that token. At the same time, your license plate number is recorded in the car park database of currently parked cars, together with the time you entered. This record is linked to the parking token given to you. When you later present your parking token to the payment terminal, the corresponding database record is retrieved, and your payment is recorded in it. As you drive to the exit, your license plate is scanned again, and the number recognized is looked up in the database. If the database reports you paid the parking fee, the exit barrier is raised and you are free to leave the car park.

So why was I surprised—yes, even annoyed—by the fact that my license plate number was printed on the parking token? Because it made me realize that the owner of the car park keeps a database record of when my car is parked in the garage and for how long. Now, the car park might argue that this is not at all sensitive information and that it isn't collecting personal data at all. After all, what's in a license plate?

But this is my own car that I usually drive myself. So with the help of the national license plate registry, the owner of the car park (or any other party with access to both databases) could in fact determine when and how long I am in the vicinity of that car park. Moreover, in this particular case the car park stood next to the hospital without any other significant places of interest in the area. In other words: when I park my car there, I do so to visit the hospital. This information in itself is already sensitive: the number of times I visit the hospital says something about my medical condition (or about the medical condition of a friend or relative of mine). No definite conclusions about my medical condition can be drawn from this small piece of personal information, of course. But according to the *mosaic theory*, a more definite and complete picture of my medical condition can be drawn with every additional data point.[2] This theory derives its name from stone mosaics, the intricate patterns and gorgeous images of which are made up of small, plain-colored stones that are insignificant and bland individually. If we fail to protect the individual stones, the innocuous individual data points, we allow a detailed picture of our private lives to be drawn in the end.

To further drive the point home, let's assume for a moment that the hospital is engaged in a longitudinal research program in which it collects anonymized health data, recording for every patient enrolled in the program a detailed but anonymized report of every visit, including the day the visit took place. Combining the data in the car park database with this anonymized data set from the hospital could allow someone to deanonymize the patients in that supposedly anonymous data set. Simply look up the dates of visits recorded in the medical data set for a particular anonymous patient in the car park database to retrieve the license plates of all cars that parked there on all those dates. If the number of hospital visits is sufficiently large, this matching process will return the license plate of exactly one car (or none, if the corresponding patient didn't use their car to visit the hospital). A quick lookup in the governmental license plate registry is all that is left to reveal the owner of the car and hence the likely identity of the anonymous patient.

I also wondered for how long the car park would keep the records in the database of parked cars and who (beyond the car park owner) would have access to this data. Unfortunately, that information was not readily available.[3] First and foremost, this is because most car parks do not even inform you of the fact that they are recording your license plate, let alone that they provide any additional information about this (if only by providing a link to a web page with additional information).

1.1 A LOT OF DATA IS PERSONAL, ACTUALLY

The preceding example serves to illustrate that even registering something as innocuous as the license plate number of a car can reveal something sensitive about yourself, because the license plate number can be linked to you. This makes a license plate number an example of personal data, corresponding to what is called *personally identifiable information* (PII) in the United States.[4] *Personal data* is a legal term used to define all data that, legally speaking, should be considered privacy-sensitive and that therefore requires legal protection.

What is considered personal data depends on the jurisdiction. In Europe, where the General Data Protection Regulation (GDPR) applies, personal data is defined as "any information relating to an identified or identifiable *natural person* ('*data subject*'); an identifiable natural person is one who can be identified, directly or indirectly, in particular by reference to an identifier such as a name, an identification number, location data, an online identifier or to one or more factors specific to the physical, physiological, genetic, mental, economic, cultural or social identity of that natural person."[5]

This definition should be interpreted broadly.[6] Not only information directly linked to names or social security numbers is considered personal data. The fact that the definition also covers identification of natural persons by indirect means implies that things like home addresses, postal codes, phone numbers, IP addresses, or license plate numbers (and all the information linked to those) are considered personal data as well. The reasoning is that as long as there is a legal way to link some piece of data to a natural person—for example, by querying several databases, even if held by other independent organizations—then this piece of data is considered personal. This is why Europe considers a license plate number personal data: the car park itself may not be able to link it directly to its owner, but the national registrar (individual states in the United States, the Driver and Vehicle Licensing Agency in the UK, or the Regional Transport Office of each district in India) definitely can. Similarly, an arbitrary web server itself may not be able to link an IP address to a natural person directly, but in many cases (even for dynamic IP addresses) the network issuing that IP address to a user typically *does* have a database linking the IP address to a name or email address of the user. In the case of an email address, an additional request for more information to the email provider will eventually identify the natural person involved.

Even if the actual natural person associated with a unique identifier cannot be determined, so long as the unique identifier can be used to single out that person (i.e., recognize the same person at a later date), it is considered personal data by some.[7] This makes a media access control (MAC) address (which uniquely identifies a smartphone or smart watch) a personal data item as well, even though no database exists that links device owners to MAC addresses. In fact, this makes any pseudonym that is specifically meant to single out a person without knowing who they are a personal data item. (We will discuss pseudonyms in detail later in this chapter.)

A company or organization may think that small, innocuous, pieces of information they are collecting are not personal data at all. But in all likelihood the opposite is true. The web server logging IP addresses? Collecting personal data. The car park using automatic license plate recognition? Collecting personal data. The website using cookies to recognize returning visitors? Collecting personal data. The smart meter in your home recording your electricity consumption? Collecting personal data. Traffic flow monitoring systems using Bluetooth or Wi-Fi signals to measure congestion? Collecting personal data. The research institute analyzing pseudonymized health data? Collecting personal data.

The myth, upheld by companies, that "we are not collecting personal data" can perhaps be attributed to different interpretations of what it means to be identifiable. If we stick to a very shallow, narrow definition of identifiability through names and addresses alone, then all the preceding examples in fact would *not* constitute personal data. But there are multiple types of identifiers, as the examples given already illustrate.[8]

An identifier is a *lookup identifier* if there is a registry, directory, or database that can be used to look up the corresponding named individual. Telephone numbers, IP addresses, and license plates are examples of such lookup identifiers.

Another type, *recognizable identifiers*, allows a person to be singled out—that is, recognized again after some time—without the ability to determine the real, named individual associated with that identifier. It's like recognizing someone on the street who you don't know by name, but who you often see walking in the city. Other examples include authentication cookies (which are set as soon as users have authenticated with an online service and which allow the user to return at a later date without the need to enter their credentials again).[9] Properly generated pseudonyms, and MAC addresses discussed earlier, are also recognizable identifiers.

Classifying identifiers allow people to be classified as belonging to a certain group, instead of recognizing and discerning each and every individual person. Cookies that store a language preference are an example of a classifying identifier. In more general terms, the profiles compiled about you—and in particular, demographic classifiers (like age groups, affluence, level of education, specific interests)—are examples of classifying identifiers as well. The difference from other identifiers is that classifying identifiers are typically not issued to users directly but instead are determined, maintained, and stored on the server offering the service.

Finally, *session identifiers* are ephemeral and only exist during a short time frame (called a *session*) in which an individual is interacting with a service. Session cookies (which allow a web server to determine which web requests belong to the same browsing session, and which are used to implement a virtual shopping cart in e-commerce websites) are the prime example of session identifiers.

Any data linked to a lookup, recognizable, or classifying identifier is personal data (in the sense of the GDPR). Data linked to a session identifier is not necessarily personal data: if, while interacting with a service, I reveal my age (and nothing else), there is nothing that allows the service to link that age to me. But if a session contains a nonsession identifier, then any other data in that session is linked to those identifiers through the session identifier and hence becomes personal data. If in the same session in which I reveal my age I also (perhaps accidentally) reveal my name or email address, then the service provider *can* link that age to me personally. In other words, if a particular session identifier is linked to some other identifier, then any other data linked to that same session identifier becomes personal data.

1.2 THE RISK OF MODERN CAR PARKS

In the Netherlands, owners of a company car (i.e., employees that drive a car provided by their employers for work-related travel) discovered a totally different use of the data collected by modern car parks like the one I parked in at the hospital. In fact, it led to an interesting legal battle between the tax authorities and SMSParking, a Dutch company offering a service where car owners can pay their parking fees by SMS or through a smartphone app. Let's discuss why.

In the Netherlands, owning a company car is considered a taxable part of your income, *unless* you use it almost exclusively for work-related travel. Private use of a company car (driving more than five hundred kilometers per year) is considered a form of tax fraud if you do not declare (and pay for) that use up front. A few decades ago, the risk of getting caught was relatively low, but with the proliferation of automatic license plate recognition technology, this has changed in recent years. In fact, at some point in time, someone at the Dutch tax office had the brilliant idea to use the license plate information collected by car parks to detect this form of tax fraud. They contacted several companies operating car parks that use license plate recognition in the Netherlands and requested an excerpt of their databases, containing the dates, times, and license plate numbers of all cars parked in their car parks during a whole year. The idea was that anyone with a company car claiming to use it exclusively for work-related travel would have some explaining to do when the car was found to be parked in car park close to a concert hall in the evening or close to the city center on a Saturday afternoon.

SMSParking challenged this request in court. The lower court ruled that the extent of the request was excessive and disproportional in light of article 8 of the European Convention on Human Rights, which lays out the right to privacy and justifies exceptions to this fundamental right only in the case of significant collective interests.[10] Motivating the verdict, the judge expressed concern for the fact that this exception to the fundamental right was in general invoked too often and on overly frivolous grounds. Unfortunately, this line of reasoning in this particular case was overturned by a higher court that argued that it is the duty of the state to ensure fair taxation and that this includes detecting tax fraud, which necessitates collecting this information from the car park companies.[11]

1.3 PERSONAL DATA IS COLLECTED EVERYWHERE

Many day-to-day activities that originally did not involve the collection of personal data at all suddenly do when they are automated and implemented by some kind of digital system. The car park scenario described earlier is one example, but there are many more.

Payment is an obvious one. Cash payments are untraceable in practice. Although bank notes do have serial numbers on them, they are not routinely used to track your spending patterns. This is absolutely not the case for debit or credit card payments. Your bank or credit card company sees all your transactions: when you shop, where you shop, and the amount of money you paid for the goods you bought.

These companies use that information to prevent fraud. Many of you with a credit card probably have been called at least once by your credit card company to confirm a transaction the credit card company found suspicious. This suspicion could be based on the pattern of your previous payments or on the distance between the current location your card is used in and the location where you last used your card. In the latter case, if the time between both transactions is short while the distance is long, the transaction is suspicious.

Your transaction profile contains a wealth of information that is useful beyond mere fraud detection. It turns out that credit card companies can predict whether you will get a divorce based on this profile.[12] Banks and credit card companies also use your transaction history to offer you specific financial advice or to allow other companies to target their advertising based on your spending patterns.[13] The UK government tracks the use of debit cards by asylum seekers to verify that they do live where they claim to be living.[14] Moreover, the new European Payment Services Directive (PSD2) forces banks to allow third-party financial service providers access to your transactions, albeit only after you give explicit consent.[15] Originally intended to boost competition in an otherwise very closed market, PSD2 has opened the doors for large data companies like Google, Facebook, and others to access this treasure trove of transaction data simply by registering as financial service providers in any of the European member states.[16] Finally, note that virtually all digital forms of transaction processing insert an intermediary between the payer and the payee that has full control over the transaction. This intermediary can block certain transactions (PayPal and credit card companies blocked donations to WikiLeaks, for example) or decide to reverse transactions.[17]

Such profiling and censoring are not inherent characteristics of digital payment schemes in general. Chapter 7 will show that it is in fact possible to implement a form of digital money that is secure and as privacy-friendly as traditional cash.

Another example of a day-to-day activity that, when implemented digitally, collects personal information is traveling by public transport. The original system involving paper tickets that were verified and invalidated by the ticket inspector on the train or the bus did not leave any trace of your journey. This has fundamentally changed now that public transport companies in many countries use some kind of electronic ticketing system in which you prove that you paid through electronic means, typically using a small, credit card–sized smart card. Well-known systems include the Oyster card to pay for trips on the bus and the underground in London; the OV-chipcard in the Netherlands to pay for trips on the bus and the train throughout the country; and the Octopus card in Hong Kong, which originally was used to collect fares in Hong Kong's mass transit system, but which was later extended to allow payments in stores, supermarkets, and restaurants. These systems are designed with little privacy protection in mind. Instead, they use the unique serial number stored in the smart card to log all your transactions and hence to keep a record of all trips you ever made by public transport in some central database.[18]

Driving a car used to leave very few traces. But now automatic license plate recognition is increasingly used to automate the enforcement of all kinds of traffic-related regulations. Moreover, cars themselves have essentially become computers on wheels, collecting large swaths of data about your trips, your driving style, and traffic conditions encountered while you drive. Increasingly, car manufacturers are looking for ways to monetize this data, to the point where the real profit of selling a car is only made once the manufacturer starts selling all this data.[19] "The future of profitability for the company [Ford] is all the data from its 100 million vehicles (and the people in them) they'll be able to monetize."[20]

Reading books or newspapers has also turned into a digital endeavor, with more and more people reading their favorite novels or the daily news on a smartphone, tablet, or e-reader. Back when books and newspapers were purely paper-based affairs, nobody could keep track of the books or newspapers you bought. Back then, no one ever imagined that at some time in the future people would be able to tell which of the books you bought you actually read all the way to the end, or which articles in the newspaper you read, how fast you read them, and when. Notes you took in the margin with a pencil were private; this is not the case for the annotations in your ebook. Today all these statistics (and many more) are collected in real time with every e-book you read or every news(paper) app you use. And this data is starting to influence which books are being published and which news stories are being written, and thus how novelists and journalists write their stories in the future.[21]

Similarly, email has essentially replaced paper-based snail mail (exposing your correspondence), and people now watch Netflix instead of traditional broadcast TV (exposing your viewing habits and preferences and allowing companies to deduce your sexual and political preferences from them).[22] All these examples show how the gradual and seemingly innocent transition to a digital world results in the collection of vast amounts of information about our behavior. And, contrary to common claims by companies, all this data should be considered personal data.

1.4 NECESSITY: PURPOSE, PROPORTIONALITY, AND SUBSIDIARITY

The fundamental questions underlying the examples offered previously are as follows: Should this transition from the analog to the digital world really be accompanied by such massive generation and collection of personal data? Is the collection (and processing) of all this personal data really *necessary*? Is this the only way to make this transition? Isn't it possible to take a less privacy-invasive approach?

Is it really necessary to retain the itinerary of every individual traveling by public transport (if the goal is to pay every public transport operator their fair share)? Is it really necessary to track how and when an e-book is read? And is it really necessary to register which movies we watch? Or where we drive our cars?

To faithfully answer questions about the necessity of something, one first needs to be clear about its purpose. Without specifying a purpose, it is impossible to argue (or counterargue) that processing certain personal data is necessary. It should come as no surprise then that *purpose binding* is a fundamental cornerstone of the European data protection framework—namely, the General Data Protection Regulation (GDPR), to be discussed in more detail in section 2.7)—specifying that "personal data shall be collected for specified, explicit and legitimate purposes and not further processed in a manner that is incompatible with those purposes."[23] The key word here is *legitimate*: for every possible processing of personal data, one could come up with a purpose that would necessitate this processing, thus voiding the data protection regime. Indeed, if, say, world domination is the purpose of a company, it could argue that processing all the data in the world is simply necessary. Clearly, world domination is not a legitimate purpose. But then the question becomes: When exactly *is* a particular purpose legitimate? Is collecting personal data for direct marketing a legitimate purpose? The GDPR says it may be, but data subjects have the right to object.[24] Are other, broader, advertising-related purposes legitimate? This is already less clear.

We see that data protection is a carefully crafted house of cards that collapses as soon as one of the cards is removed. Each card corresponds to a carefully defined concept or mechanism. As soon as one of these concepts or mechanisms is improperly interpreted, poorly applied, or insufficiently enforced, the whole protection framework collapses. It is therefore of the utmost importance that the legitimacy of the purposes specified for certain types of data processing is challenged in courts, to clearly delineate what we, as society, really consider legitimate purposes. Unfortunately, this is not really happening yet. Enacting the GDPR was only the beginning. The real level of protection it offers will only become apparent in the coming years, when it gets applied, enforced, and challenged in practice.

Once the purpose is specified and considered legitimate, the necessity of the processing can be studied. In fact, necessity can be broken down into two different aspects. The first aspect is *proportionality*; it considers whether the amount and type of personal data that is processed is proportional to the purpose for which it is collected. The second aspect is *subsidiarity*; it considers whether there is a less privacy-invasive method to achieve the same purpose. This is why privacy by design matters. Its main objective is to design systems that retain the same functionality through less privacy-invasive means.

Recent judicial rulings offer some guidance on how proportionality should be interpreted. In 2014, the Court of Justice of the European Union (CJEU) struck down the Data Retention Directive. This directive required telecommunication service providers to retain certain traffic data related to telephony services and internet services for all citizens in the European Union for a period between six months and two years. Although the objective of the directive was to support the investigation, detection, and prosecution of serious crime, the indiscriminate retention of all this data—without clear, objective criteria to determine who has access to this data and its subsequent use, and without a clear justification for the retention period in relation to the specific data being retained—was ruled to be not proportional for these reasons.[25] The Dutch court recently ruled that a system called SyRI, used by the Dutch government to detect various forms of fraud—including social benefits, allowances, and tax fraud—was disproportionally invasive in the private lives of people.[26] The main argument of the court in this case, as far as proportionality was concerned, was based on the observation that the amount of data that can be used in the application of SyRI is substantial and that it is in fact hard to imagine any type of personal data that is not eligible for processing in SyRI given the exhaustive list of data categories provided. In a more commercial setting, the Dutch high court ruled it disproportionate that banks automatically report outstanding down payments to the central credit rating agency, without taking into consideration specific circumstances. Such a rating at the credit agency can have negative consequences for future financial arrangements (like applying for a mortgage).[27]

Companies can no longer bury their heads in the sand and pretend they are not collecting personal data. In fact, the question is no longer "Are you collecting personal data?" but "Is the personal data you collect necessary for a legitimate purpose?"

1.5 DIFFERENT APPROACHES TO PRIVACY BY DESIGN

There are many different approaches to designing more privacy-friendly systems, which we will describe and discuss throughout this book. What constitutes a good approach in a particular context is sometimes fuel for a heated debate, as there are diametrically opposing views on what it means to be privacy-preserving.

Consider again the car park case that we started this chapter with. One school of thought opposes the very idea of a parking system registering license plates and would only consider a system privacy-friendly if it does not process any personal data at all. Others do not oppose the fact that the system collects and processes license plates as such, but do demand that the personal data that *is* collected is processed responsibly—for example, by deleting it as soon as the data has become irrelevant.

As Seda Gürses points out, privacy by design approaches can roughly be grouped into three quite separate categories: the *hard privacy* approaches based on the privacy as confidentiality paradigm, the *soft privacy* approaches based on the privacy as control paradigm, and a third group of *contextual privacy* approaches based on the privacy as practice paradigm.[28]

The privacy as confidentiality paradigm considers any exposure of personal information as a loss of privacy that must be averted at all cost. Strong unlinkability and anonymity guarantees are considered of paramount importance and should not depend on a single point of failure. Centralized solutions, especially those that involve the central collection and processing of personal data, are frowned upon because they are fraught with risks like involuntary data breaches. Such solutions also require a fair amount of trust from their users because of a real risk of *function creep*—that is, the (ab)use of these centrally collected and therefore easily accessible data beyond the original purposes for which they were collected. The privacy as confidentiality paradigm is very much focused on purely technological approaches to privacy by design as it instead wishes to *minimize* trust (in anything but technology, that is).

The privacy as control paradigm, on the other hand, acknowledges the fact that in an increasingly digital age, personal data simply will have to be disclosed. In this context, privacy means that people will have to be offered tools to control the disclosure of their personal information and given guarantees that the information they do disclose is not abused by those they disclose it to. In fact, the whole legal data protection framework is essentially constructed to offer people these guarantees. The GDPR is the pillar on which soft privacy is built. The privacy as control paradigm is much less technologically oriented; it instead very much relies on developing appropriate processes and oversight mechanisms to keep organizations that process personal data in check. It assumes that, in principle, organizations processing personal information can be trusted to do so responsibly, especially because there are oversight mechanisms in place. Once disclosed, people delegate the responsible processing of their personal information "to the machine," so to speak.

The privacy as practice paradigm recognizes that there is more to privacy than offering hard-core confidentiality guarantees or simply delegating the responsibility for the processing of personal data to the data controller after a binary "I do or do not agree" control decision. Instead, it views privacy as a negotiation of social boundaries, as something that is dynamic and develops in interaction with other users. Systems designed within this privacy protection paradigm aim to closely follow and support these privacy practices and to offer a direct and natural feedback loop to allow its users to gain a clear understanding of the consequences of their interactions with the system. Instead of an a priori assumption of trust (underlying the privacy as control paradigm) or a total dismissal of trust (underlying the privacy as confidentiality paradigm, at least with respect to trust in organizations and processes), privacy as practice acknowledges that trust is the result of past interactions, something that cannot be forced on users for them to accept blindly, nor something that should be disregarded as a useful construct outright.

The risk of function creep is real, however, and something that troubles the discussion considerably. Function creep is "the gradual widening of the use of a technology or system beyond the purpose for which it was originally intended."[29]

A car park system deleting license plate data immediately after your car leaves the car park is a good privacy by design approach according to the privacy as control paradigm. But it fails to offer any real protection if at some point in the future a shift in government suddenly results in a much stronger stance on tax fraud, after which car parks are forced to change their data retention policies and keep, for several months, a record of all cars parked there. Centralized solutions that process personal data without additional technological safeguards are especially prone to function creep, as the additional functionality can be realized relatively easily. Thus the risk of function creep depends on how the system is designed: certain designs make it very easy and therefore very tempting; other designs make it harder and therefore incur a significant cost for adding new functionality.

This means that privacy by design is first and foremost rooted in the privacy as confidentiality, hard privacy school of thought. Certain aspects of the privacy as control paradigm, especially data subject rights and compliance obligations, do have an influence on the design of the system as well, to ensure these rights and obligations are properly accommodated. More generally speaking, we will illustrate throughout the book that purely hard privacy solutions do not really exist, except at significant costs and/or with significant performance penalties and a degraded user experience. In those cases, a combination of hard and soft privacy approaches is appropriate. We will have much more to say about this in chapter 8.

1.6 SPECIFICATIONS: SEPARATING THE WHAT FROM THE HOW

With this understanding of what privacy by design means, companies must (re)consider their past choices carefully and ask themselves whether they really need all the personal data they are collecting and whether they really need to process it the way they are. Is it really impossible to offer the required functionality without that data? Does the system really become that much more efficient or easy to use because of the way they process the personal data? In other words: is there room to apply privacy by design to create a more privacy friendly version of the system the company needs?

Let's use the example of the car park to explore these questions in practice.

In computer science, we clearly distinguish the *specification* of a system from its *design*. The specification precisely describes the system requirements and thus documents the desired functionality of a system. In other words, the specification says *what* the system should be able to do. The design then describes *how* to implement this specification and achieve the desired functionality. For example, the specification of a lock could say that a lock can be used to restrict access to something to only those people who have the corresponding key to unlock the lock. There are many different lock designs, varying in how they look, how they work, how strong they are, and so forth.

We have much more to say about the system design process in chapter 8, but one thing worth stressing here is that writing a proper specification is hard. It is especially hard to write a specification that does not unnecessarily favor a particular design over other (possibly better) alternatives. Often specifications are written with a particular design in mind. More often than not, specifications are only written when the system is already halfway designed. In fact, this is quite understandable as in many cases a new problem can only really be understood (and thus be properly specified) after you try to solve it. However, framing the problem in a particular way and thus steering the design in a particular direction is already considered problematic in general, but is especially an issue in the context of privacy by design. Many specifications frame the problem in such a way that the collection of personal data appears to be simply unavoidable. It is for this reason that it is of paramount importance to consider privacy at the very start of the system design process and to be careful not to specify the system in such a way that it implicitly or explicitly infringes upon the privacy of its prospective users unnecessarily.

Car parks can be viewed as a very simple system, the specification of which boils down to enforcing two rules. The first rule states that everyone parking their car is forced to pay the parking fee. The second rule states that this fee may depend on the time people enter and leave the car park. The car park system needs to compute this fee and ensure that it is paid for every car parked in the car park. Framing the car park problem in this particular fashion might lead the designer to believe that in order to solve the problem it is necessary to register every car entering and leaving the car park and hence that a license plate–based system is necessary.

But the traditional car park system using a parking token with just a random bar code on it solves the exact same problem without actually registering any cars. When you enter the car park, the system issues a parking token with a printed bar code that encodes a unique sequence number (which is totally unrelated to your car's license plate). At the same time, the car park database registers the date and time of entry for that particular sequence number. After that, the barrier rises and you can enter the car park. When you later return to exit the car park, you insert the parking token in the payment terminal. The terminal scans the bar code, looks up the sequence number in the database to retrieve the date and time you entered, and calculates the parking fee based on that information. After payment, you receive the parking token back, while the car park database registers that for this particular sequence number the parking fee has been paid. If you then insert the parking token into the terminal at the exit, the barrier rises and you can drive out of the car park.

The parking token (encoding the sequence number) together with the entry and payment terminal is used to compute the correct parking fee (thus implementing the second rule). The physical construction of the car park, together with the entry and exit barriers, ensures that all cars pay this fee (thus implementing the first rule). As the sequence number encoded in the parking token is totally unrelated to the license plate of your car, this system is totally anonymous (provided it offers you the option to pay the parking fee by cash, there are no security cameras registering cars entering or leaving the car park, and so forth).

This system seems perfect when only considering the two basic rules the car park system needs to enforce. So why do car park companies opt for a different, less privacy friendly system that registers license plates? There are actually a few good reasons. Some companies do it to reduce friction. Drivers do not need to do anything specific when exiting the car park: the barrier rises automatically if the driver paid. Many drivers appreciate this. If the system does not dispense a parking token when entering (and instead requires drivers to enter the license plate of their car manually when paying or to pay a subscription-based fee linked to their license plate), thus removing the entrance and exit barriers, this increases the throughput considerably. Finally, it may even help to combat fraud as some drivers try to avoid paying the parking fee by driving dangerously close behind a car whose driver did pay the parking fee, exiting together through the open barrier.

These are all nice additional properties to have for both the driver and the company operating the car park. So the question becomes: Can we implement this in a more privacy-friendly way, without registering license plates for all cars ever parked? The answer is a qualified yes: indeed we can, but the privacy risk is only reduced, not really eliminated. The essential idea is not to register the license plates of all cars entering, but instead to register a unique code for each license plate that cannot be used to recover the license plate itself (much like the sequence number on the old paper token–based approach). This unique code then serves as a *pseudonym* for the license plate.

1.7 USING PSEUDONYMS TO MAKE DATA LESS PERSONAL

The use of a pseudonym is an age-old method to conceal one's true identity from the general public, used by artists, activists, criminals, celebrities, lovers, terrorists, and others alike. Reasons to use a pseudonym vary widely. Within a criminal gang, resistance group, or terrorist organization, pseudonyms have been used as a security precaution. If none of the members of the group know the real names of the other members, capture of one member does not immediately endanger the other members. The use of pseudonyms by artists and activists serves a similar need to protect their reputation when their works or opinions deviate widely from what is considered the accepted norm or as a form of actual personal security when there is a real danger of persecution for the opinions or beliefs expressed in their works. Street artists similarly have used nicknames because of the illicit nature of their work.[30]

But there are other important reasons to use a pseudonym as well. Sometimes a real name simply carries too much baggage, revealing the gender or ethnicity of the person and thus predetermining, priming, the perspective from which the work is perceived by others. In the past, female authors like Mary Ann Evans (using the pseudonym George Eliot) or the Brontë sisters (who first published their works using the male-sounding pseudonyms of Currer, Ellis, and Acton Bell) have used their pseudonyms to be judged without prejudice, allowing them to successfully enter a male-dominated publishing scene. Other authors have used pseudonyms to escape their notoriety or fame and to start afresh, like J. K. Rowling (itself a pseudonym of sorts), who, after having become world famous for her Harry Potter novels, used Robert Galbraith as a pseudonym to write crime fiction.

In fact, many people use different names in different contexts: some are exclusively known by their surname in one context while being known by their first name in others. Some have a pet name by which they are known to their partner or family members. Many use made-up names as handles in online environments like chat rooms, discussion forums, videoconferencing apps like Skype, or social media accounts.

More formally, a pseudonym is any *identifier* (like an email address, a nickname, or a random string of letters and/or digits) that uniquely belongs to some person and allows others to single out that person, while preventing anyone from recovering or determining the true identity (often called the *real name*) of that person.[31] Pseudonyms are therefore an example of the recognizable identifiers we discussed earlier. Pseudonymization can also be applied to other things, like license plates, that otherwise would be identifying for their owner.

People may have different pseudonyms, and indeed many people typically do. Ideally, pseudonyms are unique—meaning that no two people share the same pseudonym in a given context. This is, for example, the case for email addresses and account names, but not necessarily the case for freely chosen nicknames. The fact that pseudonyms are unique allows them to be used to single out a person: every time a system observes a certain pseudonym, it knows this pseudonym belongs to the same person, even though it may not be able to tell who that person is (yet). Pseudonyms allow us to link events or data that belong to the same person (without knowing their true identity). Using a pseudonym in our car park example allows us to link the event of a car entering the car park with the event of the same car leaving the car park (without knowing the license plate). Using pseudonyms in databases allows us to link records that belong to the same person—again, without knowing the true identity of that person. In other words, pseudonyms can be used to create profiles of people and can be used to impact real people, even if the system only recognizes them through their pseudonym. In that sense, pseudonyms offer only a limited amount of privacy protection, especially if the same pseudonym is used in many different contexts. The latter would allow someone to construct a very detailed profile relating activities and data over all these different contexts to a single (unknown) person. In fact, this is exactly how cookies work and how Facebook uses its Like button to construct such profiles. Moreover, there is always a risk that a pseudonym becomes linked to the true identity of the holder of that pseudonym (like when you use your real name in association with your pseudonym).

Pseudonyms can be generated by people themselves (e.g., when choosing a username for an account, picking an email address, or selecting a nickname for an online forum) or by service providers to avoid the use of true identities (like the example of the car park we are considering here, or a research center pseudonymizing health records), in an effort to make their systems more privacy friendly.

1.8 HASHING: A TECHNIQUE TO CREATE PSEUDONYMS

The question then becomes how to generate "good" pseudonyms. A common method to create pseudonyms from other identifiers (like names or license plates) is to use a method called *hashing*.[32] A hash function generates a unique short code for every name or license plate you feed it, with the important property that given its output, you cannot reconstruct or guess the input name or license plate used to generate that particular output.

Hashing is one of the fundamental tools in *cryptography*, the art of protecting information based on mathematical principles. Hashing is used to create a unique short fingerprint of arbitrary digital data, with the important property that although the fingerprint is uniquely tied to the data (and can easily be computed given that data), the fingerprint by itself cannot be used to recreate the data it corresponds to. Nor should it be easy to come up with some other piece of data that hashes to the same fingerprint. A cryptographic *hash function* is a function that is easy to compute but hard to invert. This is why a hash function is sometimes called a *one-way function*. It assigns a unique fixed-length *hash code* to each of its inputs (which can be of arbitrary length).[33] Hash functions are *deterministic*, meaning that given the same input, they always return the same hash code as output. In practical terms, then, a hash function is a small piece of software that given an arbitrary input (whether this is some Word document, a large movie, a name or a license plate) returns the unique fixed-length hash code that uniquely represents its input. The irreversibility or one-way property guarantees that given a hash code, it is impossible to compute the input that corresponds to it, even if hash functions are publicly known (which is typically the case).[34] In fact, there are only a few commonly used hash functions, which are all documented in public standards.[35]

It is perhaps surprising that one-way hash functions exist (secure ones are surprisingly hard to construct), but an intuitive explanation may be of help here. Given an arbitrary document, it's easy to create a table that lists for each letter in the alphabet how often it occurs in the document. Irrespective of the size of the document, this table always has the same size. Given the same document, the table will be the same. And given the table, it's hard to recover the actual document that produced it.[36] In this example, the hash function computes such a table and returns this table as the corresponding hash code for a document.

In practice, hash functions are, for example, used to secure passwords before storing them on a server for later password verification. Storing account passwords as is in plaintext in a password file on the server is really bad practice as any hack of the server would offer the hacker the passwords of all users on a silver plate. Suppose the password *petname01!* hashes to *?*hv6ba6*, while the password (or passphrase, really) *correct horse battery staple* hashes to *bsi345n&*.[37] Storing the hash of the password on the server still allows the server to verify whether the user signing in actually knows the password: the password is sent to the server, which hashes this password and compares the result to the hash of the password stored for the account. If they are not equal, the deterministic nature of hash functions implies that the password is wrong. The fact that hash functions are irreversible provides their privacy-protecting power. Although hash functions are public, given the fact that the hash function is irreversible, it is impossible to compute back the password *correct horse battery staple* given the hash code *bsi345n&* stored in the password file. This makes trying to obtain a copy of the password file much less attractive for the hacker.[38]

Next to storing passwords securely, hash functions are used to maintain integrity in data structures and for *commitments*, in which one commits to the content of a document (and thus proves that it exists at a certain point in time) without revealing the actual contents of the document. The idea is that if on a certain day I give you the hash code of a document, the contents of the document itself remain secret. But this act of giving you the hash commits me to its contents: if I later show you the document, you can verify I did not change a single letter of the document by computing the hash code yourself and comparing it with the code I gave you earlier. Moreover, this proves the document existed at or before the day I gave you the hash code. Such a time-stamping service is useful if you want to prove you had an idea for a patent without revealing the actual idea itself, for example. There are actually companies offering commercial time-stamping services. Surety, for example, has been publishing the hashes of documents as a small ad in the *New York Times* classified section every week, under the heading "Notices & Lost and Found."[39]

Similarly, you could apply hashing to license plates. To see why this is useful, consider that in Germany license plates start with a prefix indicating the city or region where the car is registered; *F* stands for Frankfurt and *HH* for Hamburg, for example. Applying some kind of hash function, the license plate *F PC 1313* could hash to *>5a39!xv*, while the license plate *HB T 184* could hash to *vjs8?42@*. Like we saw before in the context of passwords, it is easy to compute the output of a hash function given the input, but it is impossible to compute back (revert) the input that corresponds to a given output. What *is* possible is to test whether the hash code of a known license plate occurs in a set of hash codes you somehow obtained. All you need to do is to compute the hash code yourself (which is easy as the hash function is public) and look up the hash code you computed in the set you obtained. This poses a problem for things like license plates that have a low *entropy*: there are only a relatively small number of license plates in circulation in any given country, so it is quite trivial to compute for each issued license plate the corresponding hash code and put all these into a large reverse-lookup table (like a phone directory) that allows you to lookup the license plate that belongs to a particular hash code.[40] This is called a *dictionary attack*. For a million issued license plates, such a full dictionary would be around fifty megabytes in size. Even in a large country with millions of cars, such a dictionary would be easy to construct, to store, and to consult for lookups.

Even if the potential domain of values that can serve as input to the hash function is in theory very large (for instance, random first and family names), when the actual list of possible inputs is known (e.g., when you are given voter registries or birth registries), the hashes of those values offer no real protection.[41] In other words, hashing only creates good, secure pseudonyms when the number of possible inputs is sufficiently large (i.e., the entropy of the input is large enough) or computing the hash function is (artificially) made hard as this would prevent anyone from computing such a dictionary in practice.[42]

1.9 A MORE PRIVACY-FRIENDLY CAR PARK

Recall that we studied the use of pseudonyms, and the use of hash functions to create them, in a quest to design a more privacy-friendly car park that automates, as much as possible, the task of charging people for the time they park their car. The basic idea was to not register the actual license plates of all cars entering, but instead to register a unique code for each license plate that cannot be used to recover the license plate itself. Using hash functions to achieve this would work as follows.

For every car entering the car park, the license plate is scanned, and immediately hashed to create a hash code that is stored in the database of currently parked cars. This hash code is also embedded in the bar code printed on the parking token you receive when entering. When you return to the car park and insert the parking token in the payment terminal, it reads the hash code embedded in the bar code printed on the token, looks up the hash code in the database, and computes the parking fee based on the time you parked your car according to the database. If payment is successful, this is recorded in the database. When you drive out of the car park, your license plate is scanned once more, again converted to a hash code using the same hash function, and, if the database reports that the parking fee for that hash code was paid, the barrier opens.

This system still processes license plates, but they are immediately converted to hash codes by the license plate scanners and never stored. Instead, the corresponding hash code is stored in the parking database.

As discussed earlier, applying a hash function to a license plate only provides a limited amount of privacy protection as the entropy—that is, the size of the known set of possible license plates—is too small. In theory, anybody could create a large dictionary that allows them to look up the license plate corresponding to a particular hash code stored in the database, provided the hash function is public. One way the car park could prevent this is to use a secret hash function. But the hash function is not secret to the car park company itself, of course (or to the manufacturers that supplied or installed the car park payment system). Given that it has to be embedded in the license plate scanners at the entry and exit gates of the car park, there is a significant risk it will become public after some time (e.g., when someone steals a scanner or when the system is replaced and the old one is discarded improperly).

Besides the limited protection offered, there is another issue that crops up when such a system is used nationwide and when the same hash function is used in each of these car parks. As the hash function is deterministic (i.e., it always returns the same hash code when given the same license plate as input), if you park your car in several car parks throughout the country, the same hash code will be recorded in the databases of these car parks. In other words, the hash code used actually is a recognizable identifier that allows your car to be recognized and singled out in every car park in the country. This is not very privacy friendly yet. When someone sees the hash code *>5a39!xv*, he may not be able to tell it corresponds to license plate *F PC 1313*. But he will be able to tell that the same license plate that visited the car park next to the hospital was visiting another car park at Disneyland Paris.

This scenario is easily prevented by making the hash code context specific: by adding the unique name or location of the car park before or after the license plate before hashing it, the hash code corresponding to *Q-Park-Alexanderplatz/F PC 1313* will be totally different from the hash code corresponding to *IKEA-München/F PC 1313*, so visits of the same car to different car parks can no longer be linked. This still leaves the smaller problem that visits of the same car to the *same* car park can still be linked, but this is easily solved by also adding the current date to the input, like *IKEA-München/2019-02-05/F PC 1313*. Adding context in this way also makes it much less useful to construct a dictionary to try to revert the hash function and to find a license plate corresponding to a hash code. The reason is that this dictionary has to be different for each and every car park and be different every day. In other words, such a dictionary would have to be constructed for each car park separately and be recreated every day afresh. By further increasing the time necessary to compute the hash for a given input, using *key derivation functions* like scrypt, the time needed to build such a dictionary could be made prohibitively expensive—not something someone is willing to do unless very motivated.[43]

Another approach is *salting*, in which instead of a fixed and known string, a long, random, and possibly secret string called the *salt* is added before or after the value to be hashed. By keeping the salt secret (which is not necessarily easy because it's used in several pieces of equipment that can be stolen or tampered with), one can prevent such a dictionary being constructed in the first place.

It's good to step back for a moment and reflect on what we have achieved here by applying hash functions to pseudonymize license plates. One could argue that this reduces the amount of personal data being collected and thus reduces the risk of unwanted data leaks: only the license plate scanners process the real license plates, and they immediately hash them and throw away the actual license plate data. This is better than storing the actual license plates in plaintext in the car park database, even if they are deleted from the database as soon as you drive out of the car park (something that should also be done when only hash codes are stored in the database). No matter how you look at it, though, in the end people parking their cars in the car park simply have to trust the car park to process this information exactly as it claims to do. Also, in terms of function creep, the question whether the car park can be forced to retain license plates for a longer period of time pretty much depends on how easy it is to modify the retention time in the database (Is there a simple configuration option that can be changed locally, or does it require the installation of a whole new version of the software?) or how easy it is to bypass the hash function in the license plate scanners so that instead of hash codes actual license plate information is sent to the database. Is that also as easy as simply flipping a switch (perhaps remotely), or is the use of the hash function hard-coded inside the scanner so that bypassing the hash function requires the car park to install a new circuit board in the scanner (not an insurmountable problem, but definitely requiring more effort)? The answers to these types of questions influence how sensitive a particular design is to function creep.

1.10 BUSTED: A LOT OF SYSTEMS UNNECESSARILY COLLECT PERSONAL DATA

In this chapter, we studied the myth upheld by many companies and organizations that they are not collecting personal data. But the definition of personal data is much broader than many people commonly believe. In Europe, the General Data Protection Regulation defines personal data as any data about a natural living person that can be singled out or that can be directly or indirectly identified. As such, the myth is easily dispelled.

Much more interesting, then, is the question whether companies and organizations *need* to collect personal data. Many common activities, like parking your car, paying for something, traveling by public transport, sending paper snail mail, and more, traditionally did not involve the processing of your personal data at all. During the transition to our current digital age, privacy was an afterthought (if a thought at all). As a result, now that we do these activities digitally, they suddenly involve the collection of significant amounts of personal data in surprising ways.

The question is whether this state of affairs is truly necessary. This question of necessity requires us to critically assess the primary purpose of these systems and establish whether the stated purpose is legitimate in the first place. If so, we then need to study whether the current ways these systems process our personal data are really proportional to their primary purpose and whether there aren't other, less invasive means to achieve the same goal.

This second question really is the core of the privacy by design philosophy: Can a certain goal be achieved in a more privacy-friendly manner? We have seen that there are several fundamentally different approaches one can take to answer this question. The hard privacy approach treats privacy as confidentiality and considers any exposure of personal data as a loss of privacy. Another school of thought is more in line with data protection as enshrined in the European GDPR. This soft privacy approach acknowledges the fact that in our digital society personal data simply will have to be disclosed, and thus considers privacy as a form of control over this data once it is disclosed to others. We will mostly focus on the hard privacy approach in the remainder of this book as it offers the strongest guarantees against function creep, but we will not overlook more pragmatic soft privacy approaches where appropriate, if only because at the end of the day the average user may not really be able to distinguish whether she is trusting technology or trusting the actors and processes behind it. And perhaps for the average user this should not even matter. The solution to the car park problem studied in this chapter is an example of our pragmatic approach.

We then turned to the traditional use of pseudonyms as a means to separate contexts, prevent linking of events, and protect privacy to some extent. We studied hash functions as a means to create digital pseudonyms from true identifiers. Their one-way property (i.e., the fact that hash functions are hard to invert) makes them ideal for this application. The car park example used throughout this chapter shows that although the use of pseudonyms does reduce the privacy risk, their use is fraught with possible pitfalls in practice and should therefore only be used with care and proper consideration for the residual risks. This is in fact a general observation that can be made about many of the privacy-enhancing technologies and privacy by design approaches to be discussed in this book. They are by no means a silver bullet magically solving all privacy problems. As such, they should be applied in practice with appropriate care and sensitivity to the particular problem at hand.

2

YOU HAVE ZERO PRIVACY ANYWAY—GET OVER IT

Even in the late nineteenth century, people witnessed tremendous technological developments. The commercial use of telegraphy exploded in the 1860s. Alexander Graham Bell invented the telephone in 1876. Photo cameras, initially large, complex, and expensive devices that could only be operated by experts, had become portable and inexpensive. And they had also become much easier to use, allowing ordinary people to make pictures without anyone necessarily noticing. Earlier improvements in printing technology had made printing less expensive and more efficient, allowing newspapers to be more widely circulated. In particular, it made it commercially viable to print cheap, penny press newspapers that targeted a different (read: a larger, poorer, and less-educated) audience.

All these technological developments combined, together with the new business practices they enabled, caused the intimate details of Boston's notables to appear in the society columns of the *Saturday Evening Gazette*, a Boston tabloid at the time. One of these notables was Samuel Warren, son of a well-off paper manufacturer, married to the daughter of a senator, and one of the founders of the Warren and Brandeis law firm. Samuel Warren and Louis Brandeis (Warren's Harvard Law School classmate, long-time friend, and business partner) recognized this direct influence of technological developments on our privacy and feared that soon "what is whispered in the closet shall be proclaimed from the house-tops."

In response, they wrote their seminal paper defining the right to privacy, arguing that every individual should have a "right to be let alone."[1] This is the first example of how technological developments change our understanding of what privacy is and how it should be protected.

Like Warren and Brandeis and their contemporaries, we are also witnesses to enormous technological changes with a profound impact on our privacy.[2] So much so that Scott McNealy, then CEO of SUN Microsystems, famously proclaimed in January 1999, "You have zero privacy anyway. Get over it."[3]

In the next few sections of this chapter, we will explore these technological developments, which on the face of it appear to justify McNealy's blunt statement. In the second part of this chapter, however, we will zoom out to bring the bigger picture into full view. This allows us to argue that technological developments are not inevitable, as McNealy claims, and that privacy can and must be protected.

2.1 OUR DIGITAL AGE

The invention of the computer turned administrative and computational chores into an automated task that could be performed much faster, and with much more precision, than humans ever could. Soon all kinds of information (documents, balance sheets, music, pictures) were stored and processed digitally. Storing this information in digital form in a database allows it to be searched very efficiently. The profound impact of this should not be underestimated. Before the invention of the computer, information was mostly recorded on paper, and searching for some information in a book or a library was tedious work. If you were lucky, the information you were looking for could be described by a single keyword that was part of an index (referring to the pages or the books in which the keyword you were interested in occurred). Because compiling and maintaining a paper index is resource intensive, only keywords deemed important would be part of the index. If the thing you were looking for was not part of the index, you were out of luck: the only thing left for you to do was browse the books or pages in the hope of stumbling upon some relevant information (or to ask someone else who might know where to find what you were looking for).

Compare this to the free text search that computers allow (without the need of compiling an index altogether) or the ability to automatically compile and store an index for every word occurring in a document to speed up this search even more. Everything you want can be found in an instant—provided you know exactly what you are looking for. Smart algorithms are getting better and better at guessing which of the gazillion possible results are the most relevant to you. And they show these results to you first. Misplacing a book or a report is no longer a problem either. These days most computer systems automatically index all text-based documents you store. Soon they will also index music and pictures based on the instruments or melodies they contain or the objects or people they portray.

External storage grew with demand, both in terms of storage space and speed of access. Slow magnetic tapes were quickly replaced with faster floppy disks and hard drives. These days we have even faster solid-state drives that can contain terabytes of data (a *terabyte* is a thousand billion bytes, equivalent to a billion pages of text). With that much storage space abundantly available, making copies of data is cheap and effortless. For most data, a copy of it is available somewhere. In fact, truly deleting a document, a picture, or a video requires some specific effort as most computers do not actually erase an item when instructed to delete it. Emptying the recycle bin only hides the items it contains without actually erasing the data from the external storage device itself. This is precisely the reason that specialized software can undelete files you thought were gone forever. We live in a time when nothing is ever really forgotten.

The privacy impact of computers and databases is exacerbated when these systems become interconnected. The invention of the internet in the seventies and the subsequent commercialization of it in the nineties has had a tremendous impact. By using a network to interconnect computers, one can easily share huge amounts of data within a single organization or among other organizations. Data hitherto stored in separate databases can now be linked to discover new patterns and new insights, especially using data-mining algorithms that have become ever more sophisticated over time.

Some have proclaimed data to be the new oil.[4] The internet makes it possible to share these new insights with anybody else anywhere in the world. All that is needed to get access to this data is an internet connection and a basic computer with a browser that allows you to surf the web. What's more, internet users not only consume information but can also contribute information, through websites they set up themselves, by joining internet discussion forums, or via collaborative environments like Wikipedia. In this "upgraded" version of the web (sometimes referred to as Web 2.0), file-sharing sites allow us to share music and videos with the world. Social networking sites allow us to share intimate stories, pictures, and home videos with a smaller circle of friends or acquaintances. Sites like YouTube or Facebook curate the content we contribute, determining the order in which we see each other's contributions and offering recommendations for related content to read or watch. These developments blur the traditional distinction between communication service providers (like telephony) that are not responsible for the content they transmit and publishers (like newspapers) that are.

Traditional computers were inert and numb: they could not (easily) be moved or carried with you and almost completely relied on their users to provide their input and to act on their output. Now we have fully autonomous robots assembling cars or fulfilling your Amazon order. And we have smartphones and smart watches that are with us all the time and that we carry everywhere we go. Equipped with motion sensors, GPS technology (which measures location), microphones, and cameras, they sense the world around us when we sleep, walk, work, talk, make love, and so on. Smartphones thus become the first concrete and tangible steps toward the *Internet of Things* (IoT), in which everything around us (our fridges, our thermostats, our cars, the lights and switches in our houses) becomes connected to the internet while the computer slowly disappears, "weaving itself into the fabric of everyday life."[5]

All this sensing is building an even more intimate, 24-7 picture of our lives. And IoT doesn't only notice us, monitor us, or surveil us. It also influences us. It adjusts the temperature in the room, the amount of light in the street, the routes we drive in our cars. Some smart watches or fitness wearables can even tap our wrists to warn us. With IoT, the difference between the real world and the virtual world slowly disappears. And any bugs in the software or successful hacks of such systems will immediately have real-world, perhaps irrevocable consequences.[6]

2.2 LEAKY DESIGN

Computers make it easy to search anything you want in massive data sets. Digital data is never forgotten, and networks make it easy to share and combine data, making that data accessible and searchable for anyone in the world with a network connection. Moreover, users not only consume information but can also contribute and share their own. Finally, smartphones and wearables sense us, nudge us, influence us, and can even act on behalf of us, essentially letting us connect ourselves to the internet and blurring the distinction between the real and the virtual world.

But this is only half of the story.

It not only matters *what* new things computers and networks make possible but also *how* they do so. This separation in *layers*, like distinguishing the what (the outside, the visible, the known) from the how (the inside, the invisible, the unknown) is very common in engineering as it helps to solve complex problems. One can build a financial administration system on top of a basic database system. To do so, you do not need to know how the database system itself works internally. All you need is access to functions that allow you to add or manipulate records and functions to query the database. In general, we can view a complex system as a stack of layered components, in which components in a higher layer rely on services or functionality offered by lower layers, comparable to a firm in which higher management relies on reports and services offered by lower-layer departments like finance or human resources. A central theme throughout this book is that particular design choices or implementation decisions in lower layers of the stack may have an impact on the behavior or performance of the overall system, both in terms of the purely technical functioning of the overall system, but also in terms of secondary effects. This is the case in particular if the original intended use of a layer does not fit the current context in which it is used or if a particular requirement that is highly relevant now was completely irrelevant when the layer was originally designed. Such incompatibilities may have surprising consequences in terms of privacy, as we will discuss ahead, and can in general have substantial consequences for our society at large given the planetary scale of current digital platforms.[7]

For the moment, we will focus on one of the lowest layers in this stack and describe how computers and networks work to explore some important leaks in their designs that directly affect our privacy. For a thorough yet down-to-earth treatment of how computers and networks actually work, we refer to Kernighan's excellent and down-to-earth description in his book *Understanding the Digital World*.[8]

2.2.1 COMPUTERS

Everything is a computer these days. There are obvious computers, like a personal computer (PC), laptop, tablet, or smartphone. A company web server or Amazon cloud server, "serving" its users web pages or stored data, is a computer too. But other devices, like your smart watch, the thermostat in your living room, your Internet modem, your washing machine, even a light bulb—they all contain a computer as well. Although the looks, sizes, and capabilities of computers have changed dramatically over the years, the basic *architecture* of a computer—a term coined by *John Von Neumann* back in 1945 and describing how the different *hardware* components are interconnected—has never really changed since (see figure 2.1).

The *central processing unit* (CPU) is the heart and soul of the computer. It runs all software, executing the instructions in the software to perform computations (adding or multiplying numbers) and manipulate data (comparing or moving data items). The CPU fetches both its instructions and the data to operate on from main memory. This *random-access memory* (RAM) is

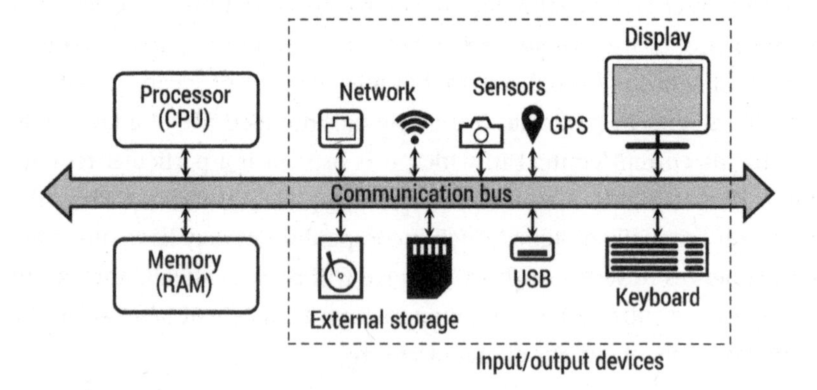

2.1 The components of a computer.

fast but small and volatile (losing its contents as soon as you switch off your computer or remove the battery of your smartphone). For long-term storage, hard drives or solid-state drives are used. Such external memory is large and permanent, yet slow. External memory (which indeed used to be external to the computer, storing the data on floppy disks or large hard drives) is one example of the many input/output devices from which the CPU receives input (mouse, keyboard, camera, network) or to which it sends its output (display and speaker, as well as a network). The CPU coordinates all input and output activities, communicating with the different input and output devices over the *bus*, which processes all input and orchestrates all output.

All the applications you use on your computer or your smartphone (like your word processor, browser, calendar, maps, messaging apps, games, etc.) are executed by this single CPU and share the same memory and the same input/output devices. The *operating system* (OS) allows all these applications to safely run simultaneously on your computer. Well-known operating systems include Microsoft Windows, Apple's MacOS, and Linux for servers and laptops, as well as Google's Android or Apple's iOS for smartphones and tablets. The operating system has several tasks that each has a critical impact on the overall privacy (and security) properties of the computer it operates.

First and foremost, the operating system is a layer between the applications and the actual computer hardware. Applications are prevented from accessing the hardware directly. Instead, the operating system mediates all hardware access requests issued by the applications (see figure 2.2). In this way, it tries to do its best to separate these applications from each other, to ensure that they do not interfere with each other or access each other's data stored in memory. The operating system is also the gatekeeper for all data and sensors found on your device. Modern smartphones in particular contain many different sensors: a microphone (sound), a camera (vision), GPS (location), a thermometer (temperature), an accelerometer (motion, direction), a gyroscope (tilt, angle), a magnetometer (magnetic field), a barometer (air pressure), a proximity sensor (how far the phone is from your ear), and an ambient light sensor (light). A poorly designed operating system would allow all apps or applications indiscriminate access to all this data and all these sensors, which would allow these apps

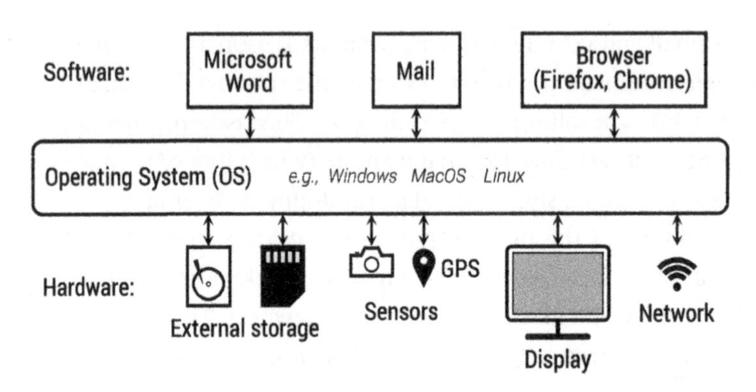

2.2 The operating system.

to spy on you in real time. With such apps installed, it's no exaggeration to call a smartphone your own Stasi agent in your pocket.[9] This is why the design of the *permission system* (which restricts the access apps have to the data and the sensors on your smartphone) matters.

To understand what an operating system is, it's perhaps helpful to think of it as a butler in a large country house serving the members of the family (and their guests), overseeing the housemaids and kitchen staff. The house and its amenities correspond to the basic computer hardware. The family members and their guests are the software applications. Instead of making their own coffee or turning the heater on, they ask the butler to do everything for them. This way they don't need to know how to make coffee or where the thermostat is (assuming the house even has a thermostat). This will also prevent them from accidentally breaking the coffee machine or overheating the mansion. Moreover, replacing the coffee machine with a different model or upgrading to a central heating system is easy: only the butler needs to be informed of the change. The butler also prevents guests from entering the master study. And the butler welcomes every new guest, while keeping the riffraff at bay.

Indeed, the operating system provides the user interface through which the users of the computer interact with it. It is the operating system that asks you to login to your computer account or to enter the passcode for your smartphone. It thus protects access to the computer, granting access only to those users that have an account. If the access control mechanism fails, privacy is at risk: unauthorized persons would be able to get access to a lot of personal data that you store or process on your computer or smartphone, if it's stolen or you lose it. Finally, at least on smartphones and tablets, the operating system also imposes stricter control over which apps can be installed on the device (compared to normal computers and laptops). On Apple phones and tablets, the only way to install apps is through the App Store, which vets all software before it becomes available. This allows Apple to keep the most blatantly insecure and privacy-invasive apps off of everyone's devices. It also allows Apple to censor certain types of applications, like those that offer pornographic materials or other content deemed unacceptable by Apple. The vetting process for Google Play, Google's app store, is less strict. Moreover, Android allows users to install apps that are not available in Google Play simply by downloading them from websites. This is not possible on Apple phones (unless their restrictions are bypassed by "jailbreaking" the device, something that Apple tries to make harder with every new update it releases).

Eight years ago, a big scandal broke out when a popular flashlight app for Android turned out to send users' precise locations and unique device identifiers to third parties.[10] The situation seems to have barely improved. Although Android enforces a much stricter permission system these days, an app like Brightest Flash LED Lights still (as of July 2019) requests a stunning amount of permissions, like access to accounts and contacts on the device, your precise location, the ability to send SMS messages and to place outgoing calls (!), access to all your stored data and pictures, the ability to record audio, the ability to connect to the network, the right to create accounts and change passwords, and more (see also figure 2.3).[11] This is clearly ridiculous for an app that is only supposed to enable the use of a flashlight. Yet millions of people have installed the app and apparently agreed to the permissions requested when their Android phone asked them to do so. Recent investigations show that even on Apple's iOS platform, mobile apps can and do track you and collect a lot of personal information, like your location, device name, and so on, and share this info with third parties.[12]

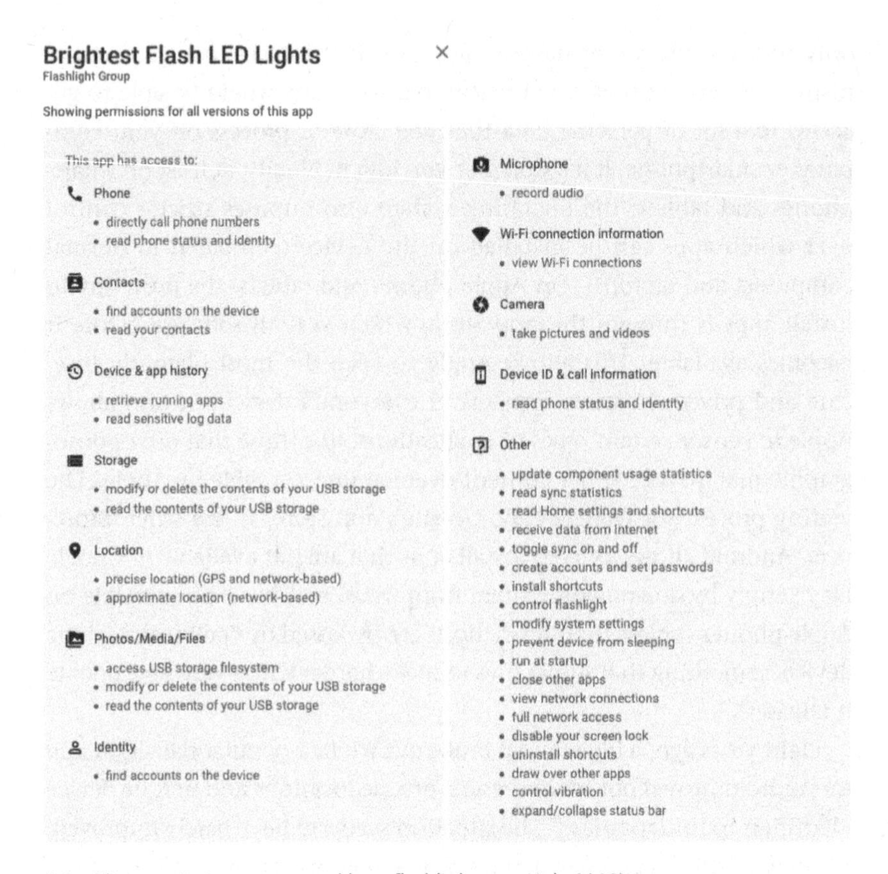

2.3 The permissions requested by a flashlight app (July 2019).

Thus, the way the operating system regulates access to data (and other resources) has a profound impact on the overall security and privacy properties of the systems we use. And the manufacturers of the devices and operating systems we currently use could do more to raise the bar.

2.2.2 NETWORKS

Networks are almost as old as the earth itself and come in many different guises. Rivers transport melting water from the mountains to the sea. Paths, roads, and highways connect dwellings, mountains, villages, wells, towns, and cities. The railway system interconnects cities, harbors, and industrial zones. The telephone network allows us to speak to our friends or relatives, whether they live a few blocks away or on the other side of the globe.

The internet interconnects computers, allowing them to exchange data. On the internet, data to be transmitted (an email, a document, a video) is first split into a number of *packets* (which each contain a fixed number of bytes) before each individual packet is submitted to the network by the sender for delivery to the recipient. Such a *packet switching* network functions, in a crude metaphorical way, very similarly to the ordinary postal mail system.

In particular, an internet packet can be visualized as a postcard (see figure 2.4). A long email is split into several packets, much like a long letter would have to be written on several postcards. The header of an internet packet specifies the *IP address* of the *source* (the sender) and the *destination* (the recipient) of the packet.[13] Like the postal address determines the route a postcard travels (from postbox to sorting center, perhaps then into a plane to another sorting center, all the way to the final delivery step when the mailman drops it in the letterbox of the recipient), the route of an internet packet is determined by its destination.

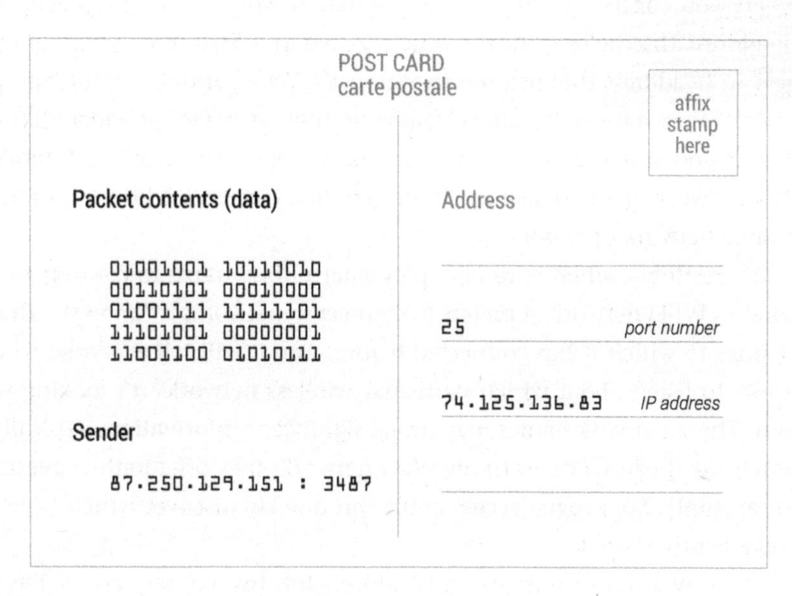

2.4 An internet packet envisioned as a postcard.

The route may differ depending on network conditions or (arbitrary) local routing decisions: like postcards sent to the same address, internet packets with the same destination do not necessarily travel the same route and may not arrive in the same order they were sent. In particular, the postcard analogy implies that internet packets can be read by all intermediate nodes on the route from their source to their destination, similar to the people at the sorting center and the mailman being able to read all postcards addressed to you. This is something to be aware of as the route an email or message you send to your neighbor does not necessarily travel along the shortest possible path: it may cross a significant part of the globe before arriving at its destination next door. In fact, the route such a packet travels can be influenced by outsiders, effectively allowing them to harvest its content even if they are not originally on the route. A large fraction of all internet traffic travels through a handful of transatlantic cables and large internet exchanges that interconnect different countries or even continents.

Every computer, smartphone, or other device on the internet has such a unique IP address, which it gets automatically as soon as it connects to the network. It does not always get the same IP address; this depends on where you connect to the network. When at work, your laptop gets an IP address that belongs to the office. When at a Starbucks, your laptop gets an IP address that belongs to Starbucks. When at home, your laptop typically gets a fixed IP address from your internet service provider (ISP).[14] And if you surf the web with your smartphone over a cellular/mobile data network, then your smartphone gets an arbitrary IP address from the mobile network operator.

Interestingly, when your laptop or smartphone wants to connect to a wireless Wi-Fi network, it prefers to connect to networks it "knows"—that is, ones to which it has connected before. And it will tell everyone who wants to listen about which particular wireless networks it's looking to join. These network names may reveal significant information. Typically hotels use the hotel name in the Wi-Fi networks they offer to their guests, for example. So a rogue access point can quickly discover which hotels you recently visited.

The way a device obtains an IP address has two consequences. First, devices with a fixed location, like wired PCs, or your smartphone or laptop that mostly connects to your Wi-Fi network at home, have a fixed and unique IP address that by itself already allows them to be recognized by the websites you visit.[15] It also implies that a particular IP address is permanently bound to a particular network at a particular location. Using this property, several databases have been constructed over time that record the known location for a particular IP address with uncanny accuracy.[16] In other words, the IP address of your computer or smartphone can be used to determine your location quite accurately through a process called *geolocation*, even if it does not have GPS. This in particular allows the websites you visit to determine your current location, because your IP address is part of every packet you send to it. You can easily test this yourself by visiting the local version of Amazon's website—for example, amazon.nl if you live in the Netherlands—where the top left of the page will show its rather accurate estimate of your location.

The servers of the internet services you use—like Google, Facebook, Twitter, and in fact all websites you visit—have IP addresses as well. These IP addresses are publicly known. This means that by simply looking at the destination IP addresses of all internet packets your computer generates, an eavesdropper can determine which internet services (Google? Grindr?) you use. Potential eavesdroppers are your ISP (which by default sees all your internet traffic) or the free Wi-Fi access point you connect to in a Starbucks. But law enforcement agencies or intelligence services that have the authority and capability to monitor large amounts of network traffic can do so as well. They need not even be very close to your own computer or network in order to gather this information.

2.2.3 THE WORLD WIDE WEB

With the invention of the World Wide Web by Tim Berners Lee in 1989, the internet exploded. Just like email, the web is yet another application that runs on top of the internet: all information exchanged between your device and the website you visit is exchanged using IP packets traversing the internet. On the World Wide Web, computers called *web servers* offer access to information that they store in *web pages*. Users can retrieve these pages, over the internet, with a piece of software called a *browser* (like

Microsoft Explorer or Edge, Google Chrome, Apple's Safari, or Mozilla's Firefox) and subsequently display their content. To retrieve a web page, you need to know its *hyperlink*, like https://en.wikipedia.org/wiki/URL. This hyperlink (the technical term is *URL*) uniquely determines a particular page offered by a particular web server (as specified by the domain name at the beginning of such a hyperlink; in the example, wikipedia.org is the domain name). The browser sends the hyperlink to the web server, after which the web server responds with the contents of the corresponding web page (or an error if the link points to a web page that does not exist). Web pages can contain hyperlinks to images to include on the page or hyperlinks to other pages that you can visit by clicking those links, creating a web of interlinked pages.

But the World Wide Web is much more complex than what this innocent-looking, basic description reveals. It truly is a web in a much more sinister sense.

2.2.4 BROWSER FINGERPRINTING

When requesting a web page, your browser also sends some additional information to the web server. For example, the browser tells the web server which browser you use, what version of that browser you use, and which operating system your computer is running. This allows the web server to adapt the contents of the web page to the particulars of your system: older versions of browsers may not support certain features, and different types of browsers may interpret web pages slightly differently, which would make the web page look bad when displayed without taking care of this. But this information is rather specific and allows your computer to be *fingerprinted*: surprisingly, your particular choice of operating system and browser, together with some other settings, may actually be unique among all other users of the web.[17] You can check whether you can be uniquely identified based on this information by visiting https://panopticlick.eff.org, the web page for the Panopticlick project of the Electronic Frontier Foundation (EFF). To my own surprise, I found that even my setup, with some tracking prevention installed, still allowed my computer to be more or less uniquely identified. The risk of browser fingerprinting is that websites may be able to identify you based on your browser fingerprint, even if your IP address changes as you connect at work, at home, or in some lunchroom, or if you disabled cookies (discussed in section 2.2.5) because of the tracking risk these impose. Browser fingerprinting (also known as device identification) is being used in practice, although it is hard to measure how often.[18]

2.2.5 COOKIES

When visiting a website, the web server may ask your browser to store some information on your own computer for later use. These small pieces of information are called *cookies*. When your browser receives a cookie from a web server, it stores it in its cookie jar. And whenever you later visit a page on that same web server again, your browser will send back the information stored in all cookies in the cookie jar that it ever received from that particular web server.

Cookies are actually useful and sometimes downright necessary. First and foremost, cookies allow websites to remember logged in users and allow e-commerce sites to keep track of the items you select for purchase for their virtual shopping carts. Without cookies, this would be impossible. Cookies also allow websites to remember the preferences of otherwise anonymous users, like your preferred language or the region you live in. After selecting such a preference the first time you visit a website, the web server will send your browser a cookie storing this preference for later visits.

But cookies are also used for much more nefarious purposes. They can be used to assign you a unique identifier the first time you visit a website. From then on, your browser will send that cookie with the unique identifier with every request for a page on the same website. This enables the website to single you out and recognize you (or rather, your browser) whenever you visit the website again.[19] It also allows the website to maintain a database that records, for every issued unique identifier, all web pages on the site the visitor with that identifier ever visited. Fortunately, this profile of your browsing preferences is still limited, covering only your visits to a single website. However, cookies can also be used to link your visits to *different* websites, thus allowing the creation of one big profile of your browsing preferences across the *whole* World Wide Web.

2.2.6 JAVASCRIPT

The first web pages were simple static text documents with some formatting information specified using hypertext markup language (HTML). They quickly became more complex and dynamic with the possibility to add JavaScript code. Web pages with JavaScript are now ubiquitous. JavaScript allows single web pages to be interactive (responding to user actions) and to synchronize information in real time with back-end systems. This latter feature allows companies like Google or Microsoft to create online collaboration sites (like Google Docs or Office 365) that allow multiple users to edit a document, a presentation, or a spreadsheet together in real time.

But scripts on web pages can also be used for other, more vile purposes, like monitoring your mouse movements while visiting a page or trying to steal information from the cookie jar. Scripts on web pages are as dangerous as macros in documents: they turn a web page into an active object with behavior that is hard to constrain or contain. This is why Microsoft Word asks a user to explicitly confirm whether they want to enable macros when opening a document that contains them. And this is also why many browsers offer their users the option to disable JavaScript.

2.2.7 LEAKY DESIGN INDEED

One could argue that from the perspective of websites that use JavaScript to make their web pages dynamic, the browser is an operating system—with all the possibilities, weaknesses, and responsibilities that come with that important role (as we discussed earlier). One way to act on that responsibility is for some browser to offer the option to block scripts, reject third-party tracking cookies, or empty the cookie jar every once in a while.

Fingerprinting, cookies, and scripts allow websites to collect a lot of additional information surreptitiously about their visitors. Your surfing behavior can be monitored to learn, for example, the sites you visit, the items you searched, the pages you read (and how long it took you to read them), the banners you clicked or were about to click, and more. All this metadata, this intimate information about your behavior, which we will discuss in depth in chapter 4, turns out to be an excellent predictor of your age, gender, race, religion, wealth, health, hobbies, interests, and so on. It's literally worth gold.

It should come as no surprise, then, that I consider all this technology *leaky*. From a very basic engineering perspective, it may make sense to broadcast all kinds of *identifiers* (i.e., unique numbers that allow you to be singled out) or other data that reveal where you have been, simply because it makes the protocols easier or faster. But from a privacy protection point of view, this practice is absolutely disastrous. And even a slightly more critical look at the engineering decisions made decades ago quickly challenges the idea that using such identifiers is actually useful. Why does a laptop that wants to access an available wireless network need to broadcast all the wireless networks it knows about, when it is clear that most of these networks won't be available at the current location? Why can't it wait for the wireless access point to disclose its name and decide based on that whether to join the network automatically?

Indeed, why does your laptop or smartphone even need to send any signals (and thus reveal its unique MAC address) when it wants to connect to a Wi-Fi network or Bluetooth device in the first place? It should be perfectly possible to design the network discovery protocol in such a way that the connecting devices are in receiving mode by default (not sending any signals and thus not revealing any identifiers) and waiting until they receive a strong enough signal for a network that they want to connect to. In fact, local area network connections do not even need to use a globally unique and persistent identifier like a MAC address: modern iPhones actually randomize the MAC address to prevent long-term tracing of the phone, although the actual implementation is far from perfect.[20]

2.3 THE IMPACT ON OUR PRIVACY

The previous sections explored how computers and networks open up new ways to erode our privacy far beyond what Warren and Brandeis could imagine more than a hundred years ago. We have also seen that the particularly leaky design of these new technologies facilitates even more detailed and peculiar ways of collecting personal data. It's time now to investigate the actual impact on our privacy of all these technological developments and to explore how and why these new technologies have been adopted by individual people, by governments, and by businesses.[21]

2.3.1 INDIVIDUAL PEOPLE

We (people, citizens, or users) now live in a digital world.[22] We increasingly shop online, instead of going to the shopping mall, the local bookstore, or a fashion boutique. As a result, our shopping preferences (including the items we looked at but never bought) are kept, shared, and analyzed by online retailers to personalize future offers. As we will see later, our preferences even allow them to guess that we are pregnant, while the prices we pay for their offers depend on the types of computers we use or the places we live. Many of us bank electronically and pay by card or smartphone even, instead of using cash. Our transactions are mined to prevent fraud, to offer financial advice, or even for direct marketing purposes.[23] We are tethered twenty-four hours a day through our smartphones, wearables, and tablets. All the information in the world is at our fingertips, a single swipe away. We can talk, chat, or connect to anyone in the world with an internet connection, which at the end of 2019 was estimated to be 4.2 billion people: 54 percent of the world population.[24] Fewer people read newspapers, at least on paper. Instead, we use social networks like Facebook, Instagram, Twitter and the like to stay informed about what's happening with our friends and loved ones and the world at large. More and more we use social networks to share our most intimate details with them—*and* with the social networking company that offers us this great service for free. The information we see is curated by social networks. Algorithms decide which status updates we see, in which order, and suggest new connections to people that are deemed similar to the people we are connected to now or that seem to share a similar interest to our own. These algorithms are optimized to maximize engagement with the social network platform, which does not necessarily correspond to the individual interests of its members. This *attention economy* keeps us captured in filter bubbles and allows fake news to spread. [25]

We (those of us that can afford it, and have fully embraced our digital lives, that is) confidently travel all around the world, navigating our way using online travel guides, navigation systems, or online maps. Google, Here Technologies, and telecommunication operators know exactly where we have been and where we are likely to be tomorrow.[26] So do dozens of other location data companies using software slipped into mobile phone apps.[27] We never miss a bus. We hail an Uber or a Lyft. We sleep in someone else's house thanks to Airbnb or Wimdu.[28]

We own less and rent or pay per use more. Everything is turning into an online service. Fewer people watch the same TV show (anonymously) at the same time. Instead, we binge-watch a Netflix series whenever we feel like it (while Netflix learns when we watched and which parts we skipped or watched more than once). Instead of buying a CD or record, we have Spotify subscriptions that allow us to listen to "all" the music in the world whenever and wherever we like. In the meantime, Spotify collects an enormous amount of very detailed information about our listening habits.[29] Instead of buying real paper books, we increasingly "buy" e-books that we never actually own. Instead, we buy licenses that allow us to read these e-books only on a secured e-reader or tablet that enables publishers to revoke that license at any time—leaving us without access to all those books we read and destroying all the notes we added to them.[30]

2.3.2 THE GOVERNMENT

Governments have become digital. Instead of talking to a government official in person, more and more we interact with our government through a website or a smartphone app. We no longer need to visit the police station but can report a crime online. We submit our tax forms digitally and apply for welfare online.[31] Sometimes the forms are prefilled with detailed information the government already has on us. Governments turn to these new digital technologies to perform their tasks more efficiently, to improve our security and well-being, and to combat fraud. But as a consequence, we are increasingly being surveilled and subjected to the logic of automated decision-making.

Consider the following more or less well-known examples.[32] The Snowden revelations revealed that the US National Security Agency (NSA) engaged in routine and worldwide surveillance of both American and foreign civilians alike.[33] It obtained the cooperation of the big internet companies like Facebook, Google, and Apple (or otherwise coerced them to cooperate), or hacked their systems to obtain access to the gigantic troves of very personal data processed there.[34] It cooperated with other security agencies, like Government Communications Headquarters (GCHQ) in the United Kingdom, to get physical access to network infrastructure otherwise beyond its reach.[35] The NSA set up an automated attack infrastructure to infect targets with malware, using vulnerabilities in operating systems of smartphones, laptops, routers, and the like.[36] It's important to stress that the fact that we live our lives more and more digitally, using the online services of the internet giants, is exactly what made it possible for the NSA to engage in such far-reaching, global, dragnet surveillance. In fact, back in 2001 the US government launched a plan for indiscriminate surveillance on average citizens called Total Information Awareness (TIA). The goal was to combine and extend several distinct government intelligence and surveillance programs and to apply private-sector data-mining techniques to create a resource for the intelligence, counterintelligence, and law enforcement communities. The program received tremendous criticism and was quickly scrapped two years later. Ten years later, commercial data brokers have more data on every American citizen than the TIA program could ever dream to have collected, at a fraction of the original cost.

Government surveillance is not restricted to the virtual world. Camera surveillance systems have been in use for decades. The capabilities of these systems have increased tremendously over the years, however. Improvements in facial-recognition software, for example, allow *verification* of identity (answering the question "Is that you?"—namely, determining whether a picture taken of you now matches a previous stored picture of you) with near 100 percent accuracy.[37] Combined with other sensors and enriched with intelligent background processing, totally different forms of surveillance become possible. A particularly striking example of the capabilities of such systems is provided by the Dutch Stratumseind Living Lab. Stratumseind is a street packed with bars and restaurants in Eindhoven, a major city in the south of the Netherlands. The street is mostly (in)famous for its nightlife and is densely packed on Friday and Saturday nights. The Living Lab captures video streams obtained from cameras and audio streams from microphones, both placed along the street, and combines them in real time with weather information, Twitter feeds, and occupancy rates of nearby parking garages. It even uses (aggregate) information of cell phone data of visitors to the bars and restaurants in the street. All this data is used to measure the "atmosphere" in the street and to alert the regional police if required. It also influences the atmosphere by changing the light intensity and color of special LED armatures attached to existing light poles as a modern form of crowd control, nudging people into more responsible behavior. All this aims to make the neighborhood more safe.[38]

A really different, politically motivated intrusion of our privacy is the use of detailed personal data during governmental elections. This really took off in the United States with Barack Obama's presidential campaign in 2012, but it had already started in 2008 when individual voters were surveyed to gauge their attitudes and preferences. The resulting profiles were used to determine which talking points would resonate best with each voter, thus guiding Democrats canvassing for Obama to which political messages to stress during the conversations. "The campaign didn't just know who you were; it knew exactly how it could turn you into the type of person it wanted you to be."[39] The 2012 campaign also used a specific Facebook app. It asked supporters (who had previously registered by email) to install the app and grant it access to certain pieces of their profile (such as their posts, likes, photos, demographics, and similar information about their Facebook friends). This information was not used to build complex profiles. Instead, it was used to determine which friends to ask to vote or ask to register to vote and to ask the supporters who installed the app to ask these friends to do so.[40]

In the 2016 US presidential campaign, both the Democrats and the Republicans turned to profiling to optimize their campaigns, not only encouraging clear Trump voters to vote, but discouraging clear Clinton voters to vote or even to register to vote.[41] The Trump campaign hired a company called Cambridge Analytica, which claimed to be able to identify likely political persuasions and personality traits by analyzing Facebook likes.[42]

A few years earlier, psychology researchers from Cambridge University discovered that they could predict ethnic origin and gender (with 95 percent accuracy), political views (distinguishing Democrats and Republicans with 85 percent accuracy), and sexual orientation (with between 75 percent and 88 percent accuracy), as well as score people on intelligence, openness, extroversion, and other psychological traits with a reliability similar to standard psychological tests for these traits, using *only* information about the things they like on Facebook.[43] Cambridge Analytica subsequently set up a venture (Global Science Research) with one of the colleagues of these researchers, who had developed a Facebook app that featured a personality quiz. The app not only recorded the results of each quiz but also collected data from the Facebook account of the person taking the test and their Facebook friends as well, including their Facebook likes. It was commonly known that developers of apps on the Facebook platform had access to Facebook account data of people that had installed such an app. What was not widely known outside Facebook was that such app developers had access to the account data of all their friends as well (although Facebook platform rules prohibited app developers from sharing this data with third parties). Using this method, Cambridge Analytica (through Global Science Research) surreptitiously harvested data from fifty million Facebook profiles in 2014.[44] When Steve Bannon was taking over as campaign manager for Trump in 2016, he brought Cambridge Analytica (and the data it collected in 2014) with him. The Cambridge Analytica models were subsequently used to make day-to-day campaign decisions and also helped drive decisions on advertising and how to reach out to financial donors.[45] In a similar setup, Cambridge Analytica also advised the Leave.EU campaign, likely tipping the vote in the UK Brexit referendum in favor of leaving the European Union.[46] And there is evidence it was involved in vote manipulation in many different countries across the globe.[47]

One could say that we are slowly moving into an era of personalized politics, in which we no longer have political parties campaigning based on a single consistent political program. Instead, we have individual politicians who sell each of us our own personalized political program, tuned to what we ourselves believe and think is important. The thing that makes politics what it is—namely, the weighing of stakes and making difficult long-term choices—no longer matters.

2.3.3 BUSINESSES

Companies like Google, Facebook, and the like are sitting on a huge treasure trove of personal data that they can analyze for patterns.[48] Not only do they know everything we search for or everything we share on their own platforms, but using techniques we mentioned earlier, they know our full surfing habits across most sites on the web. They know exactly which websites we visited, which pages we viewed, and how long it took us to read them. This allows them to offer advertisers the ability to target specific ads to very specific target groups, defined by their ages; incomes; interests; their political, cultural, religious, or ethnic orientation; and even their current emotional state.[49] It's instructive to see just how detailed the profiles these companies collect are by visiting their customer pages, the ones they use to sell their products to their advertisers.[50] (Remember: if you are not paying, you are not the *customer* but the *product being sold.*) Facebook, for example, allows you to target advertisements to people that visited particular websites. Politicians use this to reach people that showed interest in their competitors.[51] Facebook even uses phone numbers and email addresses provided for security purposes (such as two-factor authentication), numbers provided to the Facebook Messenger app for the purpose of messaging, and numbers included in friends' uploaded contact databases to allow advertisers to target users, even when users have the most private settings.[52]

All these personal data and the personal profiles derived from them are not only used for microtargeted advertising. They are used to personalize the content that we see, the search results we obtain, and the order of our Twitter feeds or Facebook status updates. This subtly nudges you into certain desired behavior.[53] And just like the social credit scoring systems in China, these profiles are used to grant or deny you access to certain services. They are used to grant or deny your loan application; they are used to decide whether or not to invite you for a job interview.[54] They are used in more or less subtle ways to admit you into a particular insurance program or to determine the fee you pay to be insured.[55] Car insurance companies used to determine your insurance fee based on the place you lived. These days, they offer a discount on the fee if you agree to your driving patterns being monitored.[56] Additional health insurance packages are often inaccessible to people that fit a particular profile.[57] This personalization of insurance terms, conditions, and fees leads to a situation in which the expected cost of insuring a particular individual is estimated with such accuracy that the total amount of fees paid by an individual will soon equal the cost made by covering all claims for that individual by the insurance company. This is no longer insurance, but a monthly installment on a mortgage instead. In the long run, solidarity is at stake: the people that somehow were dealt a bad hand of cards cannot afford insurance fees and live their lives in extreme poverty or poor care conditions.

Personal profiling is also used for *price discrimination*: offering goods or services for a price that depends on a person's circumstances, including the propensity to pay more (or less) for a particular product.[58] Proving price discrimination is hard, however. Traditionally, dynamic pricing depends on many factors, including the time of purchase or whether there is an increased demand for a particular product or service. Airlines (often accused of basing their ticket prices on your personal profile) have complex pricing strategies and increase the ticket price based on available seats and the number of days until departure. A few cases of actual personalized pricing have been proven, however. Staples, a large office supplies retailer, determines the price offered to you online based on your location.[59] The further you are from a physical store offering the same product, the higher the price you are offered online.[60] Customers trying to book a hotel online on their Macs were presented with more expensive default options compared to customers using other devices.[61]

The amount of personal data being collected and the level of detail in which it is collected is mind boggling.[62] Data brokers like Equifax, Acxiom, and Experian (companies you probably never heard of before, at least when you live outside the United States) distinguish seventy-five thousand data element types.[63] In 2013, Acxiom's database alone contained information about seven hundred million consumers worldwide, with roughly three thousand different pieces of information for nearly every American consumer.[64] They know when you are getting married, buying a home, or sending a kid to college. They know your hobbies, the purchases you made across 1,400 brands. They even know whether you are into reading romantic novels. They know your income and financial status and whether you donate to charity. They know whether you suffer from allergies, depression, diabetes, high blood pressure, insomnia, obesity, Parkinson's disease, multiple sclerosis, Alzheimer's disease, cancer, or are on a diet. They know whether you smoke or own a pet, whether you purchased a particular soft drink or shampoo product in the last six months, used laxatives or yeast infection products; whether you visited a doctor within the last twelve months, how many miles you traveled in the last four weeks, or the number of whiskey drinks consumed in the past thirty days.[65] Data brokers hardly ever obtain this information directly from consumers themselves. They get the data from the government, other public sources, or commercial parties (including other data brokers). Their stealthy way of doing business has ensured that the people at large have little idea of the extent of the data collection taking place.

Of course, the elephant in the room is the business model underlying all these free online services: in return for their use, we, the users, are the product being sold.[66] Our privacy will continue to be eroded unless existing laws are tightly enforced, or new laws are enacted, such that the economic incentive structure changes. We will return to this issue in chapter 6.

2.4 COUNTERPOINT

Do we have zero privacy anyway? Should we get over it? I don't think so.

Yes, we may have little privacy now. But it is not zero. And it is not just happening anyway. In fact, a guiding principle of this book is that technology does not develop in isolation, does not have an independent, inherent purpose or destiny of its own. Instead, technology is made by people and is shaped according to their agendas and beliefs, embedding these beliefs in how they function, what they afford us to do, what they prevent us from doing, and what they do regardless of our own intents and wishes. At the moment, information technology is used to invade our privacy. As we will show throughout this book, this is not necessarily so: technology can also be used to protect privacy.

If we want this to happen, though, we need to get involved and influence these agendas and beliefs. So no, there is absolutely no need to get over it. And recent developments show that we no longer want to.

Increasingly, the media is paying attention to privacy. A turning point was the release of the Snowden documents several years ago, which revealed the unbelievable extent of mass surveillance performed by US (and other) intelligence services. Apart from smaller stories that appear in the newspapers, on social media, or on TV news almost daily, recent big news stories like Cambridge Analytica's abuse of Facebook data have a global impact. Marc Zuckerberg, Facebook's CEO, even had to testify in front of senate hearings in both the US and Europe.

Privacy is becoming better protected by law, at least in Europe, with the introduction of the General Data Protection Regulation in 2016.[67] But this is starting to have a global impact as well. Enforcement has been stepped up, and so have the fines. A nice example is the case of the Court of Justice of the European Union regarding Google, which lead to the implementation of a *right to be forgotten*.[68] Or consider the recent Supreme Court of the United States ruling on *Carpenter v. United States*, which forces police to get a warrant before getting certain cellphone data.[69]

Privacy-friendly technology is starting to be mainstream. Surfing the web is getting safer as communication with websites is secure by default; WhatsApp is using end-to-end encryption now; and Apple explicitly uses privacy as a unique selling point. We will see many more examples of this throughout this book.

2.5 THE VALUE OF PRIVACY

We are starting to realize that privacy has value, both for people individually and for society at large. It is a personal, fundamental human right because it protects us against almighty businesses and omniscient governments. Privacy ensures that we feel personally safe and secure. It aims to restore the power balance between people and larger organizations. It protects our autonomy. This personal perspective on privacy dominates public discourse, which means we often forget that privacy is also of tremendous societal value. Privacy is essential in a democratic society. It creates safe spaces that allow us to think the unthinkable, to discuss it with like-minded people, and realize these dreams once the opportunity is there. It prevents unreasonable forms of self-censorship and conformance to existing norms. Labor rights, women's voting rights, and gay rights all needed this space to be developed. In other words, privacy is a necessary condition for societal innovation as well.[70] Moreover, recent meddling with democratic elections by Cambridge Analytica and Russian trolls alike highlight another *societal* risk of a lack of privacy.[71] Democracy itself is at risk through "the relentless targeting of hyper-partisan views, which play to the fears and prejudices of people, in order to influence their voting plans and their behaviour."[72] Finally, a lack of privacy erodes solidarity. Insurance as a concept is dead if the insurer can perfectly predict the future cost of insuring me and charge me accordingly. "The lesson is that privacy is public—it is a collective good that is logically & morally inseparable from the values of human autonomy and self-determination upon which privacy depends and without which a democratic society is unimaginable."[73]

Another way to see this is to observe that privacy has a common value, a public value, and a collective value.[74] It has a *common value* in the sense that people all value some level of privacy and have a common understanding of that value. It has a *public value* because it is important to the democratic political system and its processes (as explained earlier). And it has a *collective value* in the sense that it is a public good threatened by market forces that cannot be withstood by individual privacy choices and hence need protection at the collective level.

Perhaps the value of privacy is best illustrated using an appropriate metaphor. But which metaphor should that be?

For years, the phrase "Big Brother Is Watching You" from George Orwell's dystopian novel *1984* was used to warn us about the horrors of a world without privacy.[75] This metaphor does wonders in terms of warning citizens about the risk of government surveillance, but it falls short on many other accounts. First, governments themselves typically don't think that this is addressed to them (after all, civil servants tend to think they work for a good cause). Moreover, the problem is not only government surveillance but also surveillance capitalism—namely, the indiscriminate collection and (ab)use of personal data by companies for commercial purposes.[76] Finally, the issue is not only the overt collection and use of personal data to suppress a population. (If that is at stake, lack of privacy is perhaps not your prime concern.) In fact, the real risk of a lack of privacy is a society in which everybody is being evaluated, predicted, nudged, and judged in ways nobody really understands, using information that is surreptitiously collected without anybody noticing, by organizations that you've never even heard of. This might sound eerily familiar to people that read Franz Kafka's book *The Trial*, in which the main character, Josef K., is unexpectedly arrested by two unidentified agents from an unspecified agency for an unspecified crime.[77] Interestingly, the arrest does not land him in jail. Instead, he is free to go. Throughout the book, Josef K. tries to change the course of justice and to plead his case, which turns out to be impossible given that everything is secret: the charge, the rules of the court, and the authority behind the courts, including the identities of the judges. Perhaps the right metaphor for a world without privacy is one in which each of us fights our own trial in vain.[78] It is for exactly this reason that the chapter opening illustrations in this book are inspired by Kafka's work.

2.6 WHAT IS PRIVACY?

We have just discussed the *value* of privacy and will later turn our attention to the *right* to privacy (as protected by law). But what *is* privacy, really?

This apparently simple question is surprisingly hard to answer, given that *privacy* is a word that we often use and that we all seem to understand at some intuitive level. In fact, privacy is a hard-to-define, contested concept, the meaning of which is strongly shaped by technological developments and dependent on cultural contexts.[79] As we noted at the start of this chapter, advancements in photography combined with developments in newspaper circulation led Warren and Brandeis to develop the right to be let alone as a first approximation of a right to privacy.[80] They realized that these technological developments made it harder for people to withdraw into solitude, to protect themselves from interference by others.

When governments started using computers to automate administration and started collecting more and more information about their citizens in ever-larger databases, fear of a Big Brother state that could result when all these databases were interconnected changed the perspective. Privacy no longer concerned persons directly but was deemed necessary to protect information *about* persons. Alan Westin famously framed privacy as a right to informational self-determination—that is, "The right of the individual to decide what information about himself should be communicated to others and under what circumstances."[81] Up to this day, privacy (or, more accurately, data protection) laws are strongly rooted in this conceptualization of privacy.

Government databases, and later business databases, also gave rise to the idea that we not only have a physical identity, but also a digital one that is shaped (and distorted) by all the information in those separate databases. We are no longer perceived as the person that we really are, but as how that data portrays us to be. Moreover, with the advance of digital, personalized media and the tremendous growth of social networks at the start of the twenty-first century, the development of our identity and the ability to present it to others ourselves has changed considerably. The construction of our identity is increasingly mediated (and hence controlled and steered) by technology. Internet filter bubbles determine what we encounter online and thus what we think and believe. Social networks are now the digital stage on which we play out our identity; they shape the images of ourselves that we show to others and the relationships we establish with them.[82] These developments reveal that identity and privacy are closely related concepts, which led Philip Agre to formulate privacy as "the freedom from unreasonable constraints on the construction of one's own identity."[83]

Governments and businesses increasingly share data among themselves and with each other. Moreover, social networks nudge users to share intimate details beyond the small circle of friends and family. This is creating problems ranging from people applying for a job being confronted with their nightly escapades to employees finding that their intimate health data were shared with their manager. These breaches of confidentiality or trust are considered especially harmful because information that is relevant in one context suddenly is used in another context in which that information is irrelevant, could be misunderstood, or might even be harmful. Seen in this light, Helen Nissenbaum defines privacy as a form of *contextual integrity*.[84] The problem is not simply that something that was supposed to be private becomes public. Contextual integrity acknowledges that there is a much more complex set of social spheres in which subtle informational norms govern the flow of information between these spheres. To

Nissenbaum, "A right to privacy is a right to appropriate flow of information, neither secrecy nor control."[85]

The account of privacy offered in the preceding paragraphs focuses on something we could call *informational privacy*. It involves the informational aspects that in fact infringe on different, more basic types of privacy that have traditionally been recognized, like privacy of the body, of the home, of communications, decisions, and one's associations (see figure 2.5).[86] But even informational privacy is not enough to ensure proper privacy protection in the digital age. This is because in many cases, collecting or processing individual pieces of personal information does not constitute a real privacy infringement. Each individual piece of personal data is rather meaningless (e.g., what type of car I own, what time I went to sleep last night) and thus may reveal very little about myself. But once many such small pieces of data are combined into a single personal profile, this profile may be able to predict my sexual orientation, my religious beliefs, my job aspirations, and more. We already encountered this mosaic theory in chapter 1. This is why *data protection*, the protection of each of these individual, innocuous pieces of personal data, is also important.

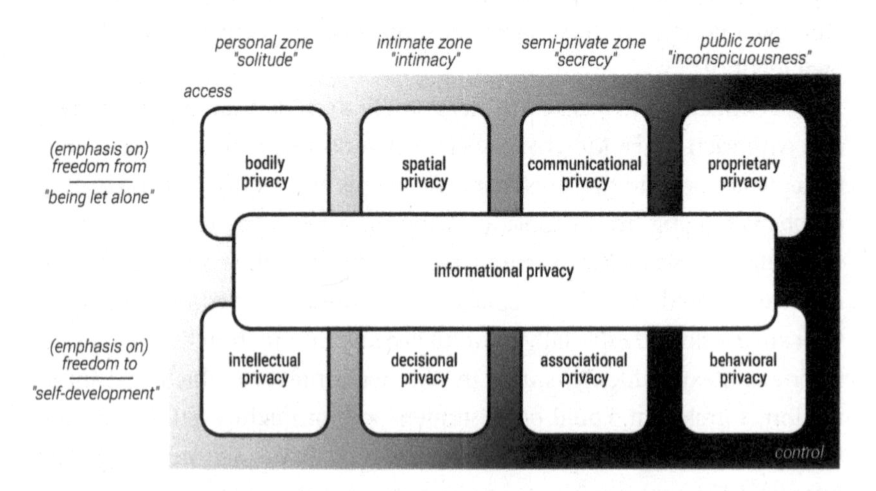

2.5 A typology of privacy.
Source: B.-J. Koops et al., "A Typology of Privacy," *University of Pennsylvania Journal of International Law* 38 (2017): 483–575.

2.7 HOW THE LAW PROTECTS PRIVACY

Both privacy and data protection are protected by law.[87] Privacy is in fact a fundamental human right since the second half of the twentieth century, both globally through the United Nations' Universal Declaration of Human Rights (UNHR) and in Europe through the European Convention on Human Rights (ECHR).[88] Data protection in itself is a separate fundamental right in Europe.[89]

In Europe, actual data protection has been offered through the General Data Protection Regulation (GDPR) since 2016, when it replaced the Data Protection Directive, with which it shares many similarities.[90] The main differences are as follows. A European *regulation*, unlike a *directive*, does not have to be translated into separate laws in each member state of the European Union. This means there will be fewer differences across member states, making it easier for companies to comply with data protection laws across Europe. The GDPR puts a stronger focus on self-enforcement of the law by organizations that process personal data. Many of them have to appoint a data protection officer (DPO), and they all have to put more effort into demonstrating compliance with the law. Also, requirements for obtaining consent are more strict. Data subject rights have been strengthened and now include a right to data portability. Moreover, the GDPR explicitly asks for privacy by design and default. And finally, the main reason that organizations suddenly started caring about privacy is that the GDPR imposes significant fines on those organizations that violate the law. In the most flagrant cases, fines could be as high as 4 percent of the total worldwide annual turnover, or 20 million euro, whichever is higher.[91]

The GDPR applies to any *processing* of *personal data* by automated means. We already discussed what the GDPR considers to be personal data in chapter 1. The GDPR distinguishes

(data) subjects, whose personal data is processed;

(data) controllers, which are responsible for the processing of the personal data of these subjects because they determine the purposes and the means for doing so; and

(data) processors, which process personal data on behalf of a controller.

The central idea of the GDPR is common sense, really: data controllers should act responsibly when processing personal data they are entrusted with. *Acting responsibly* essentially boils down to the following guiding principles laid down by the GDPR. Data should always be processed for a clearly specified *purpose*, in a *lawful*, fair, and transparent manner. The amount of personal data processed should be *limited* to what is actually necessary for the stated purpose and should always be *accurate* and up to date. Data should *not be kept longer than necessary* and should be adequately *secured* while under the care of the data controller.

A common misconception is that the GDPR makes many types of processing personal data illegal. In fact, an often-heard excuse is that something cannot be done "because of privacy rules." But there are actually a lot of grounds that legally allow one to process personal data under the GDPR. There are two grounds for processing personal data most commonly used by companies and organizations. The first is when they wish to pursue a legitimate interest (the legitimacy and the interest need to be substantiated). The second is when it is necessary for the execution of a contract (e.g., when an online store needs your address to deliver your order). Other grounds are informed consent (which applies to online services like Facebook, Google, and the like), when a legal obligation exists (like those imposed by anti-money laundering laws), if it is necessary to protect some vital interest (like offering emergency medical treatment), or to perform a public task.

Transparency is also a fundamental pillar supporting data protection. The GDPR requires data controllers to inform data subjects about the processing of personal data in a concise, transparent, intelligible, and easily accessible form, using clear and plain language. Moreover, data subjects have certain rights. They can ask the data controller a detailed overview of all the data it processes about them. They can ask the data to be rectified or erased.[92] And they can ask the data processor to restrict the processing of their personal data in certain cases, including the right to object to automated decision-making or to being profiled.

The GDPR was specifically designed to remove obstacles to the flow of personal data, recognizing that in our digital age both governments and businesses increasingly rely on the processing of personal data for their primary processes. Critics therefore point out that data protection laws in fact legitimize privacy infringements instead of preventing them.[93] Instead of downright prohibiting the processing of personal data, data protection allows such processing to take place under certain circumstances. Particularly worrying in this regard is the fact that the GDPR specifically allows such processing to take place when a legal obligation exists, introducing a loophole by which governments can simply create such a legal obligation to render the GDPR more or less null and void. This goes back to the difference between the privacy as confidentiality and privacy as control paradigms, as we discussed in chapter 1.

2.8 USING TECHNOLOGY TO PROTECT PRIVACY

The level of privacy protection the law can offer is limited, however. First, there is the problem of territorial scope: many offenders are simply not bound by laws in other countries (although the GDPR has tried to extend its scope beyond the confines of the European Union itself). Even if these companies are trespassing upon the law, trying to get them to court or to get them to comply is hard. Additional protection is necessary. We therefore believe that technology is not only part of the problem, but also an essential part of the solution.

This chapter has exposed the (technical) causes of our current lack of privacy. The remainder of this book is dedicated to show how this can be countered, by debunking a couple of persistent myths. The central message of this book is the following: The architecture of a system, the way it is designed, has a fundamental impact on whether it respects and protects our privacy or not. As a consequence, if you take protecting privacy seriously, you need to address this in the architecture of the system. This is called *privacy by design*.

Privacy by design is a engineering approach popularized by Ann Cavoukian in the 1990s, when she was the privacy commissioner of Ontario, Canada.[94] The essential idea is that privacy should be considered first as a design requirement from the very beginning and then throughout the lifecycle of a system. This is necessary for two reasons. Early design decisions (what data to collect and for which purpose) have a strong privacy impact that cannot easily be changed later on in the design process. Moreover, by considering privacy together with all other requirements from the outset, designers will be forced to think of how to meet all other requirements in a privacy-friendly way. If that turns out to be impossible (and we will see throughout this book that this is less often the case than you might think), an honest conversation about balancing all different needs will have to be had, wherein privacy is considered equal (instead of subsidiary) to all other requirements.

Privacy by design thinking does not apply just to the design of technical systems themselves. The processes in which they will be embedded and the organizations in which they will be deployed also have a strong impact on the overall privacy friendliness of the system. It is therefore crucial also to critically assess these processes and organizations and (re)design or (re)structure them using a privacy by design approach to improve the overall level of privacy that will be attained.

This book makes privacy by design concrete and shows, through its many examples, how it can be applied in practice to create truly privacy-respecting systems. Privacy by design is essential—because relying on the law, the market, or simply the good intentions of people is not enough.

Chapter 8 describes privacy by design in detail, explaining a particular methodology to make it more concrete. For now, a simple example will help to illustrate the power of the privacy by design approach.[95]

Suppose you are the manager of a popular restaurant. At peak hours, people may have to wait to be seated. Whenever a group of people enters the restaurant and there is no table available straight away, you write down a name, the size of the group, and the time the people entered your restaurant on the waiting list for today. As soon as a suitable table becomes available, you call the name on the top of the list (and mark this entry as seated, noting the time you offered the group a table). At the end of the day, you store the waiting list in a drawer for later analysis. This will allow you to determine when exactly the peak hours are, what the average waiting time is, and whether this depends on the season, or the day of the week. Also, you might be interested to learn how these figures change over the years and whether there is any correlation with, say, the staff you employed during those periods. If you do keep a waiting list like this, you process personal information: you record the names of people visiting your restaurant, and you keep these records for later analysis.

But there is another way to keep a waiting list, a way that does not process any personal data at all and allows you to perform the exact same analysis as the waiting list that records names. In fact, the idea is trivial: keep a numbered waiting list. Instead of recording a name for a group that enters the restaurant, you enter the size of the group (and the time of arrival) in the next available entry on the waiting list, and you ask the group to remember the number of this entry. When a suitable table becomes available, you call the number of the next group waiting to be served (and mark this entry as seated and record the time the group was offered a table). At the end of the day, you again store the waiting list for later analysis.

In this case, you do not process any personal data at all. All you record is the size of the group, the time the group entered the restaurant, and the time the group was seated. All this data is anonymous.[96] And all this data allows you to answer the same questions that the names-based waiting list allowed you to answer—except, of course, questions pertaining to the visits of particular groups of people, which you really have no business asking to begin with.

This simple restaurant waiting list system (that in principle could also be used for advance reservation by phone) shows the importance of a separate subsidiarity test. Whereas it may certainly be deemed proportional to maintain a reservation list using people's names, the subsidiarity principle rules out this approach on the basis of the existence of a more privacy-friendly approach (recording only sequence numbers and no personal data at all). In fact, the power of privacy by design mainly rests on this subsidiarity principle: as soon as a more privacy-friendly approach has proven to work in practice to achieve a certain purpose, other, more privacy-invasive approaches no longer pass the subsidiarity test. Barring excessive implementation costs, a very strict interpretation of Article 25 of the GDPR on privacy by design and default would render the more privacy-invasive approach unlawful.

2.9 BUSTED: WE CAN AND SHOULD RESIST

Confronted with the consequences of the technological innovations of their age, Warren and Brandeis did not just "get over it." As lawyers, they knew that the law always needs to be adjusted to keep the protection of the individual on par when challenged by political, social, and economic developments or by new inventions and business methods.[97]

We have seen that throughout history, technological developments have had an impact on our privacy and have shaped how we define and think about privacy as a result. The invention of the computer was the start of a digital revolution that took our world by storm and changed our lives profoundly. Now that half of the world population is connected to the internet and many carry a smartphone with them day and night, we are all surveilled, profiled, and nudged twenty-four hours a day and have become increasingly transparent, predictable, and hence digitally predestined. We indeed have little privacy, but like Warren and Brandeis, we do not need to sit idle at the sideline and get over it.

It's time we claim our own seat at the table. We can, and indeed we should, start to resist.

More and more people are growing concerned. Stronger legal protection of privacy has now been enacted in Europe, with other continents following suit. But legal protection is simply not enough.

Just as technology can be used to erode our privacy, it can be used to protect our privacy as well. Through a process called *privacy by design*, privacy requirements are taken seriously from the very start of the development of a new technology, system, or service. This ensures that privacy requirements are treated on equal footing with all other system and business requirements. This is not hard, although it sometimes involves making tough choices. But often it's possible to reconcile seemingly conflicting requirements. Perhaps it requires some effort, some thinking, or some creativity. But most of all, it requires awareness of the mere possibility of resolving the conflict.

Technology never develops in a vacuum but is developed by people for a certain purpose. If that purpose is not to our liking, we need to take technological developments into our own hands. We need to ensure that technology no longer trespasses upon our privacy but instead develop technology that respects and even protects our privacy. The rest of this book is devoted to explaining how this can be achieved.

3

I'VE GOT NOTHING TO HIDE

Nothing is more pervasive than the "I've got nothing to hide" myth. It comes in many different guises, like, "If you've got nothing to hide, then what do you have to fear?" Even stronger variants of the myth simply paint a distorted image of privacy as the shelter of evil. More nuanced versions are perhaps more compelling, claiming that giving up a small amount of privacy for a significant national security gain is a fair exchange in a civilized society. The underlying reasoning is that national security can be upheld and terrorism can be countered if a selected number of vetted government officials, or perhaps just some data-crunching government computers, get access to a tiny fraction of our private life. What could possibly be the harm in that? Wouldn't that be a fair price to pay to assure homeland security?[1] Or to improve public health or prevent fraud (as other, milder interpretations of the myth argue)?

A common response to the nothing-to-hide argument is to list things that people do want to hide and have every reason to hide. But such a response actually falls into the trap that this argument cleverly sets up: it subscribes to the frame that privacy is about hiding bad things. As Daniel Solove puts it: "The problem, in short, is not with finding an answer to the question: 'If you've got nothing to hide, then what do you have to fear?' The problem is in the very question itself."[2]

So what, then, is the problem with the question itself?[3]

3.1 YOU DO HAVE SOMETHING TO HIDE

First of all, hiding is natural. It's part of being human. It makes us human, even. We all hide our bodies, our thoughts, to one extent or another. Without the possibility to hide our thoughts and feelings, the whole idea of having an identity separate from someone else would fall apart. There is no *I*, no *self*, without privacy, without privileged access to one's thoughts and feelings.[4] What goes on in your mind is private by default. And it is up to you, either consciously or unconsciously, to decide what you share with others. One's person, the *I*, is a permanent manifestation of privacy. One could almost argue that hiding is the default human condition and sharing is the choice (instead of the other way around). Some, like Søren Kierkegaard, even believe that no one can really completely know everything about himself.[5] In other words, the myth is a philosophical contradiction: it's impossible *not* to hide something.

Being fully transparent in your thoughts would make your life simply impossible. There is no freedom of thought if all your thoughts are out there in the open for everyone to read as soon as they pop up in your head. Imagine that you have a decent job but that every time you are contemplating to apply for a job elsewhere your boss immediately reads this in your mind. He might decide to fire you and hire a more enthusiastic, dedicated employee instead. Every once in a while, people have doubts about their relationships with their friends or partner. This is entirely normal. But imagine the sense of insecurity you would experience if you were immediately aware of even the slightest doubt felt by your significant other. And all this is not even considering the more inappropriate, uncomfortable, or simply obnoxious thoughts that may occasionally pop up in your head (whether you like it or not).

This establishes another reason that having privacy is an inalienable part of being human: it is a necessary condition to establish and build social relationships. Sure, many of us have Googled or Facebooked dates before actually meeting them in real life. But now imagine knowing everything, and I mean really everything, about your first date as soon as you see him or her. Imagine he or she knowing the same about you. There would be no questions left to ask. There would be no answers to surprise. Without the possibility to hide—or rather, the possibility to decide what to share and what not—social relationships become meaningless. If there is no difference in how you are perceived at home, at work, or in the sports field, then in essence all your relationships with others are the same. This denies the social reality that not only you are different in different social contexts (you behave differently among your friends, at a party, than at work), but your thoughts, beliefs, and behaviors actually change over time. There are many *yous*, both in place and over time.

Apart from these objections against the myth from the social perspective, which focus on legitimizing the act of hiding itself, one can also argue against the myth from a normative or legal perspective. This perspective shifts the focus from the act of hiding itself to the question of what should or should not be hidden. From this perspective, the fundamental problem with the argument is that it assumes that there is never a problem sharing data, irrespective of the data that is shared. The myth assumes that data is either harmless (so indeed, why would you fear?) or incriminating (in which case, "you did something you shouldn't have done in the first place").[6] In other words, saying "I've got nothing to hide" really means "I'm never doing anything wrong." But this is clearly false.

First, it assumes that it's always easy to distinguish what is right or what is wrong. But this very much depends on context and interpretation. Do you mean legally wrong, for example? If so, in which country, under which jurisdiction? For women, driving a car was until very recently illegal in Saudi Arabia. Being gay or selling drugs still is a capital sin in certain countries. Or do you instead mean morally wrong, or simply inappropriate? Then is visiting a topless bar wrong? Your wife may think so. Is wearing lipstick wrong? Your husband may think so. Evading taxes? Smoking pot? It may cost you your job or even your chance to become president.

Nobody ever does nothing wrong. We all trespass upon the law occasionally—like speeding, for example. Or jaywalking. Or forgetting to pay for something. In fact, laws and regulations are so complex that in all likelihood you've done something illegal sometime in your life without even knowing it. And even if you didn't do anything wrong, information about what you did can be misconstrued or misrepresented to make it look like you did. Illustrative is the following quote, attributed to

Cardinal Richelieu: "Show me six lines written by the most honest man in the world, and I will find enough therein to hang him."[7]

Moreover, what is wrong changes over time, both in a moral and a legal sense. Manners change. What is considered appropriate behavior changes. For example, the sexual revolution completely changed attitudes toward sexuality and relationships. Believe it or not, pedophilia was accepted in ancient Greece and openly discussed in the Netherlands in in the 1970s and 1980s.[8] What is normal and legal now may be unlawful in the future.

Finally, each individual piece of information about you may seem insignificant and harmless enough, but all these little pieces of information may be combined into one telling profile of you that can be used to classify you, judge you, and possibly predict you.[9] It may be used to put you on a watch list or a no-fly list, or cause your file to be forwarded to some other agency for further investigation. It's impossible to tell whether this happens and which small breadcrumbs of information are used when it happens. And this doesn't even consider the risks of misinterpretation or misrepresentation that may get you in all kinds of trouble (reminiscent of Josef K.'s tribulations in *The Trial*).[10]

This brings us to the lack of transparency combined with the unbalanced power relationships between citizens and governments (which is the frame of this myth). You don't know which information about you is used to make decisions about you, nor do you know who is making these decisions about you. Subscribing to the nothing-to-hide argument at least assumes you know what the personal data you are willingly giving access to will be used for: homeland security, countering terrorism, criminal investigations, fraud prevention, and so on. Once the data are collected, or the means to collect the data are in place, there is a real risk of *function creep*: the risk that the data are going to be used for other purposes because it is easy to do so and serves a worthy purpose. This is especially a concern in countries with a less stable political climate, where there is very little guarantee that in, say, a decade from now, there still will be a trustworthy government in power. An unsavory example from the Second World War comes from my home country, where the Dutch Registry of Births, Deaths, and Marriages registered the religion of all Dutch citizens. This register was used by the Germans during the occupation to quickly identify and locate Jewish people for deportation.[11]

Pitting privacy against security, as one of the more challenging interpretations of the myth does, can be countered somewhat superficially with a kind of rhetorical trick. The argument is that privacy is a form of personal security: you need to keep certain information, like your PIN or your account password, private to prevent your bank account being drained or someone taking control of your email account. At a slightly more fundamental level, shielding and protecting certain personal information is necessary to prevent forms of *identity fraud* (in which criminals use their knowledge of certain personal details to pretend to be you and thus to apply for credit, buy phone SIM cards, and so on, in your name).

But perhaps the most fundamental weakness of this myth is its apparent strength. Its main rhetorical power is derived from the assumption that privacy is an individual right, while security is valuable for society as a whole: Who would dare to maintain the egotistical position that his or her information deserves to be protected against the greater societal good of increased homeland security or radically dropping levels of fraud? But this frame is wrong, and the assumption is flawed: privacy is equally a societal value (as we already argued in chapter 2). The problem with a selected a number of vetted government officials, or perhaps just some data-crunching government computers, getting access to a tiny fraction of our private life is that it axes this societal value of privacy. If we always run the risk of being surveilled, we lose the safe spaces in which we can always speak our minds.

Having established that hiding something is entirely human and natural, the question is how to hide data in an effective manner. It is important to note that hiding something actually entails two separate, and mostly independent, concerns. The first concern deals with concealing the mere existence of data. For example, some people may engage in a contract but do not want anybody else to even know the mere fact that any kind of contract among them exists. We will address this concern in depth in chapter 4. The second concern is preventing unauthorized access to the data itself. In terms of the previous example, it isn't necessary to keep it a secret that such a contract exists, but the terms of the contract—the contents of the contract itself—should remain confidential.

In the remainder of this chapter, we introduce two structurally different approaches to keeping data confidential. We first present encryption as the main technique to keep data truly confidential whenever data is stored or exchanged. In the second part of this chapter, we then turn our attention to databases containing personal data and consider approaches (like statistical disclosure control and differential privacy) to restrict access to the data in the database while still allowing useful aggregate conclusions to be inferred from this data.

3.2 ENCRYPTION: KEEPING DATA CONFIDENTIAL

Informally speaking, *encryption* can be understood as a form of communication in a secret language that only the correspondents know.[12] It is as if two people—let's call them Alice and Bob—have agreed on a secret dictionary, using that dictionary to translate English words in the message (in cryptography, called the *plaintext*) into their corresponding *ciphertext* words in the imaginary secret language (and back when decrypting the message).[13]

Cryptography has a rich and intriguing history, of which David Kahn's *The Codebreakers* provides a thrilling account.[14] The Roman dictator and military commander Julius Caesar, for example, is known to have used a form of encryption to secure communications with his generals. Caesar's *cipher*, as it is called, replaced each individual letter in a message with the third letter following that letter in the Latin alphabet. In other words, the letter *A* would be replaced with the letter *D*, the letter *B* with the letter *E*, and so on. The plaintext message "Attack at dawn" would thus become the corresponding ciphertext "Dwwdfn dw gdzq."[15]

Ahead, we will explain what cryptography is and what you can do with it in practice. If you want to know more about cryptography, Simon Singh's *The Code Book* is an excellent introduction to the topic for the layperson.[16] There are more technical books explaining the mathematical background and implementation details as well.[17]

Two fundamentally different forms of cryptography exist: symmetric (secret key) cryptography and asymmetric (public key) cryptography. We will discuss them both in turn.

3.2.1 SYMMETRIC (SECRET KEY) ENCRYPTION

Caesar's cipher is an example of what we call *symmetric encryption* or *secret key* encryption. The sender and the recipient agree on a secret key beforehand, which allows them to encrypt and decrypt the messages they exchange with each other. In the case of Caesar's cipher, the secret is the value by which to shift each letter in the message up or down the alphabet. This secret key must be remembered by heart or stored securely by both parties to the communication.[18]

Admittedly, Caesar's cipher is insecure: there are only twenty-three different letters in classic Latin, so the number of possible shifts (and hence the possible number of different secret keys) was only twenty-two. It would have been trivial to try each of these twenty-two possibilities on an encrypted message to see if it would lead to a meaningful decryption. Luckily for Caesar, most of his enemies were illiterate.

Using a real dictionary, not substituting just letter by letter, but instead replacing full words in the plaintext with arbitrary words for the ciphertext, is much more secure. As there is basically an infinite amount of different possible dictionaries, a word in the ciphertext could mean just about anything. Again, the code book can be viewed as the secret key in a symmetric encryption scheme that both the sender and recipient use to encrypt and decrypt each other's messages. Clearly this key must be kept secret, but any code book that offers a reasonable amount of security is too large to be remembered by heart. Modern symmetric key cryptography therefore employs shorter keys (typically 128–256 bits long) that encrypt and decrypt a message in blocks of similar size (i.e., roughly thirty-two to sixty-four letters each) using a complex mathematical function. One could say that each of the possible keys selects a particular dictionary that replaces sixty-four-letter words in the plaintext with random-looking sixty-four-letter words in the ciphertext (and back). The first modern symmetric key cipher was the Data Encryption Standard (DES), released in 1972, which had a key of only fifty-six bits.[19] This was replaced by the Advanced Encryption Standard (AES) in 2001, which has 128- or 256-bit keys.[20]

Because in symmetric key cryptography the *encryption key* and the *decryption key* are the same, you need a different secret key for each and every person you want to securely communicate with to ensure that one person cannot read the messages you exchanged with another person. If Alice, Bob, and Charlie all use the same symmetric key to encrypt their messages, Charlie can read the private messages that Alice sends to Bob. This creates a *key management problem*: if Alice has, say, thirty different friends she wishes to communicate securely with, she needs to securely store thirty different secret keys. As the number of people she wishes to communicate with grows, this quickly becomes unwieldy.

More fundamentally, symmetric key cryptography suffers from the *key distribution problem* that occurs when Alice and Bob have not agreed beforehand on a symmetric key to use: How can Alice tell Bob which secret key to use to encrypt messages to her if the communication medium available to her is public and insecure? Sending the key over that medium is impossible because there is a risk that an eavesdropper will listen in and therefore learn the key as well. The only way to agree on a key is to physically meet in private, which is often impractical.

As you can see, symmetric, secret key cryptography has its problems. Is there perhaps another way to secure communications that does not suffer from these problems?

3.2.2 ASYMMETRIC (PUBLIC KEY) ENCRYPTION

Suppose Elizabeth Bennet, protagonist of Jane Austen's novel *Pride and Prejudice*, wanted to keep her communication with Mr. Darcy confidential.[21] Mail was delivered by horse and/or carriage at the time, so she could (at a cost, for sure) use a small chest instead of a sealed envelope to send him a message. Sealed envelopes can be opened and closed surreptitiously; not so with a properly locked chest. The question that then remains is how to lock the chest such that only Mr. Darcy can open it. The answer to this question is surprisingly easy, provided Mr. Darcy had given Elizabeth an open padlock at an earlier occasion while keeping the padlock key to himself. Given this open padlock, and a sufficiently sturdy chest, Elizabeth could write a letter, put it in the chest, lock it with the padlock, and send it back to Mr. Darcy. Given that only Mr. Darcy has a copy of the padlock key, he is the only person able to open the chest, and hence the only person able to read the message from Elizabeth. Provided the chest and padlock are strong enough, nobody else would be able to open the chest to recover her message. (Of course, anybody could prevent Darcy from receiving the message by throwing the chest away. But the message itself would remain confidential nevertheless.)

Asymmetric encryption, more commonly called *public key encryption*, protects the confidentiality of messages in very much the same way as chests and padlocks could have protected Elizabeth and Mr. Darcy's messages back in the early nineteenth century. Recall that symmetric encryption uses a *single* secret key shared by the sender and the intended recipient of the message. Instead, asymmetric encryption always uses a *pair* of two different (but cognate) keys: a *private key* and a corresponding *public key*. The public key is used to encrypt a message (and thus corresponds to the chest and open padlock that Elizabeth uses in our example). The private key is used to decrypt the message (and thus corresponds to the padlock key that Mr. Darcy keeps to himself).

The magic (and beauty) of public key cryptography is that even though the public and private key belong together as a pair, knowing the public does not allow anyone to compute or reconstruct the corresponding private key. This means it is safe to make your public key public (hence its name) and publish it on your website or to put it in an online directory of public keys. Once someone knows your public key—either because you gave it to her earlier or because she found your key on your website or in an online public key directory—she can securely send you messages by encrypting them with that public key. You, as the sole owner of the private key, are the only person able to decrypt and read these messages. All that is needed is the appropriate software, which, given a plaintext message and a public key, encrypts the message to produce a random-looking ciphertext. Given such a ciphertext and the corresponding private key, that same software can decrypt the ciphertext to recover the original plaintext message.

Public key cryptography partially solves the key distribution problem that plagues symmetric key cryptography: the public encryption key is allowed, even supposed, to be public, so there is no problem at all if an eavesdropper learns it. There is a snag, however: when you receive a key, you somehow have to tell reliably who it actually belongs to (i.e., who it is that actually knows the corresponding private key). When Elizabeth and Mr. Darcy exchange keys in person, this is guaranteed. But when Mr. Darcy receives a key from someone claiming to be Elizabeth, he'd better make sure it is not George Wickham trying to impersonate her. Should Mr. Darcy accept this key, it would allow George (knowing the private key for the public key that Mr. Darcy thinks belongs to Elizabeth) to read all Mr. Darcy's messages to Elizabeth.

Note that in public key cryptography, every correspondent has his or her own pair of private and public keys. This means that in order to exchange messages back and forth, *two pairs* of keys, so *four* keys in total, are in use: Elizabeth needs Mr. Darcy's public key to send him messages securely (which he decrypts with his private key), but Mr. Darcy needs Elizabeth's public key to send his responses securely back to her (which she then decrypts with her own private key). This is different from symmetric key cryptography, in which both parties use the same single symmetric secret key to encrypt and decrypt their messages to each other.

This means that public key cryptography also solves the key management problem that afflicts symmetric key cryptography, as we described previously. Using asymmetric, public key cryptography, you would need to know the public keys of all your friends, but because these keys are public, there is no need to store them securely. There is only one key that you ever need to keep secure in this case, and that is your own private key.

3.3 APPLICATIONS OF ENCRYPTION

Today, both symmetric key and public key cryptography are in widespread use, to protect both transmitted data (data in transit) as well as stored data (data at rest). They are used to set up virtual private networks (VPNs) and to secure the web, creating secure connections between your browser and the websites you visit. Popular messaging services like WhatsApp and iMessage use these methods to secure the messages you send through them (calling it end-to-end encryption). Moreover, data stored in external storage (hard disks or solid-state drives) are protected using a process called *disk encryption*—for example, via BitLocker on Microsoft Windows or FileVault on macOS.

Beyond confidentiality, many of these applications also require assurance of *authenticity*—that is, guarantees about the identity of the person or website you are communicating with. For this, *digital signatures* are used, which can be implemented using public key cryptography as well. We return to this topic in much more detail in chapter 5.

3.3.1 VIRTUAL PRIVATE NETWORKS

Virtual private networks serve two purposes (see figure 3.1): to shield your IP address and to secure the first part of your connection with the internet.

To use a VPN, you typically need a subscription from a VPN provider and need to install its software (called the *VPN client*) on your computer. Modern smartphones and tablets often have the necessary software preinstalled, so then it is simply a matter of enabling it in the settings. The software encrypts all your network traffic, redirecting it to the dedicated VPN server of the provider. This VPN server in turn decrypts all this traffic before forwarding it to the intended recipient. Responses from these recipients back to you also go through the VPN server, which encrypts them before forwarding them back to your computer. One way to view such a setup is to imagine a tunnel between your computer and the VPN server, which shields all traffic (the cars in the tunnel) from external observations. This includes, for example, your own ISP or the public

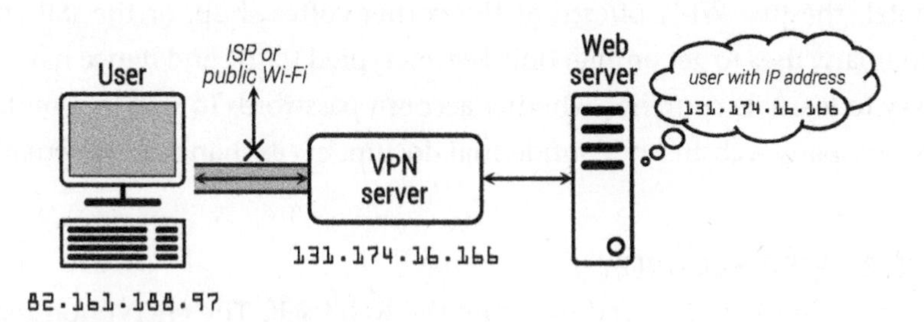

3.1 A virtual private network.

Wi-Fi you are connected to. After leaving the tunnel, the cars become visible again, and each go their separate ways. To return to you, they have to drive through the tunnel again in the opposite direction. Another way to think of it is as if your computer is connected directly, with some kind of virtual network cable, with the VPN server.

Let's say you are using a VPN and visiting a website. From the perspective of the website, it appears as if the VPN server is requesting the pages to display, which somewhat protects your privacy.[22] The web server sees the IP address of the VPN server, not your own IP address. This is because the VPN server decrypts your traffic and then forwards it to the web server *using its own IP address*. This is necessary to ensure that responses (e.g., the contents of the page to display) are sent to the VPN server so that it can forward them back to you encrypted.

On the other hand, using a VPN does not prevent browser fingerprinting or tracking through cookies. Moreover, the VPN server gets to see all websites you visit and is thus able to compile a very complete profile of your browsing habits. This means you have to select a VPN provider you can trust. Some care is warranted as not all VPN providers are equally trustworthy.[23]

Companies use VPNs to enable their employees to access the internal company network (sometimes called the *intranet*) securely. This relies on the fact that a VPN encrypts all network traffic from your computer to the VPN server by default. By setting up a VPN server within the company network, and by requiring employees to use this VPN server for work-related internet, this essentially connects all computers of all employees to your intranet over an impenetrable virtual network cable. Any nodes on the path from the computer of the employee to the VPN server within your intranet (whether this is the ISP at home, the Wi-Fi network at the hotel, the free Wi-Fi offered at the corner coffee shop, or the ISP your company uses to get online) only see encrypted traffic and hence have no way to learn its contents, whether account passwords to sign in remotely to company websites or confidential documents exchanged over email.

3.3.2 WEB SECURITY

Cryptography is also used to secure the web itself. The encryption technology used for this is embedded in a protocol called *Transport Layer*

Security (TLS).[24] The TLS protocol describes the steps necessary to establish a secure connection between your browser and the website you want to visit. Whether you can connect securely to a website is decided by the website itself (because it needs to support the necessary protocol steps); all browsers support it by default. Websites that support TLS make their pages available through hyperlinks that start with *https:* instead of *http:*, where the extra *s* stands for *secure*. And whether a connection with a particular website is indeed secure is indicated in your browser with a padlock icon next to the hyperlink in the address bar.

Often websites deploying this technology are called *secure websites*, but this a bit of a misnomer really; the sites may or may not be secure at all. All that is guaranteed is that your *communications* with such sites are encrypted (and that the site itself is authentic; that is, you are guaranteed to be talking to the right website).

To be as concrete as possible, suppose you want to visit a certain page securely and therefore enter the following URL: https://en.wikipedia.org/wiki/HIV/AIDS. Roughly speaking, such a secure connection is set up as follows. The https://en.wikipedia.org part instructs your browser to try to establish a secure, encrypted TLS connection with the server called en.wikipedia.org. The web server responds with its public key (and the browser has a way to validate that it indeed belongs to the domain en.wikipedia.org, but we will not go into this here).[25] Once the secure connection between your browser and the web server is set up in this way, your browser sends the request for the particular page (wiki/HIV/AIDS) and receives the contents of the page back. Both are encrypted.

This means that TLS not only prevents eavesdroppers from learning the *contents* of the web page you are visiting, but also prevents them from learning the specific page you are visiting. Also, if the page asks you to enter a password, that is encrypted as well. If you are visiting a medical site to obtain information about a disease you're suffering from, the pages you are visiting might reveal whether you're pregnant, recovering from pneumonia, or suffering from AIDS (as in the earlier example). But if you had visited https://aidsinfo.nih.gov/understanding-hiv-aids/fact-sheets/19/45/hiv-aids--the-basics instead, this protection would not have mattered much because the domain name itself already reveals what information you are after. What encryption does *not* prevent the eavesdropper from learning is the fact that you are visiting a medical site to begin with or that you're connecting to a dating site. This type of metadata is much harder to protect (a topic we return to in chapter 4).

Both TLS and VPN encrypt communications, so you might be a little confused and not really see any difference between the two. But there are subtle yet significant differences. A VPN encrypts *all* internet communication to and from your device—your browsing, your email, your downloads, and so on—but *only* between your device and the VPN server. Beyond the VPN server, outside the tunnel, all traffic proceeds as normal. TLS encrypts *only* specific connections, typically between your device and the web server, but does so *all* the way. Moreover, TLS guarantees authenticity of the websites you visit (using digital signatures, as we'll explain in chapter 5).[26]

3.3.3 WHATSAPP AND FRIENDS: END-TO-END ENCRYPTION

Encryption is also used by many messaging apps, like Signal, WhatsApp, iMessage, and the like.[27] Because messaging is asynchronous (Bob may be offline or Bob's phone may be switched off when Alice sends him a message), messages are sent through the server of the messaging application (Signal's, Facebook's, or Apple's, respectively) and stored there until Bob's phone is ready to retrieve them. If only the communication between Alice's phone and Facebook's server, and Bob's phone and Facebook's server, was encrypted, then the messages themselves would remain unencrypted, in plaintext, while waiting on the messaging server. This is clearly undesirable as it would allow the messaging service provider (Facebook in this case) to scan the messages and use their content to target WhatsApp users. (In fact, this was for a long time how WhatsApp worked, until 2017, but Facebook claims it never abused its potential access to these plaintext messages.) This is why it's important for messaging services to use *end-to-end encryption*. In the most basic form of end-to-end encryption, Alice's phone encrypts every message to Bob using Bob's public key before sending it to the messaging server. The messaging server stores these encrypted messages, the ciphertexts, until Bob collect them. Bob's phone is the only place where the corresponding private key (necessary to decrypt the message) is known. This allows Bob's phone—only Bob's phone, and most certainly not the messaging server—to decrypt the messages.

People often have several devices with which they communicate. A copy of WhatsApp or iMessage may be running on both Bob's smartphone and Bob's desktop computer. Each of these devices have their own pairs of keys: the private key stored securely on the device and the public key necessary to encrypt the message. If Alice wants to start a new end-to-end encrypted conversation, she needs to know all public keys of all devices of all people that are part of that conversation. End-to-end encrypted messaging services like WhatsApp or iMessage therefore maintain a central directory of public keys to use to encrypt messages for the associated user. This repository contains for each user (often identified by their mobile phone number) all public keys for each device known to belong to that user. Every time Alice sends a message, the necessary keys of the recipients are requested from this central repository, maintained by Facebook (in the case of WhatsApp) or Apple (in the case of iMessage). The full setup is depicted in figure 3.2.

In practice, end-to-end encryption is slightly more complicated and uses (like TLS and VPNs) a short-lived *session key* that is jointly generated

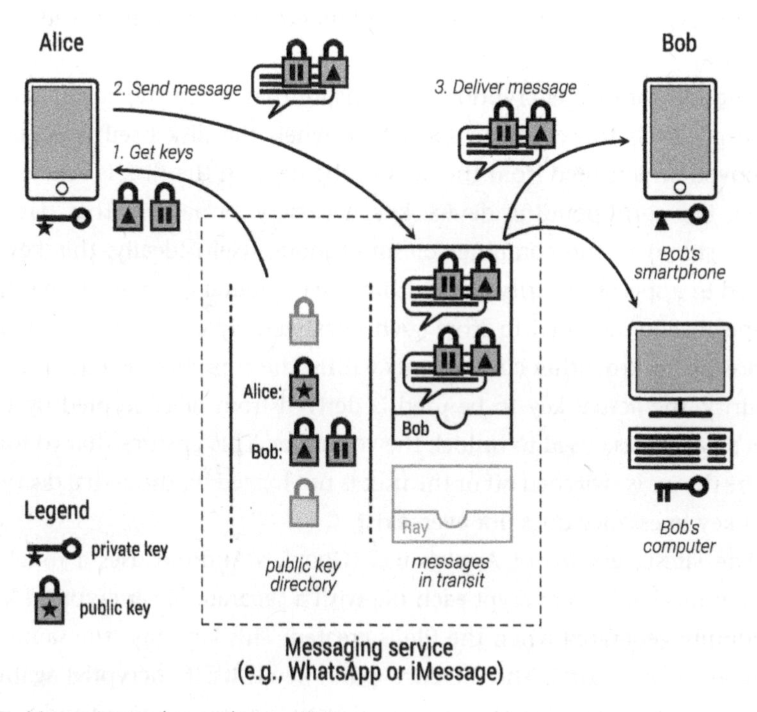

3.2 Messaging end-to-end encryption.

by all parties engaged in the conversation and used for the duration of that conversation (called the *session*) only. This means an adversary has no chance to recover such keys (and hence the contents of the session) after the session has finished. In other words, if a device is compromised, all previously exchanged messages are still secure (a property that is confusingly called *perfect forward secrecy*).

3.3.4 LOCAL STORAGE ENCRYPTION

Encryption can also be used to protect stored data.

Disk encryption is used to encrypt all data on a single storage device, whether this is an external hard disk (attached to a computer) or permanent storage inside the device (solid-state memory in a smartphone). Some disk drives encrypt everything they store automatically on the fly. Unfortunately, most of these are insecure because they implement the encryption badly.[28] It is therefore best to rely on software-based methods of disk encryption in which the device itself manages the keys to use and encrypts or decrypts the information as it is written to or read from the disk.

The idea of disk encryption is to ensure that when the computer or smartphone is turned off or locked, or when the disk itself is actually removed or detached from the device, the data on the disk is encrypted while the corresponding device key necessary to decrypt that data is safely stored in the computer or smartphone itself. Ideally, this key is stored in a special security chip within the computer or smartphone that is specifically designed to store such keys securely and is not normally accessible by any other components within the computer. For additional security, the actual key to be used is derived from or encrypted by the user's passphrase used to unlock the computer. This ensures that so long as the device is switched off or the user is not logged in, the actual decryption key in essence does not even exist.

The latest versions of Apple's iOS (Google's Android uses a roughly similar mechanism) encrypt each file with a separate file encryption key randomly generated when the file is created. This key stays the same so long as the file exists. The file encryption key is itself encrypted against the long-term device key that is derived from the user password and some

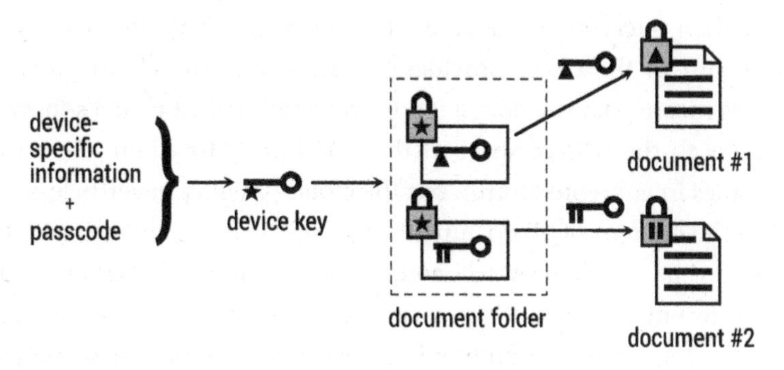

3.3 Smartphone storage encryption.

device-specific information.[29] Whenever you lock the device, this device key is discarded. This renders all file encryption keys immediately inaccessible (as they can no longer be decrypted), and therefore all files themselves become inaccessible as well. This device key is recreated again from the device-specific information and the passcode you enter when you unlock the device.[30] A more intuitive explanation of how this all works is perhaps this: Every file is encrypted with a key. This is intuitively similar to putting the file in a chest and locking the chest. The key for this chest is stored in another chest, which is stored alongside the file. This second chest can only be unlocked with the device key. The device key is stored in the main device chest, which can only be unlocked with the device passcode. To access a file, you first need to unlock the main device chest with the passcode to obtain the device key, then you need to find the file key chest, unlock it with the device key you just obtained, and then unlock the chest containing the file with the key found inside the file key chest. Without the passcode, all you have is locked chests (see figure 3.3).

3.3.5 CLOUD STORAGE ENCRYPTION

Data stored in the *cloud* also must be protected through encryption, but here we see two different approaches.

The first, dominant approach is to send a document to be stored in the cloud to the cloud server over a secure connection (e.g., using TLS as described earlier). So the document is encrypted while it is sent over the network, but it is immediately decrypted and available in plaintext for the cloud provider as soon as it receives the document. The cloud provider then encrypts the document again with a key associated with your account at the cloud provider but known to the cloud provider itself. This means that the document is protected against casual snoopers with access to the storage space of the cloud provider (there the document resides in encrypted form), but the cloud provider nevertheless has access to the content of all documents it stores. This means such a cloud provider can be subpoenaed to hand over the contents of certain documents to law enforcement. It also means that you still have access to your data in the cloud if your computer is stolen or crashes, provided you still remember your cloud service username and password. This is a usability boon (but then again, also a great point of attack for hackers, as celebrity iCloud users found out in 2014).[31]

The other, less prominent, but much more secure approach is to use the end-to-end encryption idea discussed earlier in the context of messaging apps for storing documents in the cloud as well. It works as follows. Your device encrypts the documents using a key only it knows and sends the encrypted documents to the cloud provider, while securely storing the key itself locally. Because the cloud provider does not know the key, it cannot decrypt the document. Not for its own purposes, nor when instructed by law enforcement. Your device can later retrieve the encrypted document and decrypt it locally with the key it stored earlier. The drawback of this approach is that if your computer is stolen or crashes beyond repair, the decryption key will be irretrievably lost and hence you will have lost access to your documents. They are still there, stored in the cloud, but encrypted against a key that is lost forever. Such a horrible scenario could be mitigated by using a master key (from which all other keys are derived) and asking users to make a backup copy of that key on a USB stick, or even to print the key as a QR code on paper.

Stored data is, by necessity, encrypted with a long-term encryption key: you may want to be able to access the data years after you stored it. Now each file or document may be encrypted by a different key, but in the end you will have a few master keys that allow you to (indirectly) decrypt all your documents, whether they were created minutes ago or years ago. In other words, there is no such thing as perfect forward secrecy for stored data (which is relevant for our discussion on law enforcement access to data in chapter 7).

3.4 PRIVACY-FRIENDLY DATABASES

The previous sections showed that encryption is an effective method to keep data confidential, both for data in transit and for data stored locally on disks or remotely in the cloud. This makes encryption a strong privacy-enhancing technology. It is of limited use, however, when the group of people that needs access to the data is not known beforehand or changes over time, or when the data needs to be analyzed or processed remotely. Standard encryption techniques require one to choose the keys (and hence to determine the people that must have access) the moment the data is encrypted. Moreover, such encryption techniques completely mangle the plaintext data into a ciphertext that defies any remote processing or analysis.

This is a problem when trying to improve the privacy properties of the quintessential information technology system: the *database*. In fact, one could argue that databases by their very nature are antithetical to the mere concept of privacy as they are designed to retain, relate, index, and make accessible (potentially personal) data at a large scale. Companies maintain databases to keep track of inventories, orders, and so on. Governments maintain databases with information about their citizens. Statistical offices maintain databases about all kinds of activities related to all kinds of subjects and publish the statistics derived from them. And Google maintains a gigantic database of a gazillion web pages that we can search for combinations of keywords.

As we will see in the remainder of this chapter, there are certainly methods to design databases in a much more privacy-friendly way than is currently the case. It's just that the role of encryption here is limited.

At its core, a database is a table (an Excel sheet, if you wish). For each entry (a row in the table, also called a *record*), it stores the values for the attributes listed at the top of the columns. Your address book in your phone is a database, listing for every person you know their first and last name and phone number. As described here, it would have three columns and as many rows as you know people that you bothered to enter in the address book. Typically, a database is *indexed* to speed up the search for common words or queries.

In the most general case, one can distinguish the maintainer of the database, who has direct access to all data stored in it and who also maintains its index, and the users of the database, who are granted access by the maintainer and can remotely *query* those parts of the database that they have access to in order to obtain the information they require. Such queries can be a request for all information stored in specific records in the database, but typically such queries ask the database to return aggregate information—for example, in response to questions like "What is the average income of all residents of Wedding (a borough in Berlin)?" or "How many people with Alzheimer's disease have a history of using a particular medicine, or following a particular diet?"

But what exactly *is* the privacy problem with databases? Actually, one can distinguish three different types of problems, depending a bit on the specific setup.

The prime privacy issue in databases that store personal information is of course that the database maintainer has unfettered access to all data in the database. This is especially an issue for databases that contain sensitive information, like medical records. We will see below that there are ways to protect against this threat, but these will in turn limit the type of queries one can submit to the database.

The second privacy issue is that the submitted query may be privacy sensitive itself. The database of web pages that Google maintains is not privacy sensitive directly (after all, all these pages are publicly accessible anyway).[32] But Googling for certain information may reveal my interests (when I search for recipes or a manual) or disclose my medical condition (when I search for particular symptoms). This is not unlike the situation in a company I used to work for, where employees were forbidden to query the patent database for fear of leaking information about the research that was done at the company or the patents that might be applied for.

Finally, the third privacy issue is that the answers to submitted database queries or the published statistics derived from such databases may contain too much or too detailed personal information, allowing users that do not have direct access to the database to reconstruct most of its contents anyway. The issues here are subtle because even seemingly innocuous queries like "How many people voted Republican in this district?" can be very privacy sensitive if the voting district is so small that it only contains one person eligible to vote.[33]

3.4.1 SOME BASIC APPROACHES

There are a few basic things one can do to mitigate some of the privacy issues associated with the use of databases.

To prevent the database maintainer from having access to the data stored in the database, one can encrypt the database (against a key unknown to the maintainer, of course). This would also prevent the maintainer from building an index, however, which would make it impossible to perform even the simplest form of queries, like keyword searches. Luckily, there are ways to search encrypted databases.[34] Unfortunately, a perfect system for *protected database search* does not exist. Database design must balance security (measured by how much information is still leaked to the database maintainer), functionality (indicating what types of queries are supported), and performance (expressed as the amount of computational and network resources necessary to make the system usable in practice).[35] Many different schemes exist, some of which are offered as commercial products.

To give you a feel for the type of balancing act required, consider supporting simple equality queries, in which a user can query the database for all records with an attribute or field that exactly matches the query. This can be done when each field of each record is encrypted independently using a deterministic form of encryption that ensures that the encryption of the same plaintext always returns the same ciphertext. Encrypting the query with the same key returns a ciphertext that can directly be matched with all encrypted fields in all records in the database, a process that can be sped up considerably by creating an index of all encrypted fields. Normally, one would never encrypt each field of a record independently but would instead encrypt full records (or perhaps even full database tables). Moreover, deterministic encryption is normally avoided at all cost because it leaks a lot of information: in the case of the database considered here, it would leak which records contain the same values for a field (even though the values themselves would not be leaked).

3.4.2 POLYMORPHIC ENCRYPTION

Recall that one of the problems of using encryption in a database context is that the group of people that need access to the data in the database may be unknown at the time the data is entered.

Applying encryption to data requires one to specify the encryption keys to use the moment the data is encrypted—that is, the moment the data is entered into the database. This typically fixes the keys that can later decrypt the encrypted data in the database, and hence fixes the set of users that have access to it once and for all.

Polymorphic encryption is a recently developed encryption mechanism that overcomes this limitation and allows the key that can be used to decrypt a ciphertext to be changed after the plaintext data has been encrypted against a particular encryption key (see figure 3.4). The key that must used to encrypt still has to be picked the moment the data is encrypted. But the key that can be used to decrypt the data can be chosen at a later time.[36] A *transcriptor* can be instructed to transform an arbitrary ciphertext, in a sense re-encrypting it to another key without ever seeing the actual plaintext, so that after the transformation it can be decrypted using a different key. Which key is determined by a separate agent called the *access manager*, which authorizes requests for access to the ciphertext. Clearly this access manager is a powerful agent in the system as it decides who gets access to what. The same holds for the transcriptor. This means extra care needs to be taken to ensure that these agents do not abuse their power. This can be prevented by spreading their functionality over separate components under the control of separate entities.

An example will help clarify the mechanism and explain why it is useful. Suppose you have a smart watch that you use to monitor your health. The data stream it generates is too large to store locally on the watch, so you decide to store it remotely in the cloud. Because this health data is very sensitive, you wish to encrypt it to deny the cloud provider access. Suppose you use a key that only provides you access once the data is encrypted. Using a traditional encryption scheme, the only way to provide others access is if you first decrypt the data and then show or send it to them. If in a medical emergency you yourself cannot initiate the decryption, the people in the emergency room (ER) have no access to that potentially valuable health data your watch recorded earlier and stored in the cloud. If you use a polymorphic encryption scheme, however, the access manager can authorize a request for access to your encrypted data and instruct the transcriptor to re-encrypt the encrypted data to the key of the ER so that the people there *can* decrypt your smart watch data.[37]

Daily use of smart watch:

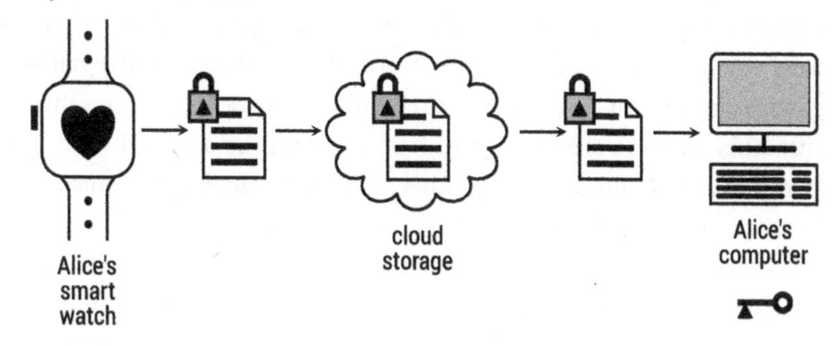

In case of emergency:

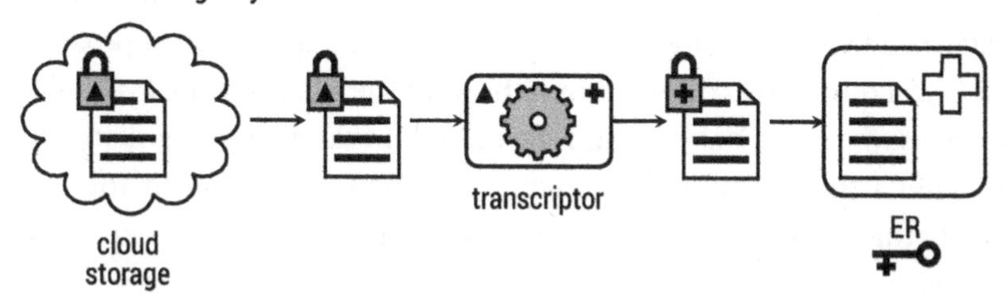

3.4 Polymorphic encryption.

3.4.3 STATISTICAL DISCLOSURE CONTROL

We now turn our attention to solving the third database privacy problem outlined earlier—namely, the risk that answers to queries or releasing aggregate statistics reveals too much and too detailed personal information contained in the underlying database.

There is an inherent trade-off between the detail with which you answer queries and trying to keep the database contents confidential. The same holds for publishing something you learn from a survey and maintaining the privacy of the participants. In fact, the database reconstruction theorem says that publishing too many statistics too accurately from a confidential database exposes the entire database with near certainty.[38]

Statistical disclosure control aims to address this trade-off and limit the privacy risks associated with publishing aggregate *statistics* derived from large data sets, as is typically done by statistical offices all over the world.[39] In the last few decades, this risk has increased as the amount of detail in the raw data sets underlying these statistics has increased tremendously.

For efficiency reasons, it makes sense to provide access to this microdata to other researchers—those at universities, for example. But unfettered access would have a negative impact on privacy. Moreover, the statistics derived from this microdata have also become more detailed, as traditional constraints on their size have vanished. They can be accessed from anywhere and can be combined with other data sources at will and more or less automatically. These forces increase the privacy risk.

Two approaches to implement statistical disclosure control can be distinguished: perturbative and nonperturbative methods. *Perturbative methods* change the data before releasing it by introducing an element of error. *Nonperturbative methods* reduce the amount of information that is published by suppressing parts of it or aggregating it. In both approaches, statistical disclosure control aims to balance the risk associated with publishing some statistical data and the utility of that data, recognizing that in general the utility increases with the amount of detail in the data, which therefore also increases the privacy risk when personal data is involved.

Statistical offices typically publish two types of statistics: magnitude tables and frequency tables (see table 3.1). *Magnitude tables* list the sum of all responses to a particular question for all respondents that belong to a certain category. For example, a magnitude table might report on total income of respondents, grouped by age. *Frequency tables* report on the number of respondents that satisfy a certain criterion from all respondents that belong to a certain category. For example, a frequency table might list the number of unemployed people, grouped per region.

Magnitude tables create a privacy risk if the number of respondents that belong to one particular category is small and sufficient prior knowledge is available about most of the contributions to the total by the other respondents. Subtracting this information from the total may reveal the contribution of another respondent. Also, if the distribution of possible contribution is skewed and publicly known—for example, when it is known that one person in a particular age group makes an insane amount of money compared to the other respondents—then the total income reported for that age group is a pretty good estimator for the income of that particular person. *Safety rules* aim to detect such situations and stipulate that statistics that do not match the safety rules should not be

Table 3.1 A magnitude table and a frequency table

Age	Aggregate income (B$)	County	Number unemployed (× 10.000)
30+	7,719	Devon	9
21–30	851	Cornwall	30
11–20	23	Somerset	11
0–10	0	Dorset	7

published. A nonperturbative approach that can be applied is to change the category to ensure it contains more respondents.

Frequency tables also create a privacy risk if the number of respondents for a particular category that match a particular criterion is small. For example, consider a frequency table grouping people by age groups and region and listing the number of unemployed people for each such group. Now assume that a second table is published, derived from the same underlying data set, that counts how many of the people who are unemployed are single (over the same age groups and regions). If one person in Devon between age thirty and thirty-five turns out to be unemployed according to the first table, and one unemployed person in Devon between thirty and thirty-five is single according to the second table, knowing a thirty-two-year-old unemployed person in Tavistock allows one to infer his or her relationship status. A perturbative approach to counter such attribute disclosure risks is by rounding each entry in the frequency table to a set of predetermined values.

The problem with many statistical disclosure control techniques is that they solely treat privacy as a property of the output alone, without considering the process by which the output was generated from the underlying database.[40] This is where differential privacy comes in.

3.4.4 DIFFERENTIAL PRIVACY

The following example serves to introduce the idea behind differential privacy.

Until not so long ago, many people were unwilling to disclose they were gay because being gay still carried many stigmata and had real-life (discriminatory) consequences. This made it hard to estimate the fraction of people that were gay using standard questionnaires. Social scientists came up with the following clever trick to bypass this reluctance to disclose sexual orientation.

To determine the fraction of gay people, they would ask respondents to answer whether they were gay, but only after they had privately flipped a coin in a separate room (so the interviewer would not learn the outcome of the coin toss). The coin toss influenced the answer in the following way. If the coin would come up heads, respondents were asked to honestly tell whether they were gay or not. However, if the coin came up tails, they were required to always say they were gay (whether this was actually true or not). This trick provided the respondents a form of plausible deniability: the fact that they told the interviewer they were gay could just as easily be caused by the fact their particular coin flip happened to return tails.[41]

Although this trick guarantees individual responses could not be used to tag someone as gay, the full list of responses still allowed the scientists to estimate the fraction of gay people in the sample (provided the sample size was large enough). The idea was that in a sufficiently large sample, roughly half of the people would see tails when flipping the coin. In other words, in the full list of responses, you would expect to see at least 50 percent of the respondents claiming they were gay (forced by flipping tails). Therefore, if 58 percent of people reported themselves to be gay, then 8 percent represents the fraction of people honestly saying they were gay *in the group of people flipping heads*. Because only half of the people (roughly) flipped heads, the actual fraction of gay people in the full sample is reasonably approximated by two times 8 percent—that is, 16 percent.

The above example is a nice illustration of how adding random noise (in this case, the outcome of the random coin flip) can help to offer true privacy guarantees to participants of a survey. The same idea of adding noise in a controlled fashion essentially underlies the principle of *differential privacy* as well.[42] Compared to statistical disclosure control (which works essentially by removing or changing combinations of variables that are otherwise likely to lead to identification in a particular database), differential privacy aims to *guarantee* privacy in a probabilistic sense, including *unforeseen* privacy risks.[43] Moreover, differential privacy can be applied both in noninteractive settings (as for statistical disclosure control, in which aggregate statistics are published) and in interactive settings in which users issue queries to a database over time.[44]

Differential privacy aims to guarantee that answering a query or releasing some aggregate statistics over a database does not reveal information that is specific to a particular person. The way differential privacy guarantees this is by requiring that whatever could be learned about a particular person from a released statistic could essentially also have been learned if the same statistic had been derived without including this person's data. In other words, it does not really matter whether the database does or does not contain the data of this particular person: the released statistic (or the answer to the query) would essentially be the same.

Notice the use of the word *essential* here: with every statistic that is released over a certain database, a small amount of information about each person present in the database is released. This *privacy loss* is unavoidable. What differential privacy does is to strictly quantify and limit this privacy loss for each released statistic, at the expense of a decreased *accuracy* of the released statistic. Moreover, with every release of an additional statistic over the same database, the privacy loss increases. The beauty of the differential privacy paradigm is that individual privacy losses add up: the privacy loss of releasing two separate statistics equals the sum of the privacy losses associated with each of the individual statistics. This means that it makes sense to define a *privacy budget* that limits the accumulated privacy losses incurred by releasing statistics or answering queries over a particular database over time. Once the budget is reached, further use of the database must be refrained from.

Clearly differential privacy poses restrictions on the way the aggregate statistic, or the answer to the query, is computed. The general strategy is to perturb the data in the database with some random noise and compute a statistic based on this perturbed data that approximates the real statistic over the real data within a certain known margin of error. This not only provides a bound on the privacy loss, but also guarantees a certain level of accuracy that is necessary to make such statistics useful in practice.[45]

There is a problem with differential privacy, though: there is no apparent strategy or agreed upon standard to set an appropriate privacy loss level. In fact, it is unclear what a particular level of privacy loss means in practice. Does a privacy loss of 0.5 provide enough privacy? How much more privacy does a privacy loss of 0.25 offer? Critics of the approach argue that to offer a meaningful level of privacy protection, the privacy loss must be set so low that the resulting accuracy of the published statistic becomes too low to be of any use. Or alternatively, any practically useful application of differential privacy actually offers very little privacy protection.[46]

3.5 BUSTED: IT'S NORMAL, NECESSARY, AND POSSIBLE TO HIDE THINGS

The "I've got nothing to hide" argument is a very common and persistent privacy myth. Its persuasiveness derives from the fact we typically associate secrecy with wanting to cover up bad, illegal behavior. In other words, if you want some privacy, this must be because you did something you shouldn't have done in the first place (to paraphrase former Google CEO Eric Schmidt).

Moreover, it takes advantage of the fact that we often feel a moral obligation to the society we live in. As we argued in the beginning of this chapter, the myth is fundamentally flawed, however. First, privacy is not the same as secrecy. There are many things that people are happy to share with *some* others but not with *everybody* else. This reluctance to be fully transparent has nothing to do with doing or wishing something illegal. Moreover, as already discussed in chapter 2, privacy is not only an individual right but also a necessity in a democratic society, and in that sense a *societal right*.

This chapter explored the possibilities for hiding. It explained how encryption works and showed how you can use encryption to keep personal data confidential when sending messages or when storing documents. End-to-end encryption in particular is useful in this respect as it guarantees that the provider of the communication service or the storage space cannot get access to your content (although it still leaves the metadata exposed; we will turn to this problem in the next chapter).

Encryption is of limited use in database contexts, where access to the data needs to be offered to different people over time, where the data need to be combined with data from other sources, and where the data need to be processed and analyzed to derive new insights. In such cases, there is little else we can do than trust the database maintainer with all these sensitive data (and strictly enforce the GDPR) and focus on technical measures that restrict user access to these data instead (although approaches like polymorphic encryption do appear to be promising). Methods like statistical disclosure control (which essentially remove or change certain combinations of data in the output that would otherwise likely lead to privacy violations) and differential privacy (which offers a stronger guarantee even against unforeseen privacy risks) are useful in such contexts but have their limitations as well.

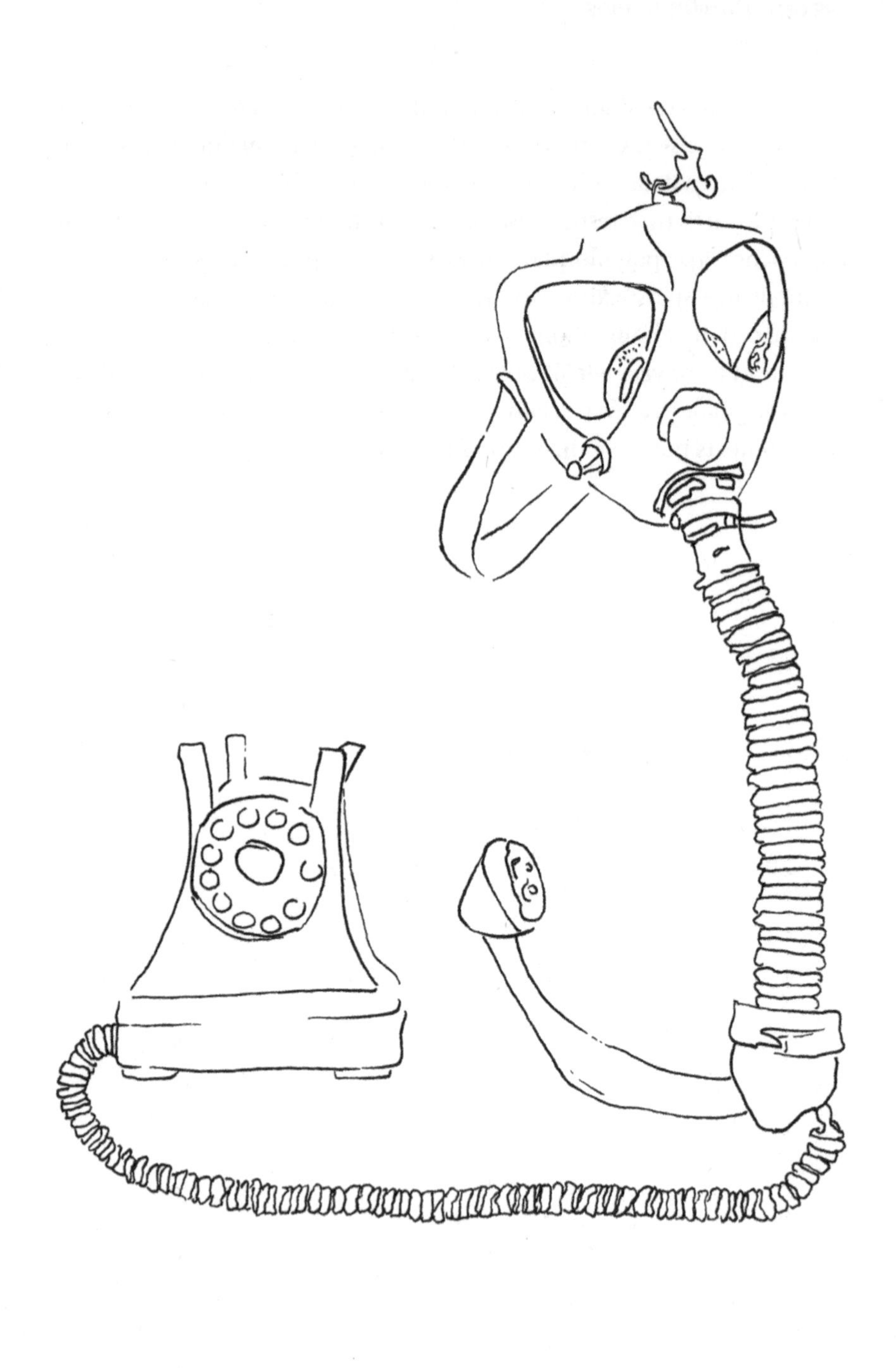

4

IT'S MERELY METADATA

Somehow there never appears to be a dull moment in the life of antivirus software pioneer, suspected drug dealer, and 2020 US presidential candidate John McAfee. In 2012, while living in Belize, he became a fugitive after the local police wanted to question him in connection with the murder of his neighbor. Having nothing to do with the murder, but fearing bad treatment from the authorities, he fled the country. He stayed below the radar for several weeks but met two journalists from VICE during that period, who bragged about this by posting a picture online.

The picture was shot with a smartphone. By default, smartphones add some additional data to the image being shot, including the location where the picture was taken. You do not see these data when looking at the picture itself, but most image-processing software will be able to retrieve them later on: the data allow, for example, the smartphone to organize the pictures you took into separate albums based on the locations in which they were taken. Unfortunately for John McAfee, the journalists forgot to remove these data before posting the picture online. This allowed the Belizean authorities to determine John's location (a resort in Guatemala just across the border), leading to his arrest just a few days later.[1]

4.1 WHAT IS METADATA?

A classical distinction in telecommunication is the distinction between data and *metadata* (sometimes called *communications data*). This distinction separates the actual content of a communication (e.g., a letter, a phone conversation) from the technical data necessary to establish the connection between the sender and the recipient (e.g., an address, a phone number, or the location of the base station to which your mobile phone is currently connected).

Traditionally, the content of the conversation itself is considered private and is offered strong legal protection: in many European countries, secrecy of correspondence is even enshrined in the constitution.

Because of its inherent technical nature, metadata has been considered less privacy invasive than the actual data being transmitted. A phone number by itself does not tell you very much: only by connecting it to other pieces of information (a name, other calls made) does a picture of the caller potentially emerge. This distinction is also made in the law. Data retention laws, for example, demanded that telecommunication services log all metadata instead of the actual conversation itself. This in an apparent attempt to strike a balance between privacy rights and law enforcement needs, and of course to limit the enormous overhead involved in fully storing all actual phone conversations. This perception has drastically changed in the last few decades, however.

These days, metadata collection is no longer restricted to mere telecommunication systems. All the digital devices and services we use potentially generate, collect, or process metadata (as we saw in chapter 2). And this starts to blur the distinction between "normal" data and metadata. To better understand what metadata really are in our current digital world, the taxonomy of personal data of the World Economic Forum is useful.[2] This taxonomy classifies personal data based on their origin, distinguishing individually provided or *volunteered* data (data you reveal knowingly and explicitly), *observed* data (data you reveal implicitly through your use of a service or device), and *derived* data (information derived from those other two types of data). When we talk about metadata, we are really talking about this second class of observed data.

Volunteered data, for example, are the pictures you post online, the text messages you send, or the information you enter in online registration forms. Observed data are the location data embedded in these pictures, the phone number you use to send the text messages, the web pages you visit, or the date and time you fill in the online form. Whereas most people are aware of the volunteered data they divulge and often think critically about whether to share that information or not, they are often totally unaware of the observed data that is collected alongside their interactions. People can hardly be blamed for this ignorance: the possibilities for this surreptitious information collection are simply staggering and beyond many people's wildest imagination. Finally, inferred data can be any useful conclusion, estimate, or belief that one can infer based on the volunteered and observed data—for example, regarding your sexual orientation, financial situation, religious beliefs, political inclinations, interests, hobbies, or whatever. For example, the status update you shared with your friends ("Had a crazy night out with my friends! OMG") is volunteered data; the fact you did so at three o'clock in the morning on your smartphone while walking home is observed data; and the fact that Facebook thinks you're gay (because of this and other metadata Facebook has about you, like your friendship connections) is derived data.

Note that the distinction between volunteered and observed data is made depending on the origin of the data, not based on the type of data itself. A phone number can be observed data or volunteered data, depending on the context: it's volunteered data if you enter it yourself in an online form, but will be considered observed data if it's collected automatically whenever you send a text message.

4.2 SOURCES OF METADATA

As we already briefly discussed in chapter 2, computers and networks radiate all kinds of information because of their leaky design, allowing for the routine collection and storage of huge amounts of metadata. In fact, a surprising amount of metadata is generated locally by the devices and applications you use and stored in documents and media files you work with, remotely collected by the online services you use, or observed by third parties that monitor the network. Let's consider these local, remote, and network metadata in a little more detail.

4.2.1 LOCAL, FIRST-PARTY METADATA

The operating system of a device logs all kinds of activity, ranging from its battery status to when the device was turned on or off, when it went online, to what networks it connected, whether a document was printed, and so on. Notably, for every document, the operating system records when you created, modified, or last opened it. Some operating systems even keep previous versions of any document by default as a kind of backup mechanism.[3] Monitoring the sensors in a smartphone allows applications to detect whether you sleep or walk or how often you use your phone.

A very creepy from of tracking involves the use of ultrasound by a company called SilverPush.[4] It allows specific ultrasound patterns (that are inaudible to the human ear) to be embedded within audiovisual content, like TV commercials. Apps on your smartphone that contain the SilverPush software library will continually listen and wait for these special ultrasound patterns to appear. As soon as this happens, the fact that you were watching or listening to this particular audiovisual content is registered on SilverPush's central servers and linked to your smartphone.

An older version of Digital Editions (Adobe's e-book management and reading software) sent information back to Adobe about the books you read, which pages of the book you actually read, and the time you spent reading.[5] Amazon uses the number of pages you read of a book on your Kindle to determine the amount of royalties to pay to the authors when you have a Kindle Unlimited account.[6]

Many applications keep a list of recently opened documents. Browsers keep a browsing history that records all the web pages you visited. Some applications remember the edit history of a document—all the changes you made to it—even when saving the document. This allows you to undo these changes at a later date. Unfortunately, it also allows others to recover things you deleted when you send them these documents without removing this metadata first. Microsoft Word was infamous for this feature, which allowed others to recover compromising texts or review comments that were deemed inappropriate and therefore deleted by the original author.[7] To avoid such errors, it's often advisable to save a document in a different format that does not maintain this kind of metadata, like PDF, before distributing it in public.

As we saw with the John McAffe gaffe, pictures you take with your smartphone or digital camera are automatically tagged with the location where they were taken, the time and date they were made, and even the aperture and shutter speed settings used to shoot the picture. Digital content (e-books, MP3s, or videos) you buy often has your identity secretly embedded in it as a digital watermark to dissuade you from sharing a copy with others. There are many, many more examples of local metadata we could give here, but you have the idea by now.

4.2.2 REMOTE, SECOND-PARTY METADATA

Online services also observe you while you are using them. Chapter 2 already described how cookies allow information about the web pages you visit to be collected by third parties like DoubleClick and Facebook. But there is much, much more service providers can do.

Facebook ran an experiment during the summer of 2012 to study self-censorship of its users. It collected information about status updates that a random group of five million users started to write out but did not actually post during the study period.[8] The Facebook researchers did not actually collect the partial messages typed (although they could easily have done so), instead only recording whether people that started writing a status update actually submitted it or not (and correlating that information with known properties of the target audience of the status update). Many websites embed special scripts in their web pages that monitor your mouse movements whenever you visit those pages. These websites literally watch you move the mouse while you are contemplating whether to click a link or button. This allows these websites to improve the design of the web page—for example, if mouse movement data suggests that certain links, buttons, or menu items on a web page are hard to find.[9]

4.2.3 NETWORK, THIRD-PARTY METADATA

Many third parties can also collect certain metadata, even though you are not directly or consciously interacting with them. Obviously, your internet service provider sees all your internet traffic. Even if the traffic is encrypted, your ISP is still able to determine which services (Google, Tinder, Facebook, etc.) you are using simply by looking at the IP addresses in your internet traffic. What your ISP is able to do, any router on the internet that processes some of the network traffic you generate while surfing the web can do as well. We have seen earlier that a device with Wi-Fi capabilities broadcasts the names of wireless networks it previously connected to. If you have Wi-Fi enabled, therefore, any access point in your vicinity could be programmed to capture that data to learn where you have been before.

Confusingly, devices not only have IP addresses but also *MAC addresses*. MAC addresses are used to distinguish different devices that are all connected to the same local area network (a Wi-Fi network, Bluetooth connection, or wired Ethernet network). Every device with a network connection (whether via Wi-Fi, via Bluetooth, or over a cable) has such a MAC address. These addresses are numbers that are (in principle) uniquely and permanently assigned to each and every networked device in the world.[10]

From a privacy perspective, MAC addresses are relevant because they uniquely identify a device (PC, laptop, smartphone, tablet, smart watch, etc.). Whenever your device wants to connect to a network, it sends signals containing its MAC address to discover potential networks it can connect to. Anybody with suitable radio equipment or anybody setting up a rogue Wi-Fi access point or Bluetooth receiver can receive these requests and the MAC addresses they contain. In other words, they can obtain a list of all MAC addresses of all devices in the immediate vicinity (up to one hundred meters outdoors under favorable conditions).[11] A number of such devices, strategically placed in a neighborhood, can trace your whereabouts in the area and can recognize when you return a few days later. This Wi-Fi or Bluetooth tracing is used in practice to track your own movements, across a shopping mall, airport, or whole town.

4.3 WHY IS METADATA SO SENSITIVE?

Metadata is much more sensitive than people used to think. Up until a few years ago, people may have shrugged, saying, "It's merely metadata." But many now have started to realize there are serious privacy consequences associated with the almost limitless possibilities of metadata collection.

Few people will worry that metadata gets people convicted of a crime, provided that the metadata is accurate and is not used to frame certain people.[12] But metadata is also putting journalists and whistleblowers at risk or denying refugees asylum across Europe.[13] Even worse, General Michael Hayden, former director of the NSA and the CIA, said during a debate in 2014: "We kill people based on metadata."[14] Metadata allows service providers to guess who your friends, colleagues, or loved ones are. In other words, it enables them to reconstruct your *social graph*. Facebook could use WhatsApp data about your contacts to suggest new people you may know on its social network.[15] This may explain how patients that were under treatment by the same psychiatrist were introduced to each other on Facebook.[16] It has also been suggested that Facebook uses location data for this.[17] This in turn would explain why people received suggestions to connect to someone they met at a bar last night or to connect to people they recently met at a gathering for suicidal teens.[18]

Metadata is also the source of most of the targeted advertising and profiling taking place online.

What makes metadata so privacy invasive and so harmful, perhaps even more harmful than the actual content of our conversations, the data we actually volunteer to share with others?

First, metadata like location data, shopping behavior, web-browsing patterns, and the like are more structured than "real" volunteered data like the emails we write, the texts we send, the pictures we share, and the conversations we have. In many cases, the meaning of this volunteered data is highly context dependent. Together with the unstructured nature of most of this data (except perhaps for the forms we fill in), this makes the effort required to distill the gist of such conversations prohibitively high. Because of their inherent structured nature, observed data, on the other hand, are much more easily analyzed and linked to other data. Metadata also require much less space to store compared to recorded phone conversations, for example.

Second, by definition, metadata is collected without you being aware that it happens. This means you have no control over what information is collected and how much of it is being collected. You have no way to review this data and are unable to tell if and when it is being used to classify you or make decisions about you. Another problem with such surreptitious collection of metadata is that people may refrain from doing things because they cannot tell whether metadata is collected or not. They may be afraid that if metadata are collected, their intentions may be misconstrued. It has been shown, for example, that people self-censor the things they search for.[19] During the 2020 COVID-19 pandemic, some people in China avoided traveling by metro as the risk was significant that the automatic contact-tracing system might flag them as potentially infected, which would require them to self-isolate for no apparent reason.

Last, but definitely not least, observed data is metadata, but should more aptly be called behavioral data: it typically reveals something about your behavior: what you do, where you are, what time you do it. For this reason, metadata could be considered even more privacy sensitive than the ordinary data it relates to. Behavior is a strong indicator of basic needs and desires. We are pretty good at concealing our real thoughts and feelings when we talk or write (over-the-top, happy, shiny Instagram posts are a dead giveaway), while we are pretty bad at suppressing certain behavior (facial expressions like looking angry or sad, giving in to impulses like eating chocolate when feeling down, breaking habits like smoking cigarettes, etc.). This makes our behavior much more revealing about our actual intentions and desires than what we say. As the saying goes: "Actions speak louder than words."[20] NSA General Counsel Stewart Baker summed it up quite nicely, saying, "Metadata absolutely tells you everything about somebody's life. If you have enough metadata, you don't really need content."[21]

4.4 QUICK FIXES

Given that metadata can be so sensitive, what can be done to prevent its collection? Later in this chapter, we will discuss two privacy-enhancing technologies (mix networking and onion routing) that have been developed to protect communication metadata and to allow users to communicate and surf the web anonymously. But there are relatively easy quick fixes that can already help significantly to prevent the collection of some other types of metadata, some of which you can apply yourself straight away. Others could easily be implemented by operating system vendors or device manufacturers instead. In fact, some have started doing so already.

The John McAfee story we started this chapter with highlighted that many documents contain possibly sensitive metadata, like location, edit history, and the like. Make it a habit to strip such metadata from your documents before uploading them to social networks or before sharing them with others over email or in the cloud. Sometimes this requires you to save documents in a different format, such as PDF instead of Microsoft Word's DOC. Instead of requiring users to remember this, it would of course be better if applications like Word or the camera app on your smartphone would not store such sensitive metadata by default and would only offer it as an option that users have to explicitly activate (preferably each time a document is saved for the first time or each time a picture has been taken).

The applications you use keep a record of the recent files you opened. Browsers keep a browsing history of the pages you recently visited. Again, make it a habit to clear these histories, or use private browsing mode (offered by certain browsers) to prevent your surfing behavior being added to the browsing history. Private browsing also typically blocks any of the cookies and scripts used to track you while surfing the web. Applications could likewise offer such a private mode so that the documents you open are not automatically added to the recently opened files list.

The sensors on your smartphone, and things like your pictures and contact list, are a valuable source of metadata. Be restrictive with respect to the permissions you give to the apps you install on your smartphone. If an app requires more permissions to install than you are willing to give it, or if some of the permissions it requests seem excessive given the functionality it is supposed to offer, think again. (Recall the example of the flashlight app cited in Chapter 2.) Operating system vendors or app store maintainers could do more to restrict access to sensors and identifying data on your phone (e.g., unique device identifiers or mobile phone subscription identifiers). They could also more carefully vet the apps they allow to be distributed.

Operating systems could be far more restrictive in what they log: Is there really a need for a mobile phone to locally log your recently visited locations, like Apple's iOS does?[22] In terms of networking, operating systems should stop broadcasting the names of Wi-Fi networks you recently visited. (You can often clear this list of known Wi-Fi networks yourself as well.) In fact, devices should stop emitting identifying information on their network interfaces all the time. They should only start to do so when connected to a network that you really intend to connect to (and therefore trust with that information). Devices should also not by default connect to networks with generic names like "Free Wi-Fi." Although you connected to such a network once in a location you trusted, this should not mean your device automatically connects to all networks around the world with the same name. Finally, MAC addresses, the unique hardware addresses associated with each type of network connection your device supports, should not be fixed but properly randomized.[23] This makes it next to impossible for Bluetooth and Wi-Fi tracking to track your movements via your smartphone.[24]

As people surfing the web are often tracked, browsers have gradually implemented measures to prevent this. Many offer the option to block certain types of cookies or to throw away cookies as soon as you quit your browser. Make sure you set the privacy-friendly preferences that make sense to you. As many people hardly ever quit their browsers or shut down their laptops or smartphones, it would make sense if browsers added an option to clear the cookie jar of all cookies older than a certain number of days. If your browser supports a private browsing mode, use it. There is an ongoing battle between online service providers—using JavaScript embedded in their web pages to track the users on their websites—and the browser vendors trying to block such use of scripts.

Finally, avoid using apps and services that are specifically designed to track you. Often, more privacy-friendly versions are available (although in some cases this may mean you either have to convince your friends to switch services as well or have a tough decision to make regarding the value of your privacy versus the value of your social life—which really is just a clear indication of the current lack of privacy we are offered online by default).

4.5 DEFINING PRIVACY IN TECHNICAL TERMS

We have so far managed to avoid the subject, but to discuss more thorough measures to prevent metadata collection, now the time has come to actually define what privacy is in more technical terms.

Personal information is information that relates to a natural person. One way to design a privacy-friendly system then is to process as little information that relates to natural persons as possible. This goal of personal data minimization (which applies to ordinary data as well as metadata, discussed earlier) can be achieved in two independent ways: by limiting the processing of the information itself or by making the data that is processed less personal by loosening the link between the information and the person to which it pertains.

This latter approach recognizes that the property *being personal* is less binary than perhaps lawyers would make us believe. Or rather, that perhaps the precision with which one can assign a particular personal property to a particular person does not always matter that much. For example, if it is known that among a group of ten particular people there are two that have an interest in cooking, but you don't know which two, it still might make business sense to target all ten persons with advertisements for, say, Ottolenghi's new cookbook. If one person out of a known group of five people is known to be HIV positive, an insurance company may choose to turn down the application for health insurance for all five of them. And if there are two suspects for a terrorist attack, but it isn't clear who is the actual perpetrator, a less scrupulous leader may decide to simply send both of them to prison (or eliminate them through a drone strike).

Crudely speaking, as the potential group of suspects becomes larger, the cost of targeting, disqualifying, punishing, or eliminating the actual suspects at some point becomes larger than the benefit. This is why some people have proposed to measure the level of privacy protection offered by a system by estimating the smallest size of such groups with a certain property that can be distinguished by the system. The official term for this measure of privacy is *k-anonymity*, applied initially in the context of databases.[25] A data set is *k*-anonymous if for every record in the data set there are at least *k* different persons known to be in this data set to which this particular record could belong. This set of people is called the *anonymity set* for this record, and in a sense it represents a cloud you hide in. A popular approach to anonymization of data sets is to make them *k*-anonymous by removing certain attributes from the data sets altogether or by making the values recorded for certain attributes less precise (e.g., instead of recording the exact age of a hospital patient, an age range such as "between twenty-five and thirty-five years old" is recorded instead). We discussed these mechanisms already in the previous chapter in the context of statistical disclosure control.

Note that applying *k*-anonymity is far from a bulletproof method of anonymizing data sets. A trivial example is a database of thousands of HIV patients. No matter how *k*-anonymous this database is, as soon as it is known you are in this database, it is known you are an HIV patient. Let's look at a less obvious example as well. Suppose a data set is anonymized in such a way that any combination of age and gender could correspond to at least ten people in the data set (making the data set 10-anonymous for that combination of attributes). But also suppose that for certain combinations of age and gender, another sensitive attribute has the same value for all records in the data set that correspond to that particular combination of age and gender. To be concrete, suppose the 10-anonymous data set happens to record for all men between twenty-five and thirty-five that they suffer from schizophrenia. Then, meeting a man aged thirty-two known to be in that data set allows one to conclude he is schizophrenic. This is not what you expect from a supposedly anonymous data set. To overcome this particular shortcoming, other privacy measures like *l*-diversity have been defined.[26] But in the end, proper anonymization is notoriously hard.[27]

To also make the privacy properties offered by *communication* systems more exact and to determine how well they prevent adversaries from using metadata to track users of such systems, concepts like *sender anonymity*, *recipient anonymity*, and *unlinkability* have been introduced.[28] All three are related to the concept of *k*-anonymity, but they acknowledge the differences between databases and communication systems. In communication systems, we distinguish senders of messages and recipients of messages. Moreover, the messages themselves are typically confidential (and therefore usually encrypted one way or another). The main thing we want to protect here is the social graph: who is communicating with whom or who is sending or receiving a particular message. Sometimes it may even be desirable to hide the mere fact that people (try to) communicate with each other, such as for whistleblowers, informants, or spies. In technical terms, this is called *unobservability*, and it's one of the hardest properties to achieve.

Loosely speaking, sender anonymity means that a sender of a particular message cannot be identified within the group of potential users of the communication system.[29] In other words, each of the potential users is equally likely to have sent the message. How large that potential group is depends on the power of the adversary and the particular way the system is designed. This *anonymity set* (observe the similarity here with the concept of *k*-anonymity) depends, for example, on whether the adversary can see at what times senders send messages and recipients receive messages. If this is the case, users known not to have sent a message at the time a particular message was received can be excluded. They are not in the anonymity set, which thus becomes smaller. *Recipient anonymity* is similarly defined as the property that a recipient of a particular message cannot be identified within the group of potential users of the communication system. On the internet, you have typically no sender and recipient anonymity as the IP addresses associated with each message are unique and often belong to a single sender and recipient. In other words, the anonymity set contains exactly one element in both cases. We see that adversarial access to metadata (like the time of sending or IP addresses) harms anonymity in this setting. The larger the anonymity set guaranteed by the design of the system (relative to the assumed power of the adversary), the better its privacy properties.

It's important to note that trying to maintain sender and recipient anonymity becomes harder as the adversary observes the system over a longer period of time. The more metadata the adversary collects, the more users it can exclude as potential members of the anonymity set. This becomes even easier when the adversary can use additional information or heuristics to further exclude users. For example, messages are hardly ever just sent as isolated events. People typically engage in conversations, responding to each other's messages more or less in real time.

This also shows that exactly quantifying sender and receiver anonymity is impossible.

Sender and receiver anonymity can both be seen as particular instances of a more generic privacy property called *unlinkability*. Two or more items are called *unlinkable* if whether these items are related or not cannot be distinguished. To be more precise, knowing the set of items, and knowing the set of all possible relationships among these items, it's impossible to determine the real relationships among them. For example, *receiver anonymity* means that for a known set of sent messages, which are known to have been received by a subset of possible recipients, the actual mapping of messages to recipients cannot be determined.

Unlinkability is not only an important property to have within communication systems. It also can be used to model privacy properties in other application areas as well, like databases (where one wants to break the link between data subjects and their records in the database), payments (where one wants to break the link between the buyer and the item being bought; see chapter 7), or attribute-based credentials (which we'll discuss in chapter 5). In fact, you could say that unlinkability lies at the core of privacy protection: by breaking the link between a data subject and his or her data, that data is no longer personal. Unlinkability underpins all anonymization techniques. The problem with metadata is that they make establishing this link so much easier.

4.6 MIXING: HIDING IN THE CROWD

Given that every internet packet contains IP addresses linking sender and recipient, you might wonder: Is there any hope of achieving any form of unlinkability on the internet? In fact, there is. We will show how mixing internet traffic of many internet users provides anonymity by essentially allowing one to hide in the crowd of others that use the internet at the same time.[30] Let's start by looking at a very basic email-forwarding service, called the Finnish remailer, which provides a basic form of recipient anonymity.

4.6.1 THE FINNISH REMAILER

Whistleblowers have every reason to stay anonymous. Yet if you are a journalist relying on a whistleblower as your source for an important story, you want to be able to ask for clarification or perhaps want to ask other questions. In other words, as a journalist, you not only want the whistleblower to be able to contact you, but you also want to be able to reach your whistleblower. How can you do that if the whistleblower wants to remain anonymous? The classical approach is to use a dead drop or dead letter box—that is, a previously agreed upon secret location (a hole in a tree, or under a seat in a church) where the journalist and whistleblower can leave their messages for each other. Even a traditional post office box would help the whistleblower to receive mail in a somewhat anonymous fashion: the journalist would have no idea who the whistleblower is unless she asks the post office or lurks outside the post office to see who opens the box.

One of the first email equivalents of such a post office box service was the anon.penet.fi system (which we'll call the *Finnish remailer service*) that Johan Helsingius, a Finnish internet entrepreneur, started running in 1993.[31] The idea behind this anonymous remailer system was simple. You could register an anonymous email alias (e.g., as123456@anon.penet.fi) at the service and specify to which real email address an email sent to that anonymous address should actually be forwarded to. This offered recipient anonymity. You could also send email from your anonymous email address, in which case any identifying information from your email was first stripped before being sent out. This also provided a basic form of sender anonymity. The Finnish remailer service ran on a small server physically located somewhere in Finland. This server stored the email address database that mapped anonymous email aliases to real email addresses. Incoming email sent to one of the registered anonymous email addresses would be received by this server and immediately and automatically be forwarded to the corresponding real email address stored in the email address database.

It's important to realize that when Helsingius started his remailer service, most people would either have a corporate, work-related, email address or a home email address associated with the ISP that provided their internet connectivity at home. Free email services like Hotmail, Gmail, and the like were not ubiquitous at the time.[32] This meant that given an email address, one could quickly determine the real identity of the owner of that address: simply look at the domain part of the email address (e.g., whitehouse.gov or xs4all.nl) to determine the company or the ISP that issued the email address, then ask it to look up the owner in its records.

The Finnish remailer service was based on a very simple idea that served its purpose at the time. It did have some very significant shortcomings, however. First, the content of the email was not protected: the remailer could read all email it processed. This also meant that a *passive adversary*, an entity eavesdropping on all the traffic sent and received by the remailer, could link incoming emails (sent to the anonymous address) to forwarded emails (sent to the corresponding real address). This adversary could, for example, be the company providing internet connectivity to the remailer service. More problematic was the fact that the whole setup relied on the secrecy of the mapping of anonymous address to real address databases, which was represented by a single database stored on a single server under the control of one single person. Too problematic, as it turned out.

In 1995, the Church of Scientology claimed that someone had used the Finnish remailer service to anonymously distribute materials over which the church claimed to hold the copyright. Scientology wanted to find the perpetrator and therefore asked Helsingius to reveal the real email address associated with the anonymous email address used for the copyright infringement. Helsingius refused but was later ordered by a judge to honor the request. As this ruling meant that he could no longer guarantee the anonymity of his users, he shut down the service in August 1996, only three years after this pioneering anonymous email service saw the light of day.

There is an important lesson to be learned from Helsingius's experience in setting up and later disbanding his remailer service: single points of failure should be avoided. It does not matter whether this single point of failure is a single server or database that can be subverted or seized, or whether this infrastructure itself is distributed but still under the control of a single person who can be tricked, coerced, or forced to cooperate and provide access.

4.6.2 A BETTER WAY TO HIDE IN THE CROWD

Over the years, several improvements to the original remailer design were proposed, all aimed at improving the privacy protection offered: by removing the reliance on a single database mapping anonymous to real email addresses and by restricting what a passive adversary could learn by observing the content, length, or even timing of incoming and outgoing emails.[33] This all culminated in the design of Mixminion.[34] The core idea is to use a mix network, a concept invented back in 1981 by David Chaum (about whom we will have more to say in chapter 7), which provides a strong form of sender anonymity.[35]

A *mix network* is an interconnected set of mixers (or mix nodes) that work together to offer an anonymous remailer service. The central idea of a mix network is to make several different servers responsible for forwarding an anonymous email to its real intended recipient. This by itself already removes the concern of relying on a single server (as the Finnish remailer did).

The sender of a message (randomly) determines the sequence of mix nodes a message will have to traverse before it reaches its intended recipient (see figure 4.1). We call this the *mixing path* for this message. For every message, a new random mixing path is chosen.[36] In essence, the message the recipient receives appears (from the recipient's point of view) to have been sent by the last mix node on this path, so the identity of the real sender is concealed. In other words, in its most basic form of operation, a mix network provides sender anonymity.

Each mix node receives the incoming messages one by one and collects them into a local mixing pool until it has received enough of them to guarantee a certain level of anonymity. It then sends out all messages in the pool as a single batch, each to the next mix network on its path. Observe how the principle of k-anonymity (discussed earlier) is applied here. Collecting messages in a pool and sending them out in batches

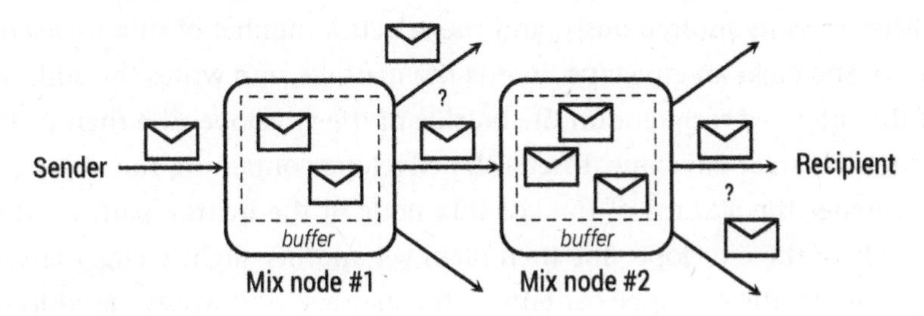

4.1 A mix network.

prevents timing attacks by a passive adversary that could otherwise link outgoing messages to incoming messages by looking at the time or order in which they are sent and received. The mix network should furthermore ensure that all incoming and outgoing messages are all the same length, by padding emails that are too short and splitting emails that are too long into several messages that each have the required length. As the individual path of each message through the network is selected at random by the original sender, messages leaving a particular mix node are not all sent to the same mix node for further forwarding. Instead, they are dispersed to be forwarded to a large number of other mix nodes. An adversary trying to trace a message through the network would quickly lose track because of the great many possible sources or destinations for a particular message. This dispersion makes traffic analysis hard.

So far, we have not discussed how a mix node knows to which next node a particular message needs to be forwarded. Care has to be taken to ensure that nobody, except the sender, knows the full path selected for a message. Otherwise, sender anonymity could easily be breached. The approach taken is to cleverly use encryption to reveal only the next node on the path, one by one. At the same time, encryption is also used to secure the content of the message to ensure that mix nodes cannot learn the contents of the messages they forward. Moreover, as mix nodes change the encryption of a message while forwarding it (as we will see in a minute), this prevents a passive adversary from linking incoming to outgoing messages by simply looking at their content: this content (or rather its encryption) is changed by the node mixing these messages.

In fact, this clever use of encryption can be visualized using paper mailing envelopes, where putting a message in an envelope corresponds to encrypting that message. Say that a sender has a message that she wishes to send anonymously, and she selects a number of mix nodes to do so. She picks an envelope, inserts the message, and writes the address of the intended recipient on the outside of the envelope. She then picks a slightly larger envelope, inserts the envelope containing the message, and writes the address of the last mix node of the mixing path on the outside of the envelope. She then picks yet another slightly larger envelope, inserts the envelope containing the message, and writes the address of the penultimate mix node on the path on the outside of this second envelope. She continues this process, inserting the current envelope in a slightly larger envelope and writing the address of the preceding mix node on the path on the outside of the envelope, until she has written the address of the first mix node on the path on the outermost envelope. She then posts this envelope. The envelope is delivered to the first mix node using the address written on the envelope. The mix node opens the envelope and stores the contents (another envelope) in its pool. Once enough envelopes are in the pool, the mix posts them all in a batch, so that each one is delivered to the mix node for which the address is written on the envelope. We see that the envelopes protect the content of the actual message from the prying eyes of eavesdroppers and mix nodes alike. Moreover, the envelopes guarantee that the nodes on the mixing path are indeed released one by one, ensuring that no one (except the sender) learns the full mixing path. In fact, a mix node only learns the address of the next mix node on the path.[37] It is this fact that offers a very strong privacy guarantee: as long as at least one of the mix nodes is honest (meaning it isn't under the control of an adversary that tries to break anonymity, does not keep records of past mixing operations, and cannot be ordered to monitor its activities), anonymity of the users of the mix network is guaranteed.

The system as we described it so far only makes the senders anonymous: the address of the recipient needs to be known. This is not what the Finnish remailer offered—namely, the possibility to send messages to anonymous recipients. Mix networks can offer *recipient anonymity* as well, through a concept called *anonymous return address*. The essential idea is that a recipient who wants to remain anonymous creates such an anonymous return address and distributes it to anyone who she thinks might want to send her a message. In particular, a sender using the mix network could include such an anonymous return address in the message to allow the recipient of the message to respond. The reply essentially encodes a path through the mix network toward the intended recipient, together with the first mix node on the network, which knows how to process the anonymous return address.

In this example, we only sketched the main idea of how mix networks work and how they help to keep our email communications anonymous. We left out many important details that, when omitted in practice, would leave such systems vulnerable to rather trivial attacks.[38] This serves as a warning that the devil really is in the details.

4.7 ONION ROUTING

Mix networks do a pretty good job of breaking the link between the person sending an email and the person receiving that email, even if relatively few people are using the mixing service. The main reason mix networks provide such strong unlinkability protection is the fact that each mix node stores incoming messages in the local mixing pool and keeps them there until enough messages have been received that it is safe to send them all out to the next mix node on the path. As a consequence, if very few people use the mix network, messages may be delayed for quite some time. And even if there are many users, the time it takes for a message to arrive at its destination (called the *latency* of the mix network) is still relatively high. This is not a problem for services like email. But high latency is definitely a problem when surfing the web, or when using messaging services like WhatsApp, via which people engage in more or less real-time conversations. So the question is how to offer unlinkability in a fast, low-latency manner that is suitable for interactive services like web browsing and instant messaging.

A quick and dirty solution to solve this problem is to use a virtual private network. Recall from our earlier discussions (see chapter 3) that a VPN hides the IP address of the user from the website. However, using a VPN allows the VPN provider to log all the websites you visit, giving it a complete profile of your full browsing activity. Moreover, like the Finnish remailer service, a VPN is a single point of failure. You need to trust the VPN server not to turn over such logs to website owners or law enforcement when they try to determine the visitors of a particular website.

A much better solution is Tor, the onion routing network.[39] Tor is a low-latency, anonymous network service that (conceptually, and very roughly speaking) improves on the idea of using a single VPN service to stay anonymous by cascading several randomly selected VPN servers in a row to ensure that none of them get to see the full picture, similar to what mix networks do for asynchronous email-like communication.[40]

Interestingly, Tor started as a research project within the US Naval Research Lab.[41] Currently, Tor is open source and is developed, maintained, and kept in actual operation by a large number of volunteers, steered by the nonprofit organization Tor Project. Anybody in the world can download the Tor Browser (a specially configured version of the Firefox browser) and subsequently surf the web anonymously using the Tor network. Users are strongly advised to use this Tor Browser to access the Tor network. Web servers on the other hand require no special configuration. In fact, they are typically unaware of the fact they are visited by users through the Tor network.[42] Tor is used by a very diverse group of users, ranging from journalists and activists to terrorists and drug traffickers to spooks and the police, each group having its own particular reasons to remain anonymous.

The Tor network itself consists of a collection of *onion routers*. These onion routers are computers of volunteers from all over the world that decided to allow their computers to be used as nodes on the Tor network. Anybody with a computer permanently connected to the internet and some bandwidth to spare can be a Tor volunteer.

Tor routes web traffic through these onion routers, using (as in mix networks) a random path of routers between the client and the server (see figure 4.2). Unlike mix nodes, however, onion routers do not keep a pool of messages but instead send out incoming traffic straight away. And unlike mix networks, which in principle route every new message over a fresh random path, Tor sets up a random *circuit* (Tor's term for a path between client and server) that is changed roughly every ten minutes. All your browsing traffic, for all the websites you visit, uses this circuit during this period of time. This minimizes delays while retaining a reasonable level of unlinkability. In fact, from the perspective of the snooping spooks of the NSA, "Tor stinks" (because the level of protection is apparently so good that they couldn't break it).[43]

Circuits in Tor typically consist of three onion routers: the *guard node*, the *relay node*, and the *exit node*, which are randomly selected by the client from a list of known onion routers. Tor splits up all traffic into fixed-length internet packets. Packets from the client enter the guard node and are forwarded to the relay node, which forwards them to the exit node, which sends them to the web server. Responses from the web server are

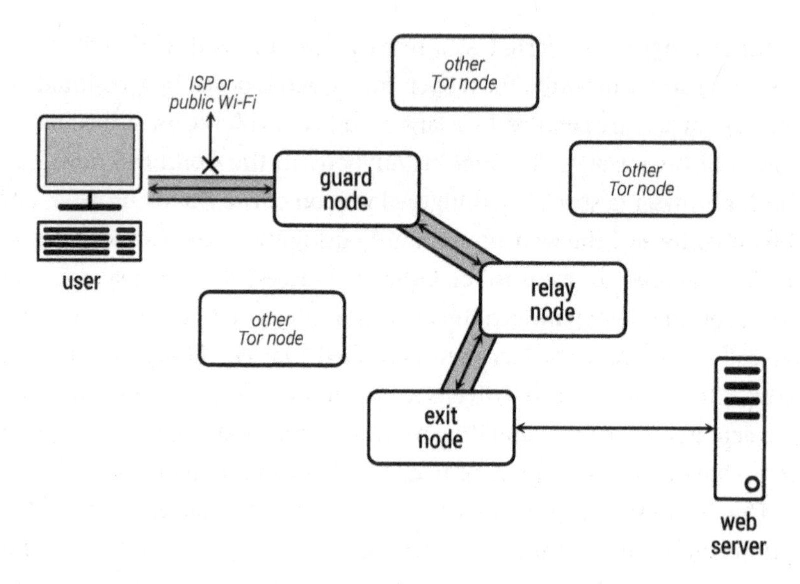

4.2 The Tor network.

channeled back to the client by the exit node through the relay node and then the guard node.

From a practical point of view, this means the exit node is visiting the website on behalf of the client. In particular, the web server will see the IP address of the exit node instead of that of the client. This is what gives the desired anonymity. But this creates a risk for the exit node, which can be blamed for any malicious or illegal traffic generated by the client (think of hacking attacks, downloading copyrighted content, distributing child pornography, or even terrorist activity). As nodes are operated by volunteers and circuits are randomly constructed from the set of all available onion routers, an unsuspecting volunteer (whose computer was selected as the exit node for some highly illegal activity) might suddenly find a SWAT team at their door. Luckily, Tor allows volunteers to specify which type of relay they are willing to support. And in fact, it is advised *not* to run an exit relay, unless "exit relay operators are affiliated with some institution, like a university, a library, a hacker space or a privacy related organization. An institution can not only provide greater bandwidth for the exit, but is better positioned to handle abuse complaints or the rare law enforcement inquiry."[44]

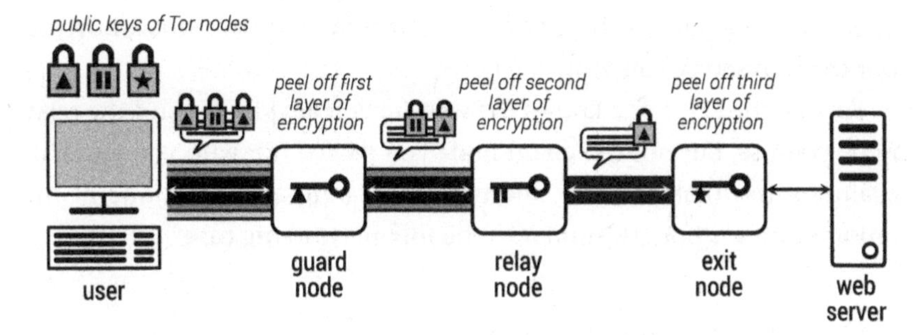

4.3 Onion encryption.

Like mix networks, Tor uses encryption to protect the content of the traffic routed through the Tor network. The client adds several layers of encryption, one for each onion router on the circuit (see figure 4.3). When setting up the circuit, it uses the (known) public keys of these nodes to establish short-lived (ten-minute lifetime) symmetric keys with each of them. When sending traffic from the client to the web server (e.g., a request for a particular web page), the client first encrypts each packet in this traffic with a key shared with the exit node. It then further encrypts this with the key it shares with the relay node. It finally encrypts this once more with the key it shares with the guard node. The result is sent to the guard node. Each layer of encryption is then "peeled off" one by one by each onion router as it forwards the packets to the web server, much like peeling off the layers of an onion (hence the name onion routers). Traffic to the web server leaves the exit node unencrypted.[45] Return traffic from the web server to the client (i.e., the web pages you request) is first encrypted by the exit node before forwarding it to the relay node. Subsequent onion routers on the circuit back to the client add another layer of encryption using the symmetric key they share with the client. In the end, the client receives a multiply encrypted packet, but because it has all the keys it shares with the onion routers on the circuit, it can peel off these layers and decrypt the packet to obtain the unencrypted traffic.

As a result of setting up a circuit and using encryption this way, knowledge of the full circuit is split over the nodes on the circuit. If you are surfing the web using Tor, the guard node knows you and the relay node you choose, but not the exit node, let alone the website you want to visit.

The relay node knows the guard and exit node but does not know you nor the web server you visit.

Finally, the exit node knows the website you are visiting and the relay node you use, but not the guard node you picked nor who you are. This again ensures that you stay anonymous so long as at least one of the onion routers is honest, similar to the mix networking case.

4.7.1 CENSORSHIP CIRCUMVENTION

The way Tor encrypts the content of the traffic and hides the final destination of the traffic from the guard node allows it also to be used for *censorship circumvention*. Governments may not necessarily like to give their citizens unfettered access to all information that is in principle freely and openly available on the web. So countries like China, Russia, and Turkey are well known for censoring the web. But even countries like the Netherlands have resorted to censoring the web to block access to known sources of copyrighted material, like the Pirate Bay.

Contrary to the idealistic beliefs held at the start of the internet boom (see John Perry Barlow's declaration of the independence of cyberspace), governments *do* have a rather tight control over what their citizens can and cannot do on the internet due to the limited number of local ISPs (which connect their citizens to the internet) and the small number of internet exchanges (which interconnect the national networks with each other).[46] Both ISPs and exchanges are bound by national laws. This means that they can be instructed to block traffic to certain sites (either by domain name or, more effectively, by IP address). But this does require the ISP to be able to see the IP address of the website you are visiting. Normally it does. But if you use Tor, the ISP is somewhere on the connection between you and the random guard node you selected, so all the ISP sees is traffic to an arbitrary IP address (that belongs to the guard node). Because the traffic is encrypted, the ISP cannot look inside the traffic and see which website you are actually visiting, making it much harder to censor. All the ISP sees is that you are sending encrypted traffic to the guard node. Simply visiting a secure website (using HTTPS but not using Tor) that also encrypts the traffic does *not* foil the censor: as explained in chapter 3, in TLS, the IP header that contains the IP addresses of the source and the final destination are not encrypted.

4.7.2 ONION SERVICES

Something else Tor is known for, or perhaps notorious for, is what unfortunately has become known in the popular press as the *dark web*. Sites on this dark web cannot be found in the normal way with a normal browser. You need the Tor browser and the Tor network to find them instead. Hence the name dark web: sites on the dark web are not (readily) visible to normal web users. Examples of sites on the dark web are Silk Road, AlphaBay, and the Hansa market (now all taken offline), which were used as marketplaces for mostly illegal trade: drugs, weapons, and the like. The term *dark web* also suggests that Tor and its onion services are predominantly used for nefarious purposes. This ignores many good uses for onion services, like whistleblowing (SecureDrop and WikiLeaks) and truly anonymous messaging or email services (Ricochet, ProtonMail) that are used by reporters and police informants alike. Social networks like Facebook are also available as an onion service, as a means to defeat censorship imposed in certain countries. These are perhaps not as newsworthy applications of onion services but are important nevertheless.[47]

In the normal mode of operation, Tor offers only anonymity to the user surfing the web. The user still visits known websites using a URL that contains a publicly registered domain. Should the website be involved in something illegal, its owners are easy to find (through the registration of domain name owners kept by the domain name registrars). But Tor also implements *onion services* (formerly called *hidden services*). This is what websites on the dark web themselves use to stay anonymous.

Tor onion services do not have a URL that contains a normal domain name like ordinary websites have. Instead, onion services are only known by their *onion addresses*, which look like arbitrary strings followed by the fake top-level domain .onion. The Hansa market used onion address hansamkt2rr6nfg3.onion and AlphaBay used onion address pwoah-7foa6au2pul.onion. (Both links no longer work as the markets have been taken down by law enforcement.)[48] Normal browsers do not understand an onion address. But the Tor browser does and uses it to find the *introduction point* (which is yet another Tor node in the network, volunteering to introduce clients to onion services) associated with an onion service. Both the client and the web server for the onion service set up Tor connections to this introduction point. Although the introduction point is known to both, the fact that both use Tor to connect to the introduction point hides the identity (i.e., IP address) of both the client and the onion service web server from the introduction point and hence from each other. In particular, this means the introduction point does not keep information that could be useful to governments, law enforcement, or other adversaries when they try to identify a particular onion service.

It's important to stress that onion services are hidden because they cannot be found using a normal browser, not because they cannot be connected to over the internet. In fact, even a onion service runs on some web server with some IP address connected somewhere to the internet. If you know the IP address of that web server, you can connect to the onion service without using Tor, using a normal browser instead. The point is that nobody knows the IP address of the onion service, thus guaranteeing anonymity for the onion service as well.

4.8 BUSTED: THERE IS NOTHING META ABOUT METADATA

A useful way to classify the different types of data is to distinguish volunteered data, which we knowingly share, and observed data, which are unwittingly collected about us. These observed data are also called metadata and are perhaps best understood as behavioral data. As we have seen in this chapter, metadata have many different sources, and their collection is hard to prevent, partially due to the leaky design of the devices and networks we use.

This is a problem because metadata are perhaps even more revealing than ordinary data that we volunteer to share, as they are more directly associated with our behavior, with what we do, and hence potentially reveal what our most basic needs and desires are. Moreover, they're much easier analyzed because of their structured nature. And last but certainly not least, they're mostly collected without us being aware of this at all.

Easy fixes, like using private browsing and throwing away cookies or being careful with the apps you install and the permissions you give them, help somewhat but really do not offer enough protection. True unlinkability—the assurance that your data and actions cannot be linked to you—requires more radical approaches. We discussed two such approaches in this chapter: mixing and Tor. Both are examples of practical applications of the state of the art in the area of privacy-enhancing technologies, a research field that traditionally has focused a lot on ways to achieve unlinkability. We will encounter more examples of this later in this book.

Having said that, systems like Tor really only treat the symptoms of a fundamentally broken system that leaks metadata like crazy. To really solve the problem, and to address the root cause, calls for a much more fundamental redesign of how hardware devices work, how operating systems work, and especially how networks work. This is an enormous challenge, but one worth taking up, given what's at stake.

5

WE ALWAYS NEED TO KNOW WHO YOU ARE

Evening falls, and you decide to go to the movies. Or perhaps you just discovered your favorite band is coming to town later this month. To secure a ticket for the event, you decide to buy one online. You surf to the online ticket shop, select the event, make sure you selected the right date and time, and choose the e-ticket option (provided the shop even offers alternative delivery options). Ideally, you would immediately proceed to checkout and pay.

In practice, buying tickets online is never this frictionless.

Somewhere along the ordering process you are required to sign into your account at the online ticket shop. If you don't have an account yet, you'll have to create one, and you will probably be asked to provide your full name, home address, and email address. In some cases, you have to provide more information, like your age and perhaps your phone number. Isn't that surprising to you? No? Perhaps you are so used to it now, so conditioned to it, that you no longer really notice this identification step, let alone question it. Apparently, you have bought into the myth that "they" always need to know who you are. But do they, really?

That is the central question studied in this chapter: Is it really necessary for service providers to know who you are?

At first sight, it appears merchants like such ticket shops need to know who you are. After all, an account is personal, and so it must be tied to a person. And for many transactions, a name, email address, or physical address is necessary to complete the transaction and to email the e-ticket or to ship the ordered items. But as we will see in this chapter, the situation is in fact much more nuanced. In many cases, merchants do not need to know at all *who* somebody is. When selling online tickets, it suffices to have an email address to send the ticket to. And in general, all that really should matter for online service providers is what their visitors are allowed to do, which can be determined in other, more privacy-friendly ways as well.

Unfortunately, we are stuck with account-based mechanisms to regulate access to online services and computer systems in general.

Traditionally, usernames or email addresses are used to unambiguously identify the owner of an account. Of course, any person can simply claim to have a certain username or email address, so a separate *authentication* step is required to ensure that it is indeed the actual owner of the account who is requesting access. There are three fundamentally different methods (sometimes called *factors*) to authenticate yourself and to prove that you are who you say are. You can authenticate yourself using something only you *know* (e.g., a password), something only you *have* (e.g., a signing key for digital signatures securely stored on a physical USB stick or your smartphone), or something only you *are* (i.e., biometrics, like a fingerprint or iris scan).[1]

We'll discuss digital signatures in a little more detail in the next section. Unfortunately, because the generation of digital signatures requires the use of additional hardware and software, they never caught on as a ubiquitous method of user authentication. As a result, usernames and passwords are still the predominant form of identification and authentication, even though they are fraught with security issues: people pick bad passwords, people use the same passwords for all their accounts, and services store passwords insecurely, giving hackers ample opportunity to steal or guess passwords and compromise the accounts of unsuspecting users.[2]

Authentication becomes stronger when combining several factors. *Two-factor authentication* means that you need two out of the three different factors mentioned earlier to authenticate yourself before you get access to your account. A common combination is a password and a physical device with which you can generate the second authenticator. A popular approach is to let users register their mobile phone number with the service, which will send a one-time access code to this number every time a user wants to log in. Another example is the use of a special authenticator app on your smartphone to generate the one-time access code. Because access to the account now requires physical access to this token, it becomes much harder for an attacker to sign into your account.

Authentication and access control are also important in an enterprise context. As the number of computer systems and networked services within companies and organizations grew, the number of accounts assigned to each individual employee exploded. The need arose to somehow more centrally manage all these different user accounts. *Identity management* systems were designed to fill that gap, in which users only need a single account to sign into all the different services they use. This approach to consolidate user accounts now also exists on the web at large, where you can, for example, use your Google or Facebook account to sign into Spotify or Expedia. Unfortunately, such identity management systems are fraught with significant security and privacy issues, as we will see later in this chapter.

This brings us back to the central question of this chapter: Is it really necessary for service providers to know who you are? Framing security in terms of *who* has access to *what* turns this question into a tautology and essentially renders any alternative, more privacy-friendly approach out of scope. But if we are willing to step out of this limited frame, we see alternative approaches are certainly possible. We'll discuss those in the second half of this chapter. But first, let's turn our attention to digital signatures, which turn out to be a core ingredient of such privacy-friendly solutions.

5.1 DIGITAL SIGNATURES

One method of authentication, which can also be used to prove the authenticity of documents, is based on *digital signatures*. Such signatures are attached to digital documents to commit to their content—a bit like ordinary pen-based signatures, but with significant differences.

Digital signatures are a different application of public key cryptography (as introduced in chapter 3). Recall that in public key cryptography, each user has a unique private key (that she keeps secret) and a corresponding public key (that everybody is allowed to know or that is otherwise easy to look up). The *public* key is used to encrypt data, and the corresponding *private* key is required to decrypt data.

For digital signatures, these two keys are used in a different manner. The private key is used to create a digital signature over a document.[3] Without access to the private *signing key*, a valid signature cannot be created. The digital signature is appended to the document and can be verified using the corresponding public *verification key* (using the document it belongs to as additional input to the verification procedure). Every different document signed with the same private key creates a different digital signature. This means that a digital signature is intimately tied to the document it signs: the slightest modification to the document invalidates the signature. To verify the signature, you need to know the public key of the person that signed the document. Because the private key is (supposed to be) private, a document with a valid digital signature proves its authenticity: we are sure the owner of the private key signed it (with some caveats, as discussed ahead).

Let's make the use of digital signatures concrete with a real-life example. Suppose Daphne wants to apply for a mortgage at Eddy's bank. To qualify, she needs to have, among other things, a sufficiently high and stable source of income. She can prove this to Eddy by handing over an employment contract that specifies her current salary and whether the contract is permanent or not. Because Daphne is not at work this week but needs the contract as soon as possible, she asks Mohammad, her employer, to send her the contract by email. Mohammad complies with Daphne's request and sends her the contract signed with his digital signature using his private key. Daphne sends this digitally signed employment contract to Eddy, who can verify its authenticity by looking up and using Mohammad's public key for verification (checking Mohammad's employer status in the process). Recall that the slightest modification to the contract invalidates the digital signature. So if Daphne wants to alter the terms of the contract and then convince Eddy (or anybody else) it was signed by Mohammad, Daphne either needs access to Mohammad's private key or needs to trick Mohammad into signing the altered contract. Note that to be convinced that it was really Mohammad that signed the document, Eddy needs to be certain he is using Mohammad's public key to verify it (and not Daphne's public key) *and* he needs to trust the fact that Mohammad kept his signing key private (and did not allow it to be used by someone else to generate a signature).[4]

Digital signatures can also be used to directly authenticate people. Suppose Daphne, after approval of the mortgage, has an account at Eddy's bank. The bank wants to be certain that only the real account holders get access to their accounts. Daphne and Eddy can again use digital signatures for that. The idea is straightforward: Eddy sends Daphne a *challenge* message and asks her to sign that particular message unchanged with her private key and return the digital signature to Eddy. Eddy verifies the digital signature using Daphne's public key (which she registered with Eddy when the account was created) and the challenge message he sent. If this is successful, he is convinced Daphne is accessing her account.

One is easily fooled into believing that because digital signatures are called signatures, they are the same as traditional ink-on-paper, "wet" signatures. There are two very important differences, however. First, digital signatures are generated by computers: the underlying computations to generate the signature are simply too complex for any human to carry out directly. This implies that there is never a direct link between the user and his or her digital signature on a particular document.

In the preceding example, it is not Daphne herself that signs Eddy's challenge: her smartphone does that for her. And similarly, it is not Eddy himself verifying the signature: his server does. There is always a computer mediating the intention of a user to digitally sign a document, meaning that the computer can decide to sign a document without the consent or intent of the user or that the computer can decide to sign a document different from the one the user intended to sign. The risk of this very much depends on the particular setup that is used to generate these digital signatures.

If the private key and the signing software are stored and running without any protection on a general-purpose computer, the risk is high. If, on the other hand, the private key is stored on a separate smart card and the signature is generated using a certified, special-purpose device, the risk is much lower. Second, digital signatures protect the integrity and authenticity of the document they sign much more strongly than a paper-based signature: whereas a minute change in a printed document doesn't change the paper-based signature at all, the same small change in the digital document would immediately invalidate the corresponding digital signature.

5.2 IDENTITY MANAGEMENT

As the number of computer systems and online services we use has grown and each of these systems and services requires us to have yet another account to sign into, people have started to be fed up with having to remember yet another account name and account password. This problem in itself could be solved by using a password manager that stores all account names and associated passwords locally on your own computer or smartphone. But the complexity has not only increased from the user perspective: service providers wishing to add a new service for existing users also have to either copy the account information from an existing service to the new service or force users to create a new account for the new service the first time they start using it.

Identity management is a concept that aims to reduce this complexity for both users and service providers alike.[5] It not only allows users to manage their online identities but also allows service providers to determine the conditions under which users get access to their services. In that sense, identity management is also a tool for access control. This should come as no surprise given the preceding discussion on identity, authenticity, and authorization: establishing identity has (unfortunately) become a crucial part of any access control decision. Identity and access management systems are therefore used in many organizations to manage access to internal applications, services, and data. Although this is a very important topic from a security point of view (an efficient and up-to-date identity and access management system is a crucial component of the overall security architecture of an organization), we will focus mostly on the user perspective of identity management because that is where most of the privacy issues lie.

Identity management at the core distinguishes between users that wish to access a service and *relying parties* that offer these services, relying on the identity information provided by the identity management system to decide whether to allow a user access to the service or not. Traditionally, relying parties did all the work themselves: they each set up a system to allow users to create an account and then to authenticate users whenever they returned at a later time. Each user account at a relying party is thus different from and independent of any other user account at another relying party, leading to what we call *identity silos* (see figure 5.1). These silos are a problem for both users and relying parties. A user cannot easily share information among accounts, so when they, for example, move to another address, they have to manually change their new home address for each of their accounts. Relying parties cannot share information about their users either, like credit scores or customer reputation.

The core insight of identity management was to separate and outsource the process of creating and managing an online identity. Instead of each relying party doing this by themselves, a separate entity called the *identity provider* is assigned this task instead. The identity provider is a separate online service that allows users to create *one* account, with *one* password (or other authenticator) that can subsequently be used to access all services of all relying parties that have a contract with this identity provider. When you want to access a service offered by such a relying party, the relying party redirects you to the identity provider. The identity provider then asks you to sign into your account, verifies your authenticity, and if successful informs the relying party of this fact and tells him who you are.[6] The relying party then decides whether to grant

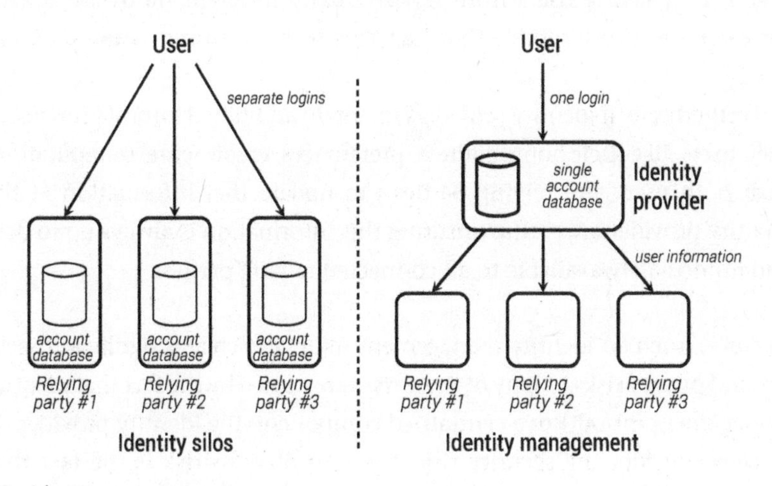

5.1 Identity management.

you access to the service based on this identity. This setup is also called *social login* and is very common today: Facebook and Google are in fact massive identity providers that allow their users to access other services (like Spotify or Pinterest) through their Facebook or Google accounts.[7] To access Spotify, you can sign into your Facebook account. To access Pinterest, you can sign into your Google or Facebook account. Similar identity management schemes are used by governments as well to provide their citizens with a government-issued eID that they can subsequently use to access several government services, like submitting income tax declarations, applying for social welfare, or submitting a change of home address. Examples of such eID schemes include BankID in Sweden and DigiD in the Netherlands.[8]

The advantages for the user are obvious: instead of having to remember separate account names and passwords for each and every service she uses, she now only needs to remember her account name and password at the identity provider. If she is smart, she picks a strong passphrase for this (as this is the only password or passphrase she has to remember from now on), thus increasing her security. The advantages for the relying party are obvious as well: it no longer needs to store passwords securely. Moreover, relying parties that want to strengthen authentication and set up something like two-factor authentication can simply ask the identity provider to do so once, thus spreading the cost of distributing hardware tokens and saving users from having many different hardware tokens for each and every service that happens to have strong authentication needs.

Furthermore, if identity providers maintain additional information about their users, like their home address, preferences, credit score, or reputation, then both users and relying parties can update that information at the identity provider once, thus ensuring this information is always up to date and immediately available to all connected relying parties.

However, such an identity management setup also creates significant security and privacy risks.[9] Many of these risks are caused by the fact that identity management introduces a centralized component: the identity provider.

Let's consider the security risks first. An obvious risk is the fact that the identity provider is a single point of failure. If it gets hacked, the attacker gains access to all accounts for all relying parties associated with the identity provider. Without a central identity provider, the hackers would have to hack each relying party separately.[10] It also makes identity providers likely targets for phishing attempts: once you manage to phish the account information of some users at the identity provider, you again have access to all their accounts at the associated relying parties. Moreover, it sets identity providers as a source of information to perpetrate identity fraud and hence an attractive target for attacks.

Having one online identity at a single identity provider to access all your online accounts is risky. It's like having a single key that unlocks your house, your car, your bike, your desk, your safe, and so on. If you lose it, or if it falls into the wrong hands, you're doomed.[11] A fundamental question then becomes: How many keys, how many separate identities should one have? So far as we know, no clear answer to this question exists yet.

A much more significant, but often overlooked, security risk of identity management is the following: the identity provider has full access to all your accounts at all relying parties.

For this point, the following analogy may be helpful. In a traditional apartment building, each resident has a key for the front door and another key to enter his apartment. Now consider an apartment building that operates like a hotel instead. There is a concierge behind the desk opposite the front door that keeps all keys to all apartments in a safe behind his desk. If you want to enter your apartment, you have to ask the concierge for your key. He will not give it to you, though: he'll walk with you to unlock your apartment and return to his desk with your key. This fundamentally changes the game in two ways: first, the concierge knows when you enter your apartment (and with whom); and second, the concierge can at any time satisfy his curiosity and decide to peek into your apartment whenever you're away. He may even take things if he is so inclined.

The same is true for identity management systems: the identity provider is the concierge that at any time can pretend to be you and decide to sign into your account at any of the relying parties associated with it. The identity provider may even be forced to do so when instructed by law enforcement officials. The only thing that prevents him from doing so is trust and reputation: any identity provider caught in the act would be out of business straight away.

There are also privacy risks associated with using identity management systems. In fact, the concierge analogy already exposed one such privacy risk: the identity provider learns when you sign into each of the online services you use. It knows how often you start listening to music and at what time. If you are subscribed to a gambling service using social login, it knows how often you gamble. If you use your Google account to access the job advertisement board, Google might infer how eagerly you are looking for a new job.

Another privacy risk is in fact one of the advantages cited earlier of relying parties using identity management in the first place: it trivially allows them to link different accounts at different relying parties that all belong to the same user. This allows relying parties to share preferences, credit scores, reputations, and the like, but more importantly it allows them to create much more detailed customer profiles based on your behavior across all the different services you sign into using the same identity provider account.

Linking accounts is much harder to do when users have really separate accounts at different service providers (provided they use a different account name at each provider and also use a different email address).

The privacy risks associated with the type of identity management system sketched earlier have two distinct causes. First, the identity provider is necessarily online all the time and directly involved in setting up a session between a user and the relying party. Second, access control decisions made by the relying party are bound directly to identity. Two decades ago, Carl Ellison had already argued that this is a bad idea (for security reasons).[12] Here we see that this setup also has undesirable privacy consequences.

5.3 ATTRIBUTE-BASED CREDENTIALS

A radically different approach to identity management is inspired by traditional paper-based credential schemes, like passports, driver's licenses, and diplomas. People have been using these for centuries to prove things like their citizenship (using passports issued by their country of residence), their aptitude to drive (using a driver's license issued by, say, the Driver and Vehicle Licensing Agency in the UK), or their qualifications (using a diploma issued by an educational institute). In these traditional systems, users can use their passports or diplomas to prove their citizenship or levels of education autonomously, independent of the issuer of the passport or the diploma. In fact, these issuers are not involved at all in the use of these documents. Moreover, these documents are used not only to establish pure identifiers (like names or social security numbers) but also to establish arbitrary qualifications about people.

In fact, in such *claims-based approaches*, the identity of a person is modeled as an arbitrary set of properties or characteristics (called *attributes*) ascribed to that person.[13] Pretty much anything you can think of regarding a person can be an attribute. Attributes can be real identifiers (like name or social security number), a description of physical appearance (like height or hair or eye color), age, martial status, address, anything related to medical history or current medicine use, allergies, information about capabilities or level of education, badges, ranks, titles, and so on. Attributes are specified by their *type* (e.g., age, town, degree) and their particular *value* (thirty-three; Mumbai, India; MD).[14]

Moreover, claims-based approaches acknowledge that people may have quite distinct identities in different contexts. In some contexts, a person's identity may contain mostly attributes related to his personal life, while in another context his identity is (better) described by a set of attributes covering work-related aspects. In fact, it is up to the person to decide which set of attributes to show in a particular context.

A *claim* is an assertion about the value of a certain attribute belonging to a certain person. For example, "The author of this book has a PhD in computer science" is a claim. Or "Donna Strickland won the Nobel Prize in Physics in 2018." Or "My brother is taller than me." A claim can be true or false. Whether we believe a claim to be true depends on many factors, not least of which is the entity stating the claim. This entity is called the *issuer* of the claim. If I tell you that I have a PhD in computer science, this may not be very convincing to you. If, however, I can show you my PhD certificate with the official red lacquer seal of the University of Amsterdam on it, you may very well be convinced. This is because the process of obtaining a PhD at the University of Amsterdam is well documented, meeting stringent quality criteria and appropriately secured to prevent fake or unwarranted certificates from being issued. Not everything the

University of Amsterdam says about me should be relied upon, however. For example, a driver's license with the seal of the university should be as meaningless as a PhD certificate issued by the Driver and Vehicle Licensing Agency. So the validity of a claim not only depends on the trustworthiness of the issuer itself and the process by which it issues its claims, but also on whether the issuer is considered to be an authoritative source for the information provided by the claim—that is, for a particular attribute. This by itself is a subjective decision of sorts that each relying party has to make for herself. Ultimately, it's up to the relying party—which relies on the validity of the claim—to accept or reject it.

That is not the end of the story, however. After the accepting the claim as valid—that is, accepting the authority of the issuer over the contents of the claim and trusting that claim was issued by an appropriate process—the relying party has to interpret the claim and tell what it really means. For example, the value of university diplomas is not universally agreed upon. It makes a difference whether I got my degree from, say, Harvard, DeVry University, or the University of Amsterdam. The criteria for issuing a degree vary wildly among academic institutions, both within countries and across continents. Other claims may involve a professional judgment (like claims about medical conditions) or involve language that is interpreted differently by the issuer of the claim and the parties relying on that claim. This makes it all the more important to clearly specify the *semantics* of an attribute—that is, to specify as exactly as possible what a particular attribute really means and to ensure that both issuers and relying parties stick to these semantics.

In summary, a claim is an assertion made by an issuer about the value of a particular attribute belonging to a certain person.[15] In other words, claims have the following general structure:

Issuer I asserts that attribute A of person P has value V.

For me to be able to use such claims and convince somebody about the value of some of my attributes, I somehow need to be able to present or show this claim. Traditionally, this is done by printing the claim on some kind of official document that is not easily forged, like a passport, a sealed certificate, or a signed and stamped piece of official paper. The issuer issues this official document to me once, after it has ensured that the stated values for the attributes are correct. I can subsequently show this document to anybody that needs to establish the value of some or all of the attributes printed on the document. I can show my passport or identity card to prove that I am over twenty-one when buying alcohol, for example. Sometimes I need to show two different documents at the same time to prove a combination of attributes that are not all printed on one of them. Sometimes I need my passport to prove my name in order to prove that I indeed have a university degree (using my university diploma that states my name).

In the digital domain, claims can be securely stored in digitally signed documents called *credentials*.[16] The idea is that just as in the traditional paper-based domain, users can obtain credentials from issuers in the digital domain once and subsequently prove some attributes about themselves for relying parties later on. Users store their credentials in a digital *wallet*, which can either be an app on a smartphone (or a similar application on a tablet or PC) or a hardware token like a secure USB drive or smart card (see figure 5.2).

In fact, a credential is a secure container for a limited set of attributes all issued by the same issuer. The typical structure of an attribute-based credential (ABC) is shown in figure 5.3. Apart from the attribute values (for four different attributes in this case) it contains an *expiration time* and a *user key* as well.[17] It is secure because it's digitally signed by the issuer (using her private key) and can therefore be verified by any relying

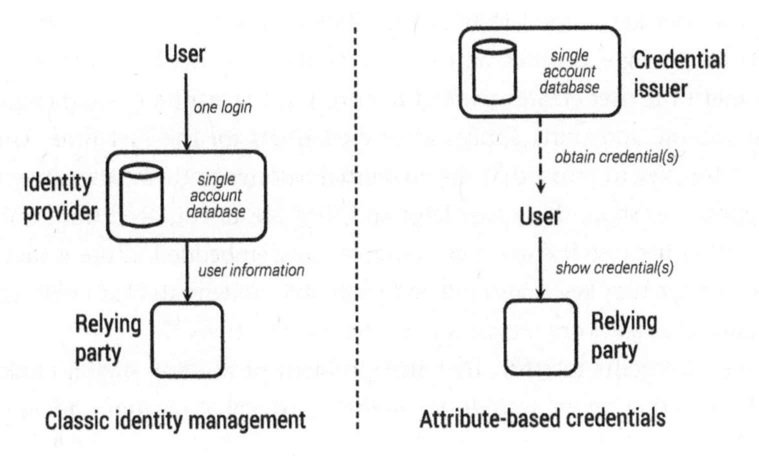

5.2 Identity management versus attribute-based credentials.

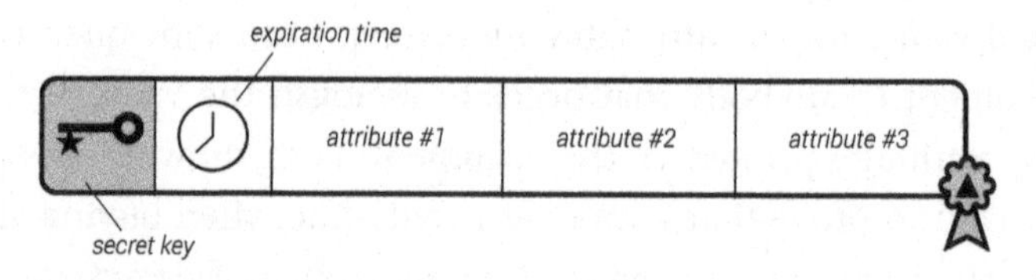

5.3 An attribute-based credential.

party (in fact, by anybody) using the corresponding public key. The signature ensures that nobody can alter the contents of the credential. In particular, this means that I cannot change, add, or remove attributes assigned to me by the issuer (although I *can* choose not to reveal certain attributes, as explained later). The signature also ensures that the relying party verifying the signature also knows which particular issuer issued the credential. We saw earlier that this information is necessary to determine the validity of the claim, or rather the attributes, contained in the credential.

The expiration time is set by the issuer: the attributes are only valid before the expiration time. For credentials with dynamic attributes that change relatively frequently, like medicine use, subscriptions, or memberships, the expiration time is set relatively shortly after the credential is issued. For credentials with more static attributes, like date of birth or citizenship, the expiration time is set for a longer period. Expiration times are important because attribute-based credentials are not as easily revoked as other, more traditional certificates.[18]

The user key is used to bind the credential to a particular user. Each user has a single, distinct, and secret user key. This user key is created the moment the user creates a wallet to enroll in the attribute-based credential scheme and starts applying for credentials for the first time. Users need this key to prove that the credential belongs to them. Users are not supposed to share these user keys and they are discouraged from doing so, either because the user key is inaccessibly embedded in the wallet or because the user key is also linked to valuable credentials (like credit card details) that users are less willing to share with others.[19]

It's important to stress that this problem of binding digital credentials (whether more traditional digital certificates or more advanced credentials) to natural persons is a problem in general: the security of such digital certificates or credentials is typically guaranteed through cryptographic means, involving long cryptographic keys that people cannot remember by heart and that cannot really be tied reliably to one particular natural person.[20]

Ideally, we want to use such credentials in a privacy-preserving manner, to improve upon the traditional identity management architecture that relied on true identifiers. In fact, we would like the use of digital credentials to be very similar to the experience of using paper-based credentials. If I have to prove my age in a shop using my identity card, I take that card out of my wallet and show it to the cashier. The cashier can compare me with my picture on the card and then verify my age using the date of birth printed on it, but unless he has perfect photographic memory he will have forgotten about me right after I paid and left the shop. Such forgetfulness by design does not exist in the digital domain, where everything is perfectly copied (and often kept) all the time.

So how can we construct such a scheme that on the one hand guarantees that the identity of the owner of a credential remains unknown while on the other hand guaranteeing that credentials are not (ab)used by people to which they were not issued? What would prevent a relying party from making an exact digital copy of all the information contained in a credential? How do we prevent the unique details in a credential from being used to link different uses of the same credential? The magic happens by using a special kind of digital signature for the construction of attribute based credentials and by using special protocols to *issue* credentials and subsequently *show* a selection of the attributes they contain at a later time.[21]

The issuing protocol runs as follows. At the start, the issuer identifies and authenticates the user and uses that to determine the values for the attributes in the credential to be issued.[22] The issuer also sets the expiration time. Then a special method for signing the credential is used to ensure that the issuer creates and signs the credential with the set attributes and expiration time, but without learning the secret user key that is also part of the credential. This is necessary because the user key needs to remain private to the user in order to guarantee the security of the scheme.

The showing protocol consists of a sequence of steps involving only a user and a relying party, which allows the user to prove to the relying party that it has some attributes contained in one or more credentials. The showing protocol is special for two reasons.

First, it allows a user to select which attributes to reveal to the relying party. In other words, it allows a user to hide certain attributes contained in a credential from the relying party. For example, if I have a digital credential mimicking my passport, containing my name, date of birth, and social security number, then the *selective disclosure* property allows me to reveal my date of birth while not disclosing my name or social security number. In fact, the showing protocol is even more advanced in that it allows me to prove a property about any of the attributes contained in a credential without revealing the actual attribute value itself. To return to the passport example, the showing protocol would allow me to prove to the relying party that I am over twenty-one (if that follows from my date of birth, of course), without actually revealing my exact date of birth.

Second, the showing protocol is *unlinkable*. This means that even though I use the same credential many times to prove certain properties about myself at the same relying party, the relying party considers all these proofs to be generated by different users using different credentials (albeit with the same properties). This is quite a feat, given the fact that the showing protocol somehow must also involve my secret user key linked to the credential to guarantee that this credential really belongs to me. This is what makes the credential scheme anonymous. If I use a credential to prove I am over twenty-one, there is no way for the relying party to tell that I am the same user that proved the same statement an hour ago or yesterday. Of course, when I use a credential to reveal my name, the unlinkability provided by the protocol offers no anonymity whatsoever because I choose to reveal my identity myself. This inherent unlinkability property of attribute-based credentials is their main privacy-protecting feature, and it prevents relying parties from profiling their users. In particular, the unlinkability property even holds when relying parties would try to collude with credential issuers to try to identify holders of certain credentials. Such collusion is pointless for both relying parties and credential issuers. Note that any metadata leaked by the network or other parts of the system using attribute-based credentials may destroy unlinkability (see chapter 4).

We see that the seeming paradox between guaranteeing privacy while at the same time assuring that a credential is securely tied to a particular user can be resolved with a fundamental paradigm shift. Instead of actually showing or handing over the digital credential itself (which almost by default would mean that a digital copy is made by the relying party), the idea is to allow the relying party to ask the user questions (like, "Are you over twenty-one?" or "What is your name?") that the user can reliably answer using the credentials she owns. She can do using a fundamental tool called a *zero-knowledge proof*, discussed later.

5.4 ABC IN PRACTICE

Attribute-based credentials were an active area of research around the start of this century, based on earlier work by David Chaum.[23] Microsoft developed U-Prove based on earlier PhD work by Stefan Brands (as a student of David Chaum, in fact).[24] IBM developed the competing Identity Mixer based on the research by Jan Camenisch and Anna Lysanskaya.[25] Practical implementations of the latter are now actively developed by the IRMA (I Reveal My Attributes) team of the Radboud University in Nijmegen.[26]

The IRMA project started off as an efficient implementation of ABC on smart cards. Now it's a complete platform, with a user-friendly IRMA smartphone app for Android and iOS devices, which you can use to obtain, manage, and show your credentials. The platform also contains ready-to-deploy server-side software to issue or verify credentials, including JavaScript for easy website integration. The full platform is open source.[27] Let's briefly consider the kinds of privacy-friendly applications that could be built on top of such an ABC platform.

Age verification is often a legal requirement when selling cigarettes or alcoholic beverages, when offering gambling services, or when streaming age-restricted content. In the offline, physical world, this is implemented by asking everybody under the age of twenty-five to show their IDs when buying such items or when entering the casino or the cinema. Online, this is much harder. In fact, few reliable online mechanisms for age verification currently exist, and the ones that do rely on credit cards, users scanning their full IDs, or users signing into an online identification service that can then reliably vouch for their age.[28] Using ABC, and IRMA in particular, online age verification becomes a breeze, as soon as a trustworthy issuer of age credentials starts offering its services on the IRMA platform. This could be the government (which is a reliable source for age information about its citizens) or a bank (which typically is required to verify the personal details of its customers before they open bank accounts). Anybody with an electronic government ID or a bank account can obtain such an age credential once and store it in the IRMA app to later use for age verification on any website accepting IRMA age credentials. The underlying ABC technology guarantees that no other personal information is collected, ensuring that shoppers or visitors cannot be traced.

Students or seniors often get discounts. For seniors, the age-verification mechanism outlined earlier can be used to offer such discounts online as well. For students, proof of being a student is required. Traditionally, this involves having a physical student ID card. In the ABC/IRMA world, this student ID card is replaced by a student credential issued by the university. The student obtains this credential (and stores it in the IRMA app) after successfully enrolling at the university. Again, online services wishing to offer discounts to students need to integrate acceptance of IRMA student credentials into their websites. And again, access to these services is completely anonymous after that.

Applications of ABC are not restricted to just the online world. Access to the university library or discounts at the campus cafeteria can be offered based on such credentials as well. In this case, physical credential verification devices (similar to the turnstiles in the metro you open with your public transport pass, using NFC readers or QR code scanners) must be installed. This idea of using ABC for access control in the physical world can be applied to many other situations as well, like access to the local swimming pool or access to public transport. ABC would replace the traditional physical tokens or passes you get with a weekly, monthly, or yearly subscription. The credential would simply encode what you are subscribed to and the period for which your subscription is valid.

One important piece of the puzzle is still missing, though: How do you prove possession of an attribute-based credential without revealing all attributes it contains, including the secret key and the unique signature of the issuer that would make your use of the credential completely traceable? The answer is to use zero-knowledge proofs.

5.5 ZERO-KNOWLEDGE PROOFS

Many applications require you to prove you know a particular secret. One example is authentication (discussed earlier), often based on secret passwords or private signing keys. Preferably, the secret really remains a secret if you use it to authenticate yourself. This is not the case for password-based authentication: you reveal your password as soon as you prove you have it. The signature on a random message does not reveal your private signing key, however. If that were the case, digital signatures would be entirely useless. But digital signatures *do* leave certain traces that may create privacy issues in certain cases. For example, the signature on a message can be verified by anyone knowing the corresponding public key. If you signed several different messages, their signatures would allow them to be linked.

Zero-knowledge proofs are the fundamental building block underlying many privacy-friendly systems, including attribute-based credentials. They allow someone to prove to a particular person that she knows a secret, while keeping the secret a secret and, moreover, *preventing that person from convincing anybody else of the fact that the prover knows the secret.* The underlying mathematical theory is very complex, and the whole concept might at first seem utterly impossible to begin with (How do you prove something while keeping the thing to prove *and* the proof itself a secret?). Yet there exists a surprisingly simple and intuitive explanation of the basic idea (thanks to Quisquater and others) that I will summarize here.[29]

The story involves Peggy (the prover) and Victor (the verifier) and the ancient cave of Ali Baba. The cave has a peculiar shape, as depicted in figure 5.4: a curved entry passage leads to a T-shaped junction, and each leg of the junction appears to lead to a dead end. Ali Baba was rumored to know

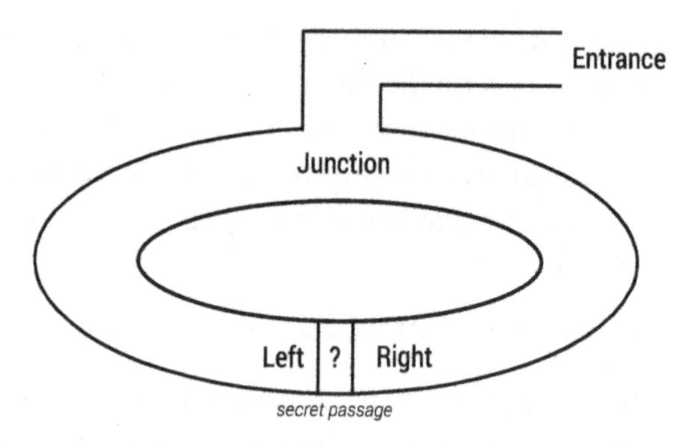

5.4 Ali Baba's cave.

the secret passphrase that allowed him to open a secret passage between the two dead ends at the left and right, allowing him to go from one dead end to the other without anyone standing at the junction noticing.

Peggy knows the secret of the cave as well, and she is willing to prove this to Victor. However, she does not want to reveal the secret itself. So whispering the secret passphrase in Victor's ear is not an option. Peggy has another concern, however. She is afraid that if anybody else learns the mere fact that she knows the secret, they might force her to reveal it. So she does not want anyone beyond Victor to learn the fact that she knows the secret. In particular, Victor should not be able to convince anybody else of this fact.[30]

To convince Victor of knowing the secret under these conditions, Peggy and Victor agree on the following zero-knowledge protocol: Victor first inspects the cave and verifies its shape. Then Peggy and Victor meet at the entry of the cave. Peggy walks in and decides to enter either the left or the right dead end, walking all the way until the hidden door. Victor cannot see which path she took, as the entry passage is curved. A few moments later Victor walks in and stops at the junction. Standing there he cannot see Peggy because she is waiting at the hidden door. He then randomly asks Peggy to meet him at the junction by walking back either from the left or the right dead end. Now if Peggy chose to go left and Victor asks her to come back from the left (or if she chose to go right and Victor asks her to come back from the right) she can simply walk back without using her knowledge of the secret. If, however, Victor asks her to come back from the right dead end while she chose to go left when walking in, she is forced to use her knowledge of the secret and open the secret door between both dead ends to honor Victor's request. If she does not know the secret, she cannot satisfy the request and is forced to come back from the wrong end (and then Victor learns this and hence knows Peggy does not know the secret).

If Peggy does come back from the correct dead end, however, there is a 50 percent chance that she had to use her secret knowledge to do so. So Victor's confidence of Peggy knowing the secret of the cave is 50 percent after executing this protocol once successfully. Clearly this is not enough. So Peggy and Victor both walk back to the entry of the cave and repeat the same steps, say, forty times. If in all forty tries Peggy satisfies Victor's request every single time, Victor is convinced she knows the secret. After all, the probability that Peggy correctly guesses upfront the dead end that Victor will later ask her to come back out of is $(1/2)^{40}$, which equals roughly one-trillionth. In other words, this is highly unlikely.

We see that the protocol outlined here would allow Peggy to convince Victor she knows the secret of the cave without revealing it. What about the zero-knowledge part, however—the requirement that Victor should not be able to convince anybody else of the fact that Peggy knows the secret of the cave?

At first sight, this property does not appear to hold at all. Consider, for example, the case in which Victor secretly records a video of everything he and Peggy do (with Peggy entering the cave and coming out of the correct end whenever Victor asks her to). Now suppose Victor shows this video to his friend Walter.

Clearly, Walter sees everything Victor saw, so Walter is convinced Peggy knows the secret of the cave. However, Walter's conclusion is naive. Even when shown this full video, Walter should not be convinced that Peggy knows the secret based on this video alone.[31] The reason is simple: Victor and Peggy may collude and agree on the sequence of forty questions that Victor will ask when standing at the junction in advance, before starting the video recording. After starting the recording, each time Peggy enters the cave she will choose to enter the dead end toward the hidden door according to the sequence of questions she agreed on with Victor. Then, even though Peggy does not know the secret at all, she will be able to respond to Victor's challenges and appear to come out from the correct dead end each and every time.

Zero-knowledge proof techniques can be used to prove statements like "I have a credential signed by issuer X containing attribute a and b" without actually revealing the credential itself (which would reveal all attributes contained in it and would allow repeated use of the credential to be linked because of the unique signature). This is exactly the kind of statement someone would like to prove when showing an attribute-based credential with certain attributes to some relying party, explaining their ubiquitous use in creating attribute-based credential systems.

5.6 WHAT IS IDENTITY, ANYWAY?

So far in this chapter, we've discussed identity management without really defining what identity is in the first place. In fact, we've been using different understandings of the concept throughout this chapter. We essentially started out with a very narrow interpretation of identity as being or having a unique identifier (a social security number, an email address) associated with an online account. We then broadened the scope by modeling identity as a set of attributes relevant and valid within a certain context. But this very technocentric understanding of what identity is fails to capture many important aspects.

We talked briefly about the relationship between privacy and identity in chapter 2, wherein we mentioned that privacy can also be understood as a freedom from unreasonable constraints on the construction of one's identity. This interpretation of what privacy means acknowledges that identity is something that is much more dynamic and social than a mere identifier or a simple bag of attributes.

In fact, this definition of privacy very neatly dovetails with sociologist Erving Goffman's conceptualization of identity.[32] According to him, identity is constructed and expressed in and through interactions with other people.[33] He says that identities are consciously or subconsciously *staged*, as an actor would do on stage. As such, identities are not a given, but a construct that is open-ended, dynamic, and exists (in different perceptions) in the minds of both the performer and the audience.

The means to construct and express our identity, and hence the range of options available to us to do so, then very much depends on the stage we are provided with or choose ourselves. The following quote from Ian Kerr summarizes this different perspective very well: "Who we are in the world and how we are identified is, at best, a concession. Aspects of our identities are chosen, others assigned, and still others accidentally accrued. Sometimes they are concealed at our discretion, other times they are revealed against our will. Identity formation and disclosure are both complex social negotiations, and in the context of the network society, it is not usually the individual who holds the bargaining power."[34] Moreover, in the network society, these social interactions are mediated by complex digital infrastructures and platforms. Our digital stages are controlled by entities usually not involved in similar negotiations in more traditional settings.

Seen in this light, attribute-based credentials do have their limitations, which one should acknowledge and address before blindly implementing this technology just because it has superior privacy-protecting features.[35] Just as any other technology changes the way we perceive the world around us as soon as we start using it, so do ABC change the way we understand our own identities and those of others.[36] Issuers, for example, will define which attribute types are available and which attribute values one can acquire for them. Available attribute types determine (and thus limit) which aspects of your identity you can reliably prove to others. The range of values a certain attribute can assume limits how you can express your identity. A binary gender attribute will not do justice to the fluid gender types some people perceive themselves to be, forcing them to be either male or female. Facebook's relationship status is famous for offering the option "it's complicated" (raising the question of exactly for whom it is complicated).

There is also a risk of function creep that crops up as soon as a fully functional and widely adopted platform for attribute-based credentials exists. The issue is that such a privacy-friendly authentication platform may create an incentive to *overauthenticate*—that is, to formally verify attributes that before were not verified at all. For example, if age verification becomes trivial and cheap because everybody carries an age-verification credential, then it may be very tempting for, say, social networks to enforce a minimum membership age. This immediately leads to the question who gets to decide the age limits for certain content; such age limits tend to vary across different cultures.

This is not to say that using attribute-based credentials as a more privacy-friendly form of identity management is bad idea. Just the opposite, I would say (and I hope you agree after having read this chapter). However, attribute-based credentials also offer a very nice example of the limits of any privacy-enhancing technologies and how they themselves may create other important issues that will have to be addressed in the final system design.

5.7 BUSTED: KNOWING YOU IS HARDLY EVER NECESSARY

Let's return to the ticket shop example that we started this chapter with. Almost all ticket shops require you to create an account, or at least require you to specify your name, phone number, and home and/or email address when you purchase a ticket. Your e-ticket is then sent to your mobile phone (by text message to the phone number you specified) or by email to the email address you specified. This is the most obvious way of delivering an e-ticket, but it is not a privacy-friendly way. Moreover, it's completely unnecessary.

Selling you a ticket should not involve your identity at all, just like brick-and-mortar box offices do not ask for your identity when you buy a ticket there. There is a simple exchange of money for tickets, and that's it.

In abstract terms, the exchange of money for tickets happens within a *session*. The session starts as soon as you approach the counter of the box office and start talking with the cashier behind the counter. The session terminates as soon as you walk away (with or without your tickets). Everything that happens within this session is relevant for the duration of the session. As soon as the session ends, however, you and the cashier can (and should) forget all about it. The way the interaction is scripted within the session (you asking for a certain number of tickets for a particular show, the cashier checking that there are still seats available before asking you to pay, you paying the requested amount, the cashier checking the amount before printing the tickets, and you checking the tickets before walking off) ensures the integrity of the transaction. If something goes wrong, it should also be dealt with within the session. If you go home after getting your tickets and only then find out you got too few, you may try to return to the box office and pray to be able to get this sorted out, but in all likelihood the attempt will fail: there may be another person behind the counter, the person behind the counter doesn't remember you, or they may simply not believe you.

This model can also be used online. Instead of asking you for personal details, the ticket shop could immediately proceed to the payment phase of the shopping process. Once the ticket shop successfully receives the payment (and yes, as we will see in a later chapter, even this step can be done in a privacy-preserving way), the ticket shop can simply display the e-ticket (whether this a PDF with a bar code or an HTML page with a QR code) on the purchase confirmation page. You can then print the PDF or, if you bought the ticket using your smartphone, ask the ticket to be stored in your wallet.[37] This session-based design for the ticket purchase process is privacy friendly: the ticket shop only learns that someone visited the shop, browsed for tickets, selected some for purchase, and paid for them, after which the tickets were displayed in that person's browser (to be printed or stored in a wallet). The ticket shop does not need to remember much after the session ends.

People might object that this approach is perhaps privacy friendly but not very user-friendly: What if something goes wrong in the purchase step? What if someone accidentally closes the browser window with the e-ticket before printing or storing it? If you have an account, all tickets you ever purchased can reside there, waiting for you for whenever you need them.

This is a very valid objection and one that many privacy-friendly approaches admittedly do not sufficiently address. One way to solve this problem in this particular case is to make clever use of transaction numbers during the payment process. Suppose every payment is tagged with a unique transaction number, for which the ticket shop knows the corresponding e-tickets that were bought during that transaction. This transaction number will be part of the transaction information in your credit card statement or the overview of your debit card payments kept by your bank (such payments could be made privacy friendly if the credit card companies and the banks would shield the credit card number and the bank account number from the merchant). This allows you to look up a transaction number for a transaction that went astray. If the ticket shop provides a way to retrieve e-tickets after entering a transaction number for which the ticket shop indeed received the payment, such mistakes can be solved. Clearly, the transaction number should be random and long enough to make it impossible for someone to successfully guess a transaction number and subsequently download the corresponding e-tickets that actually belong to someone else.

So buying e-tickets does not require the use of your name, phone number, or email address. There is no need for the ticket shop to know you. But what about other online services? Do they really need to know who you are? Let's consider a few cases.

Your real and full identity is legally *required* in certain cases—when dealing with the government, for example (filing tax returns, requesting permits, applying for social benefits), or when opening a bank account (due to know your customer [KYC] and anti-money laundering [AML] regulations). Similarly, your identity needs to be verified at general elections to ensure you are eligible to vote, but great care is taken subsequently to ensure the anonymity of your actual vote.

This last example in fact shows that your actual identity does not matter (at least not when entering the polling station). All that matters is that your eligibility to vote can be reliably established. This would be a typical example of the use of attribute-based credentials, except for the fact that people should not be allowed to vote twice.[38]

Much more often, online service providers (legally) need or simply want to ascertain certain properties about you instead of obtaining your full identity. Many services are required to verify that you are above a certain age, to establish your current country of residence, or to confirm your nationality. Some of these services rely on your honesty in this regard when creating an account. Others actually require you to submit a scan of your identity card or passport so they can verify these pieces of information. In these cases, the creation of an account is unnecessary. We have seen in this chapter that attribute-based credentials can be used to prove all kinds of properties (attributes like your age, your nationality, your achievements) about yourself in a totally privacy-friendly fashion, without revealing your identity. All online services that claim they need to know who you are because they need to know your age, your gender, your whatever are simply lying. There is a privacy-friendly (and probably even much more secure) alternative available.

In fact, a personal account for an online service need not be identifying at all. All that matters is that the service provider can reliably establish that the *same* person that created the account is now returning to access it. *Who* that person is exactly is completely irrelevant in many cases.[39] Traditional ways of accessing an account using usernames and passwords at least provided the option to create an arbitrary, silly pseudonym as a username. Moreover, you could choose a different username for each service, making it impossible for the services to link to each other's accounts. Nowadays, the use of email addresses as usernames is ubiquitous. These are in principle identifying and at least allow such linking of different accounts at different service providers. Again, we see a usability trade-off here: with an email address as a username, you are unlikely to forget the username of an account and you at least have the option to ask for a password reset should you have forgotten your password.

Subscriptions to online newspapers, video or music streaming services, and more can be perfectly anonymous while still being strictly personal—for example, by storing your preferences, your playlists, or your saved news articles. Of course, the more personal the preferences you store in such accounts are, the more likely it becomes that you are identifiable based on these preferences. This does require a certain amount of effort from the service provider, however, and thus is a far cry from services that simply require you to provide your real name, address, email address, or phone number. In any case, in the next chapter we'll discuss radically different approaches that dispense with the accounts concept altogether. Instead of having an account at each and every service provider, users maintain their own account information once, on their own devices, and share this information with service providers on request.

As we'll discuss in much more detail in chapter 7, digital payments can be made as anonymous as ordinary cash. In particular, credit card payments can be handled in such a way that the merchant does not learn the credit card number, while the credit card company does not learn the details of the goods being purchased. For this, back in 1996, Visa and

Mastercard developed the Secure Electronic Transaction (SET) protocol.[40] It never caught on, unfortunately. A simple trick would similarly shield your bank account number from the online merchant when paying by debit card online: your bank could feed your payment through a central clearing account that would then show up in the payment information on the merchant's side instead of your own bank account number.

Another interesting class of applications contains messaging services. Most of these use your mobile phone number (which is tied to your identity in many cases because mobile phone operators are also bound to KYC requirements in many counties) as the main identifier for you and your contacts. Again, this is not really necessary. In fact, in certain cases this is downright undesirable: the current state of affairs requires the contact list of an investigative journalist or foreign correspondent to contain the phone numbers of whistleblower or informants. This can be avoided. All the service needs is some kind of service-specific identifier that ensures that messages intended for me are indeed delivered to me. This identifier could even be different for each of my contacts; that is, the identifier you use to reach me does not have to be the same as the identifier someone else uses to reach me. Clearly, the service provider is still able to link all these identifiers, unless the scheme is set up in a special way.[41]

But perhaps we should look at the problem from another angle and not ask ourselves how to make privacy-invasive systems less privacy invasive by applying a certain privacy-enhancing technology (while leaving the underlying mechanisms that lead to the privacy invasion more or less intact). Instead, we should challenge these very mechanisms and assumptions and try to create systems differently from the ground up. (Admittedly, the use of attribute-based credentials is by itself already quite a paradigm shift, but it still fundamentally relies on the use of personal attributes to grant or deny access.)

As a small example of a radically different approach to access control, deciding who gets access to what, consider the use of (physical) keys. I use my house key to enter my house. I use my car key to open and start my car. I use my bicycle key to unlock my bike (and untie it from the lamppost). My house does not "know" who I am. Neither does my car, nor my bike. In fact, who gets access is determined *not* by considering identity (i.e., tying access conditions to fixed identities) but simply by who has (a copy of) the key that opens the lock. The same mechanism is used to open lockers, safes, turn switches, and so on.

As the preceding discussion illustrates: knowing you is hardly ever necessary.

6

YOUR DATA IS SAFE WITH US

Leiden, a small historic town in the Netherlands, was the first stop of a national "privacy tour" that Google organized down in the Low Countries in 2017.[1] In a colorful, Google-styled caravan, Google staff helped passers-by to do a quick two-minute *privacy check*, to verify whether their privacy settings for the Google products they used matched their expectations and adjust them where necessary. Google's message was clear: your data is safe with us.

Google's privacy tour was supported by an ad campaign in the national newspapers, wherein full-page advertisements explained what personal data Google collected, explained how users could manage the personal data collected by Google, described how Google did its best to protect that data, and stressed that it did not sell our personal data to others (although it did note it was using the data to allow advertisers to target their ads to specific audiences).[2]

Now we could of course applaud Google for its efforts to be transparent about how it treats our personal data, as a warm-up to the GDPR, which was going to be enforced a year later in 2018. A public statement that the company is not selling the personal data it collects to others is a good thing. It's a clear promise that we can pin Google to.

On the other hand, the tour, the ads, and the accompanying website are all cleverly designed to change how we understand and appreciate privacy—to, in fact, reframe what privacy is as "give all your data to us, and we will keep it private."[3] This is hugely problematic, as privacy does *not* mean that Google keeps our data private. Privacy means that we ourselves can do so. Adding insult to injury is the fact that companies like Google are actively subverting our abilities and efforts to do so.

Google is certainly not the only company advancing this frame. Facebook does the same.[4] And it uses that frame as an excuse, as a legitimization, even, to surreptitiously collect intimate details of our personal lives without necessarily asking us beforehand, believing they are entitled to do so just because our data is in their safe hands. Their whole business model is based on it.[5]

One could argue that we are partially to blame ourselves, as the legal protection of privacy through laws like the GDPR specifically allows the processing of personal data, so long as this is done in a responsible and safe manner. In fact, one of the reasons to create the GDPR (and earlier data protection laws) was the recognition that many services and applications simply need to process personal data in order to function. But the spin Google and Facebook give to data protection is deceptive: it does not create a prerogative to create a centralized data store for all our personal data. And it blatantly ignores many provisions in the GDPR, like purpose limitation and proportionality of processing. We will return to this issue at the end of this chapter.

There is a second reason to shun centralized approaches: What if the data is not as safely stored in such central places as the Googles or Facebooks of this world would like us to believe? The 2018 Polar incident is perhaps a good illustration of the potential problems that could arise.[6]

Polar, an originally Finnish manufacturer of sports training computers, offers a wearable device and accompanying fitness smartphone app popular with runners all over the world. The app allows runners to share their runs with others through a central server operated by Polar so that they can be viewed on a map. In 2018, journalists discovered that, contrary to intuition, *all* runs (even private ones) made by owners of a Polar fitness device are stored on this central server.[7] Although the user interface restricted access to only public runs, bypassing the user interface and entering URLs manually allowed them to extract all runs made by anyone since 2014.

Earlier that year, it had already become clear that indiscriminate public availability of the exact location where people exercise might create a (national) security risk.[8] This was discovered when another social network for athletes, Strava, released a global heat map of the activity of all its users. It turned out that this allowed people to identify potential military bases because the Strava app was also popular with soldiers. Their runs would stand out, especially if the soldiers were on a mission abroad and their military base in question was located in an otherwise uninhabited area or in a neighborhood without native Strava users.

The Polar leak exacerbated the issue: different runs by the same person could be linked because they were all stored for the same pseudonymous user identifier. Using this data set and looking for runs made close to military bases or known intelligence agency offices allows one to identify possible military personnel. Subsequently, looking for many runs made by the same people that start and stop at the same location will, in all likelihood, reveal the home address of these people. A little more digging (e.g., in property owner registers) will reveal names. This allowed a journalist to recover the name of at least one Dutch secret agent. He was unpleasantly surprised when the journalists paid him a visit!

6.1 KEEP IT LOCAL

Such disasters are easily avoided by keeping the data local on the device of the user herself, instead of processing them centrally. Moreover, local data processing is a natural approach to privacy protection: it essentially shields any personal data from the service provider. Whether it's possible to keep the processing of personal data local depends on the particular application at hand. Let's make this more concrete with a few examples.

Menstruation apps, also known as period trackers, allow women to track their menstrual cycle to keep tabs on their menstrual health and to estimate their fertile periods. They are quite popular, even though their usefulness and reliability is contested and even though they collect and even share some sensitive personal data with third parties.[9] Simple applications such as these really have no need to share the data they collect with the provider of the app: the model to track your cycle is really quite simple and only depends on the information you yourself provide, not on any external resources (like data or services).

Even if the app does depend on external resources, there is not necessarily a need for an online connection to provide the service. Navigation apps can perfectly function with a local and up-to-date copy of a map of your current whereabouts. There is no need to fetch this map in real time from a central server and in the process continually share your current location with the navigation app provider, like Apple Maps or Google Maps does.

Even in more complex scenarios, in which the behavior of the application does more intricately depend on external resources, local processing goes a long way toward offering a decent level of privacy protection, even though some personal data occasionally has to be shared with the service provider for the application to function. The case at hand is a mechanism to warn you when you are about to visit a fraudulent website. One such system is offered by Google and is called Safe Browsing (see figure 6.1).[10]

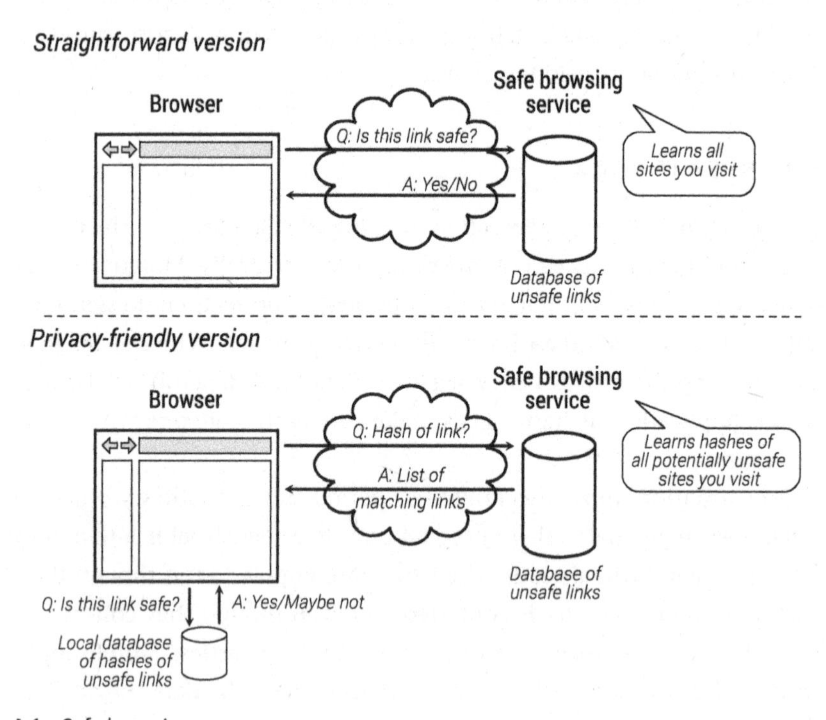

6.1 Safe browsing.

Safe Browsing relies on a huge database, maintained by Google, of links to websites known to serve their visitors malware or that are used in phishing attacks. In the original Safe Browsing system offered by Google, browsers would first send every link of every page you were about to visit to Google for verification. Browsers would only proceed to actually retrieve the page after Google confirmed the link did not occur in its database of fraudulent website links. If the link did occur in Google's database, the browser would issue a warning. This is clearly a terrible choice from a privacy perspective because Google learns about every website you visit.

The database of fraudulent websites is too big to send to users in its entirety, so this obvious approach to allow users to perform the safety check locally fails. To make the Safe Browsing system more privacy friendly, Google therefore uses the following trick: It hashes all entries in its database using a hash function (discussed in chapter 1) with a rather small output range of thirty-two bits. With such a small output range, many links will hash to the same short hash code. Therefore, the resulting database of hash codes corresponding to malicious links is much smaller and can in fact be shared with users and stored locally by the browser. Given this database of short hash codes, your browser can now do the following: It first hashes the link of a page you are about to visit and locally checks to see if the result is in this local database. If this is not the case, the page is safe to be retrieved. If the resulting hash code does occur in the database, an additional check is necessary to correctly classify the link.

The reason that this works is as follows. Every link in the original database of malicious links is hashed, and the resulting hash code is stored in the smaller database of hash codes. If the hash of the link you are about to visit is not in this smaller database, that link cannot have been in the large database of malicious links, and so the link is not known to be malicious. The additional check is necessary because there is a risk of *false positives*—that is, a risk that a nonmalicious link hashes to the same hash code as a different malicious link, which is relatively likely given the short range of thirty-two bits used for the hash codes. This check is essentially performed by asking Google to send over the small set of actual fraudulent links that correspond to the short hash code your browser just computed. After receiving this list, your browser checks whether the link occurs in this list or not. All Google learns in this case is the short hash code of the link you are about to visit, provided that hash code corresponds to a link to a fraudulent website.[11]

Resource use is another possible impediment to processing data locally: if the task requires significant computing power, time, or storage space, then it may not be feasible to run it on a small, resource-constrained device. The significance of this limitation is rapidly diminishing, however, as modern smartphones are hardly considered resource constrained anymore. In fact, current smartphones are faster than the fastest supercomputer from the eighties. Two examples will serve to illustrate what used to require central processing but can now be done completely locally.

Recent versions of Apple smartphones allow one to group pictures into albums based on the people in the picture. So you might have an album dedicated to your partner, your parents, your friends, and so on. These albums are created by analyzing each picture using facial-recognition algorithms. Unfortunately, such algorithms are quite complex and require a significant amount of computing power. Until a couple of years ago, smartphones were too slow to run these algorithms themselves, so all pictures would have to be uploaded for analysis to a central server, with all the associated privacy risks. But modern smartphones are entirely capable of running these algorithms all by themselves, and this is exactly what modern iPhones do, in order to protect your privacy. You no longer have to share your pictures with Apple or store them in the cloud to have your picture albums grouped by the people in them.

The same holds for the speech-recognition software used in many smart speakers, like Google Home, Amazon Alexa, or smart services like Apple's Siri. Again, speech recognition is a difficult problem that requires significant computing power to be handled reliably in real time. As most of the current smart speakers are relatively simple devices with only a modest central processing unit, they still rely on central processing for the actual analysis of the commands you speak to them in your home. Once activated, they stream any audio they record directly to Google, Amazon, or Apple for processing (and recording for later analysis). This explains the privacy concerns raised regarding such smart speakers every once in a while.[12] Laptops have been able to do speech recognition locally for some time now, and modern smartphones are following suit. The latest version of iOS includes Voice

Control, which allows you to dictate documents or written messages while speaking to your phone or tablet, even when you're completely offline. Similar offline speech recognition software is included with the latest Google Pixel smartphone.

Both the preceding examples involve some type of *machine learning* model, trained to recognize faces or to recognize spoken words, respectively. These examples confirm that machine learning has become more efficient, at least when we consider the use of models trained earlier. Popular machine learning platforms like Google's TensorFlow are starting to support lite versions that can be used on mobile and embedded devices, making the *use* of smart algorithms (based on machine learning technology) more privacy friendly.[13] The *training* of the models underlying these smart algorithms still requires large amounts of often personal data, however. Apart from privacy, the application of machine learning and artificial intelligence for automated decision-making raises other serious issues related to bias, discrimination, fairness, accountability, and transparency.[14]

6.2 PERSONAL DATA STORES

The previous section showed that many applications can be implemented in such a way that personal data is processed only locally. Conspicuously absent from the examples discussed thus far are governmental database systems, corporate information systems, and e-commerce applications, which each maintain a citizen record, user account, or user profile with varying levels of detail.

In certain cases, governments simply need a central database, like the register of births, deaths, and marriages, to function. Similarly, corporations need a personnel database, if only to pay their employees their monthly salary. But in many cases, we can question the necessity or even the benefit of relying on a central database. Maintaining a central database makes you responsible for its contents, both in terms of properly securing it and in terms of ensuring the data it contains is correct and up to date. Moreover, given the ubiquitous use of central databases, many of them replicate the same data, like our names, home addresses, email addresses, telephone numbers, and so on. As a consequence, when you move to a different address or change your phone number, you have to change this information in each and every central database that records it. Most of us probably forget a few, meaning that old, incorrect data lingers in many databases.

Since the turn of the century, alternative approaches that aim to reduce the dependence on centrally stored user profiles or user accounts have been advocated. One of these approaches is sometimes called *customer-managed relations* (CMR), a play on the traditional customer relationship management (CRM) systems used by commercial enterprises to collect information about current and potential future customers. The underlying technology is commonly known as a *personal data store* (PDS). The general idea is that instead of the company managing information about its customers in a central database, customers manage their information for all companies they do business with in their own personal data store. If a company needs a shipping address, it asks the customer (through the CMR system). If it needs a phone number, it can again ask. If it needs a credit score, it can ask.

For this to work, there needs to be a way for the company or organization to request this information from the personal data store in a straightforward manner. Moreover, users should be able to easily honor (or deny) such requests. They should not need to manually copy information from their personal data stores and paste it into a form provided by the company. Personal data store platforms therefore offer a service through which companies can request the information they need from the personal data store of a user. There are, unfortunately, competing standards for this, offered by different providers of such personal data store platforms.[15] Examine figure 6.2, and notice the analogy with figure 5.1 in the previous chapter.

To the user, a personal data store simply looks like a single database containing all his personal information, often grouped into categories, like addresses, health data, financial data, and so on. Users can enter new information or update existing information in this database through a web interface or a dedicated app. A PDS also contains a list of companies and organizations the user does business with. For each of the data items in the PDS, users can specify which of these companies or organizations have access to it. Often, such access is read only (i.e., companies can only access it, but not modify it). In other cases, companies can be given write

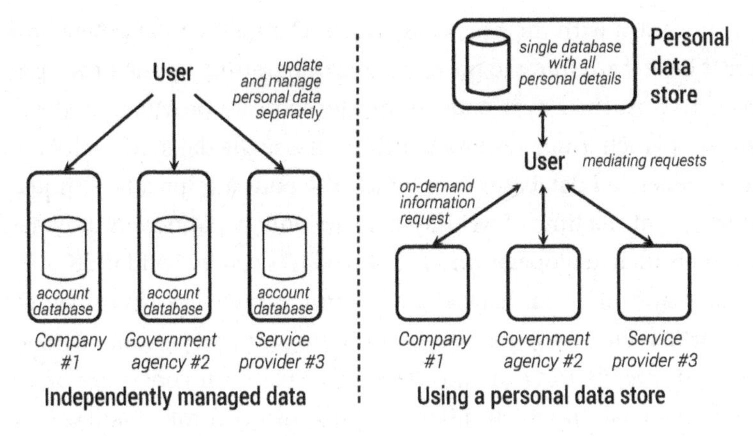

6.2 Personal data stores.

access, allowing them to update the information or add new information. Depending on the system, users get to review each request for information, giving them insights into which data a company requests at a particular time, and also offering them fine-grained control over the release of their personal data.

Now ideally (at least from a privacy perspective), the personal data store would run locally on the user device. But in practice, most platforms currently in operation instead offer a centralized data store, making personal data stores very similar to a cloud storage system. It might seem this wholly defeats the purpose of offering such a service in the first place, making the situation even worse because now *all* your personal data is stored in a single database under the control of the personal data store provider, thus turning such a *digital data vault* into a Pandora's box.[16] This can be mitigated, however, as some providers like Mydex do, by encrypting the data on the user device using a user-specified key before storing the data in the central store (similar to what end-to-end encrypted cloud providers do). The details vary across PDS platform providers, especially in terms of the mechanisms by which companies get access to the encrypted data when the user agrees to share that data with them.

Others, like Solid, use a different, more decentralized approach.[17] Instead of offering one central location to store data, the platform allows several independent providers to offer their own instance of a personal data store (called *pods* in Solid's terminology). Users can select the provider they trust most with their personal data and store their data there. In fact, there is little if anything to prevent users from setting up their own private servers to host their own pods, using the software provided by the Solid platform (which is open source). Instead of a single database, Solid creates a set of federated databases over which the pods are spread—although in all fairness, at the time of writing there are only two different providers of Solid pods in actual operation, one of which is run by Solid itself.

The vision of Solid, backed by Sir Tim Berners-Lee (the inventor of the World Wide Web), goes beyond offering a mere personal data store. It instead intends to create a collaborative platform consisting of a web of personal data, in which different apps, with controlled access to your data, can talk to each other and collaborate "to enrich and streamline your personal life and business objectives." To be honest, this does not sound entirely reassuring.[18]

Intuitively, there are many benefits to the personal data store approach: companies no longer need to store your personal data (meaning they are no longer responsible for its accuracy and security, except for the short periods of time when they actually process the data they requested from you); users have more control (as they are now in the position to decline access to certain pieces of information each time they are requested); and you only need to change any piece of information once, locally. And there is of course a general increase in privacy because no central processing of personal data is taking place any longer.

There are also downsides to this approach. For one thing, companies now need to rely on the correctness of the answers given by their customers. Customers may not have incentives to lie about their shipping address (unless they are pulling a prank), but they may want to skew their credit score in their favor. In other words, the trust relationships change: customers have to trust the companies less, but the companies need to trust their customers more. Approaches related to attribute-based credentials, as discussed in chapter 5, could be used to mitigate such issues, as customers would not be able to change, say, a credit score stored in a credential issued by a credit scoring agency. But they may still be able to withhold any information pertaining to their credit score. Trust relationships are not the only things that change: security risks change as well. A central customer database may be an attractive target for hackers, can be abused by employees, or may be the source of a data leak. On the other hand, medium and large companies typically are able to protect their digital infrastructure and the data they process better than customers can. In other words, customer-managed relations approaches move from a central single point of failure that is often reasonably well protected to a very distributed customer data store in which each individual device is poorly protected but contains only a little information. This is one of the reasons that, in practice, personal data stores are decentralized at best.

6.3 THE PEER-TO-PEER APPROACH

A particularly radical interpretation of the *keep it local* idea is to distribute collaborative tasks, those that require coordination among many different parties. The traditional method is to have one large server, or cluster of servers, that all participants connect to and that coordinates and synchronizes the actions of all participants. Centralization makes synchronization trivial, but it comes at a cost. Not only is the work unevenly distributed (the central server does all the work), but it also creates a central point of failure and a central point of control to which all the personal data flows.

Instead of doing all the processing centrally, it's also possible to do so in a decentralized or even distributed fashion (see figure 6.3). In a decentralized setting, the work is divided over several nodes that each serve a smaller cluster of users. Each of these nodes still has some control over part of the network—in particular, over the cluster of users they serve. The personal data stores discussed earlier, when not running locally, and systems like Solid are decentralized. In the distributed setting, all nodes are equally responsible for doing some of the work, and all nodes have very similar connections to nodes all across the network. This in particular means that no node controls any other node. The physical network structure of the internet (with ISPs, national exchanges, backbones, and transatlantic cables) is not really distributed but somewhat reminiscent of

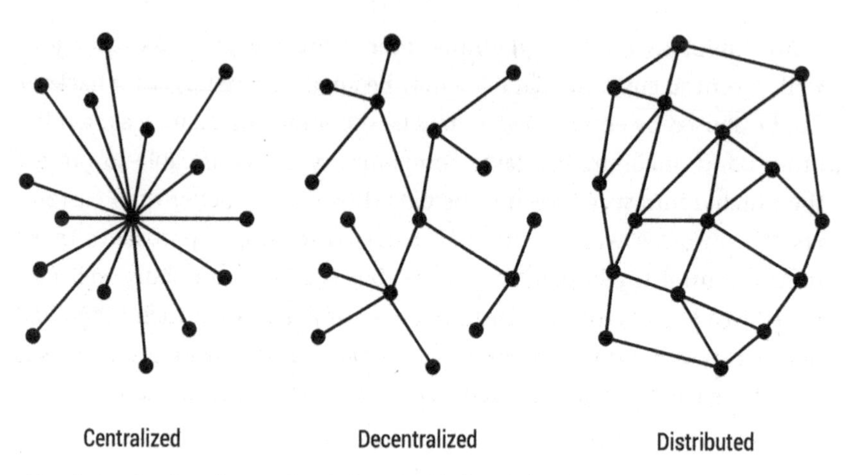

6.3 A visualization of centralized, decentralized, and distributed systems.

a decentralized topology, except that a truly central node controlling the other nodes is missing.

A recent buzzword for such distributed processing is *edge computing*, but the idea of decentralization is much older: *peer-to-peer* (P2P) networks became popular for file-sharing applications like Napster that were used a lot in the late nineties of the previous century. Such networks depend as little as possible on a centralized component, to prevent law enforcement or other actors from stepping in and preventing the sharing of (often illegal) content. Such P2P network architectures also have strong performance benefits, which is one of the reasons Skype started as a P2P network.

Taking the idea of P2P computing to the extreme, it's certainly possible to envision a social network like Facebook implemented in a completely peer-to-peer fashion. In fact, Twitter has recently expressed interest in investigating such an approach.[19] After all, the essential function of a social network is for a user to inform the people in her own personal network of any status updates and to receive updates from those people in return. If all our personal profiles are stored on our smartphones instead of on a central server controlled by Facebook, a peer-to-peer sharing infrastructure allows our smartphones to exchange status updates directly, without any involvement of a central component. (Of course, this would completely kill the business model underlying all social networks, so the app offering this model would be one you have to pay for.)

6.3.1 DIGITAL CONTACT TRACING

A very recent example of the benefits of a distributed approach in terms of privacy protection is offered by the development of *contact tracing* apps in response to the COVID-19 pandemic that began to affect the world in 2019 and wreaked havoc in 2020.[20]

These apps aim to support health authorities in their quest to quickly determine who has been in close and sustained contact with a person infected by this virus. Contact tracing (also known as *proximity tracing* or *exposure notification*) apps have been in use in China for some time.[21] The work of Feretti et al., modeling the infectiousness of SARS-CoV-2, showed that digital contact tracing could in principle help reduce the spread of the virus, provided that enough people use the app.[22]

But whether digital contact tracing actually works in practice still remains to be seen. Many of the current systems are Bluetooth-based, meaning that they use the strength of Bluetooth signals emitted by nearby phones to establish whether two people are in close contact. The product lead of the TraceTogether app used in Signapore warns that no Bluetooth contact tracing system deployed or under development, anywhere in the world, is ready to *replace* manual contact tracing.[23] The problem is that establishing whether two people that were in close contact could indeed have infected one another depends on context, such as whether the place they met was properly ventilated. Such information about a context in which people met cannot be derived or even approximated using Bluetooth (or other commonly available sensors). A human in the loop is therefore necessary.

Let's assume for the moment that Bluetooth signal strength can be used as a reliable enough proxy for proximity. Then there are two fundamentally different designs for Bluetooth-based contact tracing: a centralized design and a distributed design. In both designs, smartphones with the contact tracing app installed emit temporary pseudonymous identifiers over the Bluetooth network. Nearby smartphones that also have the contact tracing app installed receive and store these identifiers locally (if the signal was strong enough). Now the difference between the two designs only becomes apparent when a person is diagnosed as infected.

In the centralized design, the phone of the infected person is instructed to upload all pseudonymous identifiers it *received* over the past fourteen days to a central server of the health authorities. These authorities are able to deanonymize the identifiers and thus learn the identities of everybody that was in close contact with the infected person over the last two weeks. In particular, the authorities will learn large parts of the social graph of infected persons—a significant privacy risk.

In the distributed design, the phone of the infected person is instructed to retrieve all pseudonymous identifiers it itself *sent out* over the past fourteen days and upload them to a central server belonging to the health authorities. Instead of the health authorities informing potential contacts (which they can't), the phones of all people that have the app installed retrieve the list of recently uploaded pseudonymous identifiers of people that have tested positive for COVID-19. The phones compare the entries in the list with the identifiers they received earlier over the Bluetooth network and if there is a match, then they learn they have been in contact with such a person. The app instructs them to take appropriate action (but does not automatically inform the health authorities). The authorities only learn who was infected and those that report having been in close contact with such an infected person, but they do not learn who has been in contact with whom: a significant privacy improvement. This is how DP-3T and the exposure notification API, a joint project from Google and Apple, work.[24]

This does not necessarily mean that a distributed design for contact tracing is preferred in practice to fight a pandemic like COVID-19. First, a centralized solution (wherein the health authorities obtain a full and immediate picture of all people that have been in contact with an infected person) may be preferable over a distributed approach (which relies on the initiative of people to report to the health authorities themselves once the system has notified them of having a risk of infection). Second, the perceived privacy benefit of distributed solutions is debated.[25]

6.4 THE ROLE OF BUSINESS MODELS

According to its annual report, Facebook's mission is "to give people the power to build community and bring the world closer together," but it generates "substantially all of [its] revenue from selling advertising placements to marketers." Facebook had on average 1.6 billion daily users and

2.5 billion monthly users in 2019. Its revenue over 2019 was close to $71 billion, resulting in a net income of $18 billion. Almost all its revenue ($70 billion) is due to advertising.[26] Google's mission is "to organize the world's information and make it universally accessible," yet it also makes most of its revenue (84 percent of it in 2019) in the advertising business. It also generates some revenue "when users purchase digital content like apps, movies and music through Google Play or when they purchase our Made by Google hardware devices. Businesses also pay for the use of our cloud services like Google Cloud Platform and G Suite." Google products had over one billion monthly active users in 2019. Alphabet's revenue over 2019 (almost all attributable to Google, by the way) was close to $162 billion, resulting in a net income of more than $34 billion. Of that revenue, $135 billion comes from advertising.[27]

For comparison, the revenue covering the US budget in 2017 was $3.3 trillion and the revenue over 2017 for a country like the Netherlands was $361 billion (11 percent of the US revenue, a bit more than twice Alphabet's revenue).[28] Countries like Finland ($134 billion) or Indonesia ($131 billion) are completely subsumed by Google's revenue. And Facebook could, metaphorically speaking, buy Singapore ($51 billion) or Chile ($58 billion).[29]

The essence of local data processing as a privacy protection measure is that it essentially shields any personal data from the service provider. It's exactly this aspect that makes local processing less attractive for certain service providers, whose business model depends on extracting value and making money from our personal data. The revenue figures presented in the previous paragraphs seem to suggest that companies like Google or Facebook would simply cease to exist if they could no longer target us with advertisements.

But perhaps companies like Google and Facebook can actually survive such a shift to local processing. On the one hand, not all targeted advertising needs to be personalized or needs to be based on collecting a personal profile. For example, ads shown when searching can simply be based on the keywords in the search query. Ads shown on web pages (whether blogs, magazines, or newspaper sites) could be based on the particular content of those pages: car magazines could show ads for cars, the economy section of a newspaper could show ads for banks, and so on. Such ads would still be targeted but not be based on a personal profile.[30]

Moreover, true personal advertising can in fact be done in such a way that your personal profile is stored and adjusted locally on your own device and is never shared with other parties involved in the complex ad-serving business. The general idea is to send a large number of ads to the user to be matched by the user's browser based on the locally stored profile, instead of matching possible ads with user profiles on the central server of the ad network. Special care is taken to securely measure ad impressions and ads clicked and report them back to the ad network in a privacy-preserving way (as these statistics determine the amount an advertiser needs to pay).[31] Clearly, a user trades an increase in privacy for an increase in load times for every ad-filled web page visited because instead of loading advertisements that won the bidding server side, now all competing ads need to be loaded for the local bidding taking place within the user's browser.

Of course, such more privacy-friendly approaches to targeted advertising would require Google and Facebook to completely overhaul their businesses (both in an economic and a technical sense) and might still impact their revenue significantly. This is not a very enticing proposition.

6.5 LIMITATIONS

A word of warning is in order here. There is an inherent risk associated with all approaches that propose to store all personal data locally: they tend to throw all responsibility for their privacy back at the feet of the users. This assumes that people always make rational decisions, are able to oversee the future consequences of these decisions, and are actually in the position to make such decisions in the first place. Such a liberal approach to privacy, in political terms, denies the existence of power imbalances between individuals on the one hand and governments and companies on the other and ignores the societal value of privacy. Companies may decide to deny access to their services to people that refuse to answer requests for personal information. Companies can do so when they are in essence the only ones offering the service (e.g., Facebook), when all companies offering similar services all request roughly the same amount of information, or when you contact a particular company in case of an emergency (and it knows you are in need). Sometimes a privacy-friendly alternative is available, but at a cost. In those cases, people with financial constraints are excluded.

There is another, more fundamental limit to the protection offered by processing data locally. So long as a service relies on central processing to extract information from the data it collects, local processing is an appropriate defense mechanism and indeed protects our privacy as it prevents the service from learning our personal details. By moving intelligence to our own devices, however, this line of defense obviously breaks: though there is no central place where information about our personal details resides, the system as whole (i.e., the system comprised of all our own devices as well) still knows about us, and it predicts, judges, and nudges us.

Thus, relying on local processing would not solve a more general issue that looms large over the internet-based economy in general. Personalized advertising is but one manifestation of *surveillance capitalism*, defined by Shoshana Zuboff as "a new economic order that claims human experience as free raw material for hidden commercial practices of extraction, prediction, and sales."[32] But it is by no means the only one: most internet-based businesses deploy similar mechanisms. Uber, through a process called *surge pricing*, adjusts the prices for rides in an area in real time based on information about the current behaviors of both drivers and riders. Augmented reality games like *Pokémon Go* lure their users to visit particular bars, restaurants, or shopping malls by placing PokéStops and Pokémon Gyms at those locations. Game players need to physically go to these locations if they want to catch particular Pokémon, which has created a market for PokéStops and Pokémon Gyms. Proprietors of bars, restaurants, or malls offer money to Niantic (the publisher of *Pokémon Go*) to ensure placement of such game features on their premises.

As the example of local personalized advertising cited earlier shows, and as our earlier discussion on the increasing potential of running complex machine learning algorithms locally on smartphones and other consumer devices revealed, the fundamental extractive and predictive mechanisms underlying surveillance capitalism largely work unimpeded when restricted to local processing of personal data.[33] Personalized advertising is still possible. *Pokémon Go* would still work as before. And even Uber's surge-pricing algorithm doesn't necessarily need to know (in a centralized sense) where *you* are, so long as the Uber app on your phone knows you're in a busy neighborhood and can locally decide to show you a higher price as a result. It's certainly possible to compute generalized statistics like the number of people currently looking for a ride in a privacy-friendly fashion.

The excessive power companies like Google and Facebook now wield cannot be curtailed by only addressing their privacy violations. How they obtained that power and, more importantly, how it can be reduced is a fundamental question left unanswered by studying surveillance capitalism only through the lens of surveillance. Perhaps we need to shift our attention and focus on the underlying capitalist premise instead.[34]

The sudden shift to working online after COVID-19 was declared a pandemic in 2020 has made painfully clear that to remain functioning, our society completely depends on the technologies offered by a small set of powerful companies. In particular, many people have pointed out issues with Google and Apple's exposure notification API. "Instead of an app, the technology is pushed down the stack into the operating system layer creating a Bluetooth-based contact tracing platform. This means the technology is available all the time, for all kinds of applications. Contact tracing is therefore no longer limited in time, or limited in use purely to trace and contain the spread of the COVID-19 virus. This means that two very important safeguards to protect our privacy are thrown out of the window."[35] The issues with such a platform also extend into areas beyond privacy.[36] For one thing, Apple and Google dictate which forms of digital contact tracing are possible and which are not. In other words, they move from having a seat at the drawing table to having a seat at the decision-making table.

6.6 BUSTED: YOUR DATA IS NOT SAFE WITH THEM

"If you're not paying for it, you're not the customer. You're the product being sold." This infamous saying is often graphically illustrated by two little pigs discussing the free food in a pig-breeding farm.[37] A similar picture with the Beagle Boys guarding Scrooge McDuck's money bin would serve to illustrate the cognitive dissonance associated with how Google wants us to understand what privacy is. Just as the pigs are safe in their barn, and Scrooge McDuck's money is safe when guarded by the Beagle

Boys, so too is our data safe with Google and Facebook and the like. Yes, they may not sell your data to others. In fact, it would be stupid for them to do so, killing the goose that lays the golden eggs. But they will take every opportunity to extract value from it.

We have seen several examples of how data can be processed locally instead of centrally, either because a service does not depend on any central coordination or because any such central coordination can be achieved in a more privacy-friendly manner. Personal data stores offer an interesting approach to give users control back over their personal data, storing one copy of a certain piece of data locally once, instead of many times at any number of companies and organizations that one does business with.

But there are limitations to this approach. Giving users more control over their data should not make people themselves solely responsible for how their personal data is used. Strong protection, both in a legal and a technical sense, is still necessary to prevent people from shooting themselves in the foot and to protect the collective value that privacy also embodies. Moreover, several threats to human autonomy and dignity that privacy aims to protect against do not diminish by simply shifting from a centralized to a distributed form of data processing on the devices of end users. Without additional safeguards, such distributed models can still profile and influence us.

7

PRIVACY AND SECURITY ARE A ZERO-SUM GAME

Every time a terrorist attack succeeds, every time a hideous crime remains unsolved, every time a slumbering domestic problem erupts, every time people slide deeper down the spiral of debt, people blame such diverse security problems on a lack of information. They believe that if only we had known more and had known sooner, such tragedies could perhaps have been averted.[1]

You would almost believe privacy is security's worst enemy.

Privacy and security are often seen as a zero-sum game: a gain in security necessarily decreases privacy and vice versa. This point of view is not only common when discussing homeland security (like fighting crime and preventing terrorism) or societal or economical security issues (like getting to grips with domestic violence or preventing fraud) but also when considering traditional computer and information security goals in the design of information technology systems. Security and privacy are often seen as opposite, irreconcilable goals. Because the stakes involved are high, the debate is often heated and emotional. Privacy advocates and security hawks cling to rigid viewpoints, fighting each other in an aging war of trenches. As a result, measures to increase our security scorn our privacy. And privacy-enhancing technologies do very little to address legitimate security concerns. This is bad, both for our privacy and our security, and for society at large: "It is highly unlikely that either extreme—total surveillance or total privacy—is good for our society."[2]

This chapter will show that the issue is really more nuanced. First, it's certainly possible to design systems that are both secure and privacy friendly. We will illustrate this through the design of a privacy-friendly form of digital cash, via which the way people spend their money is completely untraceable. The ideas illustrated through the digital cash example can be generalized to the concept of *revocable privacy*, which can help bridge the gap between legitimate security and privacy concerns.

7.1 A SHINING EXAMPLE: DIGITAL CASH

Traditional cash (i.e., paper money and physical coins) is a very privacy-friendly means of payment. Although paper notes have serial numbers, they are not scanned with every transaction. This means that looking in someone's wallet will not allow you to tell where they got their money from. Nor can the supermarket tell at the end of the day who its customers were and what they bought. Now, suppose you want to create a digital means of payment. Is it possible to do so in a privacy-friendly fashion? And if so, what about the security of the scheme?

Digital payment schemes that allow you to pay for goods online or that allow you to pay for your coffee with a tap of your smartphone do exist, of course. But those are all very privacy invasive. That is because all these schemes are essentially *account* based. You have an account with a bank, and so does the merchant. A payment essentially instructs your bank to transfer money from your account to the account of the merchant you bought something from. The banks keep a record of all these transactions. So do the merchants. The transactions include your account number and that of the merchant, plus possible other transaction details. This allows the bank (and the merchants) to link transactions and to compile profiles of your shopping behavior. The main privacy property we want from a payment mechanism is *unlinkability* (as discussed in chapter 4): it should be impossible to link transactions—to link the money I spent to the money a merchant collects.[3]

From a privacy perspective, then, account-based systems are doomed. What about a cash-based model for digital payment? *Digital cash* aims to model traditional cash by representing money as digital tokens that can be spent directly between a consumer and a merchant, without an intermediary like a bank. The idea is that a consumer could send a few digital cash tokens (which we will call *digital coins*) to the merchant, just as one traditionally would physically hand over some cash. Because the intermediary is out of the loop by definition (at least for now), the immediate privacy risk is eliminated.[4]

But proper privacy is not guaranteed yet. What's worse, we've now introduced a gaping security hole. By their very nature, digital coins (which are just small digital documents stored on a computer or in a smartphone) can be perfectly copied at will. Physical cash is guaranteed to literally change hands (when I give a coin to you, I no longer have that coin), but when I send you digital coins, it does not by definition remove those coins from my computer. I have to explicitly delete them afterward. And why would I do that? Why would I not keep them and try to spend my digital cash another time at another shop? This is called the *double-spending* problem that is brought about by moving from a digital account-based system to a digital cash-based approach.

Apart from the need to prevent double spending, there is of course another security requirement: digital coins should be unforgeable. People should not be able to create digital coins out of thin air, and merchants should be able to determine whether digital coins are authentic and what their denominations are. These security requirements quite naturally lead to the conclusion that digital coins should be unique and somehow digitally signed. This is the most obvious way to prevent counterfeiting and to prevent tampering with the denominations encoded in the digital coins. But making digital coins unique almost by definition makes them traceable. So have we thrown the baby out with the bathwater?

The digital cash problem essentially captures the core of the security versus privacy paradox. The security requirements for a digital cash-based system are essentially twofold: (1) double spending of digital coins should not be possible; and (2) digital coins should be unforgeable. And the main privacy requirement is the following: digital coins should be unlinkable.

At first sight, these requirements seem to be contradictory. Enter David Chaum.[5]

David Chaum in fact pioneered the field of privacy protection in the 1980s and invented many core privacy-enhancing technologies, like the mix networks discussed in chapter 4. He also started the work that eventually led to the anonymous credentials described in chapter 5. And he developed a form of digital cash that was both privacy friendly and secure, squaring this circle for the first time.

His core invention that allowed him to pull this off is the *blind signature.*[6] Recall from chapter 5 that a digital signature on a document is created using a private signing key and that the signing process involves the full contents of the document (ensuring that not a single bit can be altered afterward without detection). This essentially means the signer knows the contents of the document being signed. David Chaum realized that it was possible to modify the process by which a digital signature was made in such a way that the signer did *not* have to know the contents of the document being signed. In general, this property is not useful: Who in his right mind would wish to sign a document without knowing its content? For all you know, you might be signing your death warrant! But for private digital coins, it's exactly the property you want.

The mathematics underlying blind signatures are too complex to explain in this book, but a nice physical analogy (also thanks to David Chaum, in fact) helps to explain how they work.[7] Suppose a bank wants to allow its customers to obtain special commemorative dollar bills that each customer can design by himself, without revealing their design to the bank. You (a customer of the bank) and the bank could proceed as follows. You put your design for a commemorative dollar bill together with a piece of carbon paper in a closed envelope. In exchange for a real dollar bill, the bank signs the outside of the envelope with a signature that is only used (and therefore valid) for virtual one-dollar bills. Back home, you open the envelope and take out the commemorative dollar bill inside. Because of the carbon paper, the commemorative dollar bill now carries the signature from the bank denoting this bill as a valid commemorative one-dollar bill. And because the bank never opened the envelope, it did not learn what your design for the commemorative dollar bill looked like.

Chaum's idea was that a digital coin was nothing more than a random serial number chosen by the user (like the design for the commemorative dollar bill), blindly signed by the bank using different signing keys for different denominations. This ensures that the value of the digital coin can be determined from the key used to sign the coin. Forgery is prevented by the signature. Unlinkability is guaranteed by the blind approach. Preventing double spending will be discussed in a minute.

To obtain a digital coin, a user proceeds as follows. He picks a random serial number, blinds it (i.e., puts it in an envelope with carbon paper), and sends it to the bank for a blind signature. This ensures that the bank does not learn the serial number. In exchange for real money, the bank signs it with the appropriate private signing key and sends the blind signature back. The user unblinds the blind signature (i.e., removing the envelope), revealing the serial number now signed by the bank.

To spend this coin, the user can send it to a merchant in exchange for goods. The merchant can check the signature using the corresponding public verification key and determine its value. Just before finishing the transaction, the merchant sends the coin to the issuing bank. If the coin has not been used before, the merchant receives the value of the coin in real money in return (and the transaction succeeds), while the bank records the serial number of the coin as spent. However, if the bank reports back to the merchant that the coin has already been spent, the transaction fails.

Privacy is guaranteed through the use of blind signatures. These signatures guarantee that the bank does not see the serial numbers when issuing digital coins, making the coins that merchants deposit at the bank unlinkable. Security is guaranteed by the traditional properties of signatures that ensure that digital coins cannot be forged. Double spending is prevented because merchants check the serial numbers of the coins they receive in real time with the bank. Realizing that requiring an online connection with the bank was undesirable, Chaum later improved the protocol to allow digital coins to be accepted by merchants without the need to check them immediately for double spending with the bank.[8] As this clearly cannot *prevent* double spending (so long as a merchant does not clear a spent coin with the bank, it could be spent again at another merchant), the security requirement is relaxed somewhat: if a coin is double spent, this will always detected later.[9] Moreover, for double-spent coins, and for double-spent coins *only*, the bank will be able to deduce who they were issued to.

David Chaum founded the company DigiCash to commercialize his invention in 1989.[10] Unfortunately, the company was not successful and went bankrupt almost ten years later.

7.2 REVOCABLE PRIVACY

Chaum's ideas, and especially the mechanism alluded to in the penultimate paragraph—wherein the identity of the perpetrator that double-spent some coins is revealed—eventually were generalized to a different concept called *revocable privacy*.[11]

Revocable privacy aims to bridge the two sides of the security versus privacy debate and to break the status quo. Revocable privacy is a design principle for building systems that balance security and privacy needs. The underlying principle is *privacy unless*. This means that the system must be designed to guarantee the privacy of its users unless a user violates a predefined rule. In that case, (personal) information will be released to authorized parties. This principle is enforced by technical means because laws and regulations by themselves are insufficient: they can be changed or sidestepped later on.[12] That is why the principle of *code as law* is taken as the point of departure: the rules and regulations must be hard-wired into the architecture of the system itself.[13]

Formally, revocable privacy is defined as follows: "A system implements revocable privacy if the architecture of the system guarantees a predefined level of privacy for a participant as long as they do not violate a predefined rule. If the rule is violated, some personal data of the perpetrator is released to act on the violation."[14] Moreover, the guarantees should hold for both the design and the implementation of the system.

One way to achieve revocable privacy is by using a *spread responsibility* approach, wherein several trusted third parties verify whether all conditions for releasing personal data have been met and grant access (or release the data) if this is the case. By using several such parties, one mitigates the likelihood of corruption or subversion because the power to do so is spread. No single party can act on his or her own. Techniques to ensure that the actual cooperation of a certain fraction or threshold of the trusted parties is required do exist. *Secret sharing* techniques, for example, allow a decryption key to be split into several shares such that at least a certain threshold number of these shares must be obtained to enable the reconstruction of the decryption key.[15]

The other mechanism is much stronger and is what mostly interests us here. This is a *self-enforcing architecture*, wherein the rules to release data are hard-coded into the architecture itself. If the rules are violated, the data are released automatically. If no rules are trespassed, no information can be obtained at all. Because spread responsibility–based systems are in essence still procedure based (by changing the procedures and replacing the trusted parties, one can still change the rules of the game), we believe that self-enforcing approaches to revocable privacy are the way forward. Chaum's digital cash is self-enforcing, for example.

As mentioned before, the ideas underlying revocable privacy are certainly not new.[16] But the concept has so far not received the attention and further investigation it deserves. A practical example may help to demonstrate the power and the limitations of the approach. In fact, the example cited ahead motivated the study into revocable privacy in the first place.

Canvas cutters are criminal gangs roaming the highways looking for trucks with valuable cargo. Hence their name: they cut the canvas of trucks parked at night in highway car parks to see what's inside. If the contents are worth the effort, the truck is stolen or relieved of its contents later at night. At some point, canvas cutters became quite a nuisance in the Netherlands, so the Dutch police wanted to investigate and see whether they could somehow track the perpetrators. As the modus operandi of canvas cutters involves visiting all the car parks along a stretch of highway, the police reckoned that a car visiting a lot of different car parks would be a telltale sign of possible involvement. (Clearly there are exonerating explanations for such patterns: police cars on patrol tend to visit many car parks as well, and so do the roadside assistance vans of the ANWB, the Dutch automobile association.)

The police realized that they could detect such patterns if they could collect the license plate numbers of cars visiting many car parks along a highway using automatic license plate recognition (ALPR) cameras (also used in the car park example discussed in chapter 1), mounted at the entrance of every car park along a stretch of highway frequented by canvas cutters. By collecting the lists of all recorded license plates of every monitored car park at the end of each day and counting how often each license plate appears in each of the lists, potentially suspect license plates could more or less automatically be found and further investigated. The police *also* realized that by doing so they would collect huge lists of license plates of unsuspected and innocent passersby as well. This was deemed a risk and considered too much collateral damage.

—

Could there be a less privacy-invasive approach to detect such patterns? In other words, could the canvas cutters problem be solved in a more privacy-friendly way? The problem, in abstract terms, fits the revocable privacy frame: cars visiting highway car parks should enjoy perfect privacy, *unless* they visit more than a predetermined threshold of different car parks on the same day. In that case, they are suspect. A solution to this problem would thus inform of us how revocable privacy could be implemented in practice.

Indeed, such a solution exists.[17] The idea is to encrypt the license plate numbers directly in the ANPR cameras as soon as they have been recognized (and immediately remove the plaintext license plate numbers after that). This means that a camera only stores encrypted versions of license plate numbers that visited the car park it monitors. Each camera has a different encryption key, which is constructed in such a way that an encrypted license plate can *only* be decrypted if the same license plate is encrypted with a sufficient number of different encryption keys (i.e., on a sufficient number of different cameras). This sufficient number corresponds to the preestablished threshold mentioned before. This threshold is a parameter that controls the process for initializing the keys for the camera to guarantee this property. If less than the threshold number of encryptions of the same license plate occurs in a list, the individual ciphertexts in the lists of encrypted license plates produced by the cameras are worthless: they simply cannot be decrypted.

Revocable privacy cannot always be achieved in a purely self-enforcing way. In the canvas cutters example, it *is* possible because the rule depends on information that can be ascertained in a fully automatic way. The same holds for the double-spending rule in Chaum's digital cash. In many other applications, this is not the case, however. Often the rule depends on vague, incomplete information. Or it depends on a (human) interpretation of the evidence at hand. Consider, for example, another application of the revocable privacy concept, used to combat abuse on Wikipedia.

Wikipedia is a massive collaborative online encyclopedia: people from all over the world contribute to its currently fifty-one million pages (as of July 2020).[18] Wikipedia in general does not allow truly anonymous editing of entries, mostly to keep people accountable to their actions at some level.[19] But allowing truly anonymous editing of pages would be desirable in certain circumstances—for example, when editing potentially controversial pages (whether they cover the recent protests in Hong Kong, pedophilia, climate change, fascism, or the alt-right movement). On the other hand, especially in the case of controversial pages, anonymity can be abused to perform malicious edits on pages or to disrupt discussions of their content without a risk of retribution.

An approach to this dilemma is to try to apply the revocable privacy principle here as well: editors enjoy anonymity, unless they abuse it. *Abuse* is a vague condition, however, one that cannot be established by purely technical mechanisms alone. Some kind of human judgment needs to be involved. Hence a spread responsibility approach, involving several independent moderators that create a verdict on an edit that is flagged as abusive, is the best we can aim for. It turns out that such an approach is possible, allowing the identity of the author of an offensive edit to be revealed, provided enough votes to this effect are cast by a known group of moderators. If the number of votes does not exceed the predetermined threshold, the author is guaranteed to stay anonymous. It's even possible to design the system in such a way that other edits of the same author over a limited time period (which otherwise are unlinkable) can be linked if one of his edits is deemed inappropriate.[20]

It's important now to step back a bit and see what revocable privacy really delivers and what its limits are.

By encoding predefined rules into the architecture of the system, and by guaranteeing—through technological means—proper privacy for those that abide by those rules, we reduce the risk of function creep (as discussed in chapter 3). The risk that personal data is going to be used for other purposes disappears if that data is only ever available in a very restrictive set of circumstances that depend on the predefined rules that are encoded into the system. It's simply impossible to change the rules after the fact because this would require a complete redesign and reimplementation of the system. It's precisely this fact that makes the technical protection offered through revocable privacy through self-enforcing means so strong. But it's also exactly this constraint that makes it much less desirable to apply revocable privacy in practice: systems designed using the revocable privacy approach cannot be easily modified or extended.

There are limitations too. At a more technical level, there appears to be a fundamental limitation for handling cases in which *not* doing something violates the rule—for example, a rule that requires all citizens to vote or to fill in their tax forms. The problem is that mechanisms to achieve revocable privacy typically encode a small breadcrumb of information with every action performed. This is done in such a way that even several breadcrumbs combined still divulge no information, unless the combination of breadcrumbs happens to correspond to a sequence of actions that trigger the predefined rule. Such a mechanism by definition does not create a breadcrumb if no action is performed, and hence it is unclear how the act of not doing something would then result in the final piece of the puzzle being released.

But at a more fundamental level, there are even more important questions that need to be addressed when applying concepts like revocable privacy in the first place.

First and foremost, the strength of revocable privacy stands or falls with the rules encoded in the system. Are these rules fair, do they make sense, and are they appropriate given the overall goal the system aims to accomplish? How is the rule-making process organized? Which stakeholders are involved, and in particular, do data subjects themselves have a seat at the table? Who ultimately decides on them? In fact, one of the reasons to develop the concept of revocable privacy is to force a more general discussion on such questions related to the balance between security and privacy in society. Revocable privacy forces a discussion on the rules of the game, on the rules to be encoded in the system, before the design of the system can commence. There is no escape; the discussion cannot be postponed until later. At the moment, this debate is sorely lacking.

Second, there is hardly ever a scenario in which all good and all bad behaviors are clearly separable with a set of simple rules. There will almost always be a gray area between the clearly bad behaviors and the clearly good behaviors. This means that a particular choice of rules will either lead to false positives (like the police cars and ANWB vans in the canvas cutters scenario) or false negatives (where canvas cutters avoid detection by only visiting a small number of car parks each day).

And last but not least, the question is whether a fully automatic enforcement of rules is really desirable at all. As a simple and perhaps controversial example: with the current state of technology, it's almost trivial to enforce speed limits. By forcing the installation of a speed-measuring device in every car, one can either prevent cars from speeding altogether or can ensure that anybody speeding gets fined automatically. Yet we do not do this.

7.3 BUSTED: PRIVACY + SECURITY > ZERO

Privacy and security are often seen as mutually exclusive aims: you can't have your cake and eat it too. This is a myth for reasons similar to why "I've got nothing to hide" is a myth (as discussed in chapter 3). It's creating a false dichotomy between security and privacy: both are important in a democratic society, and both have a lot more in common than we are led to believe. Privacy is a form of personal security, for example. It protects against *identity fraud* or *phishing* and protects vulnerable people and minorities against harassment and abuse. Victims of domestic violence that take refuge in a safe house depend on the privacy of their location for their personal safety. Members of religious minorities or members of the LGBTQ community likewise depend on the privacy of their religious beliefs, their sexual orientation, or their gender identity if these are repressed where they live. Consequently, there is not only a privacy versus security trade-off, but often also a security versus security trade-off at stake.

Furthermore, even in cases in which privacy and security *are* distinct goals, they can often both be achieved at the same time, as our discussion of Chaum's system for digital cash makes clear. In general, the concept of revocable privacy can be used as a guiding principle when such potential conflicts between privacy and security arise. This approach has the benefit that it forces an up-front analysis of the security and privacy requirements guiding the system to be designed and that the rules to be embedded into the system have to be agreed upon in advance. It also reduces the risk of function creep.

Finally, the trench warfare between privacy advocates and security hawks is counterproductive and even harmful: clinging to extreme points of view significantly increases the risk that we end up with systems that no one wants, which weaken our privacy and do little to increase our security (or vice versa).

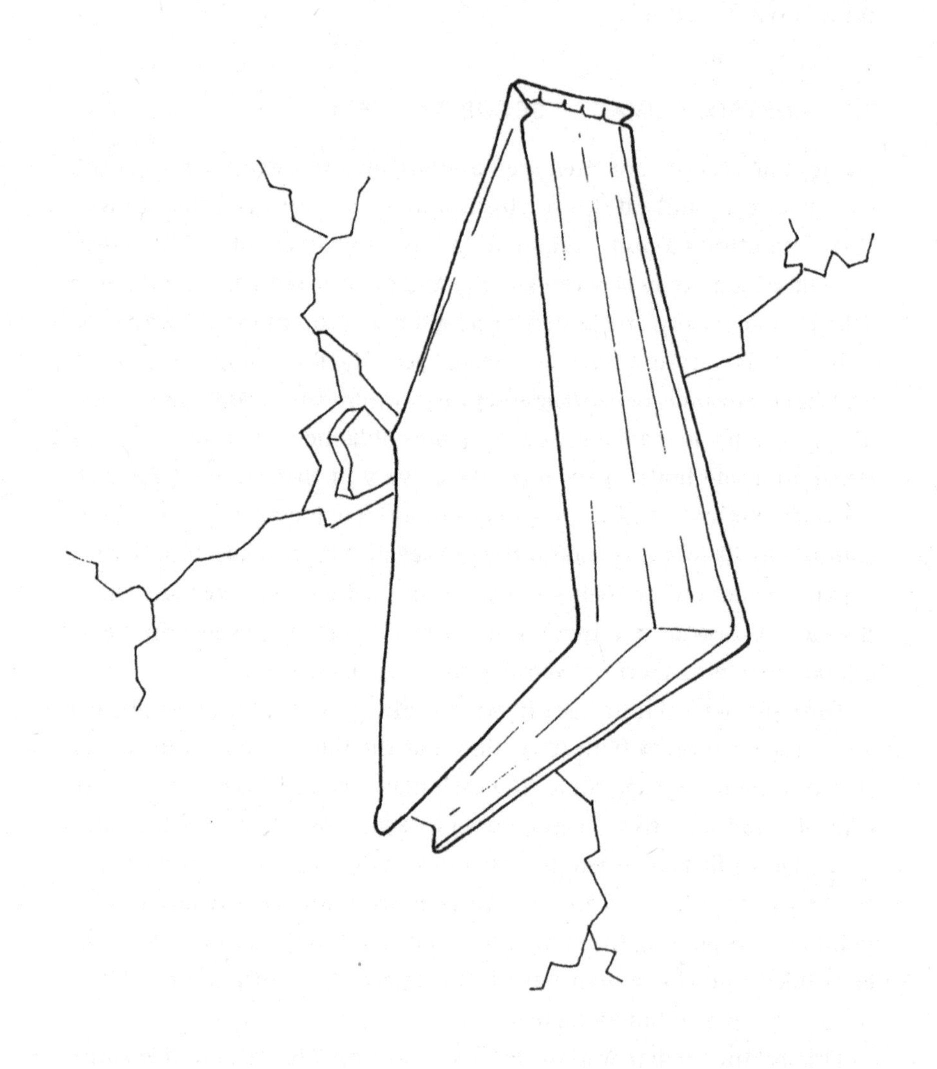

8

PRIVACY IS HARD

Even though proper privacy protection requires a fundamental shift in how systems are designed, it is really not as hard as people tend to think. Throughout this book, we have encountered many examples in which a simple shift in the underlying approach, a change of perspective, makes it much easier to cater for privacy. We have also seen that there are many privacy-enhancing technologies ready to be used for the implementation of more privacy-friendly systems.

Perhaps an important reason that privacy is perceived to be hard is that privacy is different from other requirements that system designers typically encounter (like security or performance). Privacy is a much more ambiguous, context-dependent, social normative construct, whereas these other types of requirements are typically much more concrete and technical in nature.

This chapter discusses the privacy by design philosophy at length, describing the different phases the development of system proceeds through and how in each of these phases privacy can systematically be addressed. Our particular focus is on the early system development phases, wherein important decisions that can impact privacy at a fundamental level are made continually. We show how privacy design strategies can guide system designers through the first phases of privacy-friendly system design, making privacy by design more concrete and showing that privacy can be achieved through careful design.

8.1 PRIVACY BY DESIGN

Suppose you are responsible for the development of a new system that could potentially impact the privacy of a large number of users. Perhaps you founded or joined a start-up, or perhaps you work for a large company or government organization. In other words, you are now in a position to apply everything you learned so far in this book—to actually put privacy by design into practice.[1]

As discussed in chapters 1 and 2, privacy by design is a system design philosophy that aims to improve the overall privacy protection of systems. The point of departure is the observation that privacy is a core property of a system that is heavily influenced by the underlying system design. Initial design decisions have a decisive impact on the ultimate level of privacy offered by the system being designed. We have seen many examples of this throughout this book. As a consequence, privacy protection cannot be implemented as an add-on. Privacy must be addressed from the outset instead.

The main question is how to do so in real life. The first attempts to formalize privacy by design, like Ann Cavoukian's foundational principles, do a good job explaining the privacy by design philosophy and the intended outcome, but offer little concrete guidance on how to get there, how to achieve the intended outcome of a more privacy-friendly system.[2] The fair information practice principles of the US Federal Trade Commission (FTC) or the privacy guidelines of the Organisation of Economic Co-Operation and Development (OECD) offer a little more guidance but still are not concrete enough.[3]

To understand the privacy by design approach, and see how it can be made more concrete, you need to know a little bit about how systems are usually developed. System development ideally proceeds through a number of distinct phases: ideation, definition, design, development (including testing), deployment, operation, evaluation, and decommissioning, explained further ahead.[4] These correspond to the system lifecycle (see figure 8.1).

The *ideation* (or *concept formulation*) phase starts when a need or opportunity to build a new system is identified—for example to automate a certain business process or to offer a new online service. It is followed by the *definition* phase, which delivers a clear description of the functional

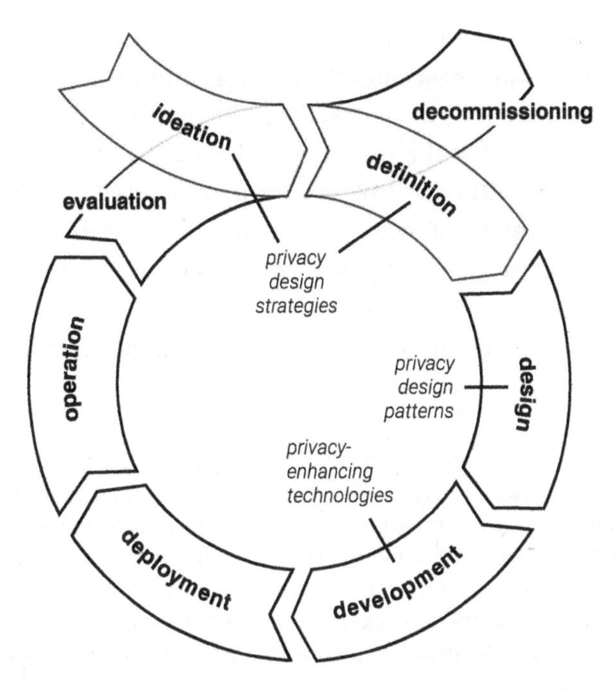

8.1 The system lifecycle, and how to address privacy in the first four phases.

requirements of the system—that is, a description of what the system is supposed to do and how well it is supposed to do it, within specified constraints. This *functional specification* (see also chapter 1) is based on a proper understanding of the needs of the end users of the system and the context or environment within which it must operate. A description of this context is part of the specification and in essence expresses the constraints within which the system needs to be designed and developed. Because it is very hard to specify *what* a system needs to do without describing *how*, the functional specification of a system will often already describe the different components and the information that flows between them. This is especially the case if the system needs to run on known devices (which is the case if, for example, you are developing a smartphone app supported by a back-end infrastructure).

The fundamental principle of privacy by design is that privacy requirements must be addressed already at the very start of the system development process. In a sense, privacy is a nonfunctional requirement, also known as a *software quality attribute*. It says something about the way in which the primary functionality must be implemented; it expresses a quality measure that the system needs to satisfy. This makes privacy similar to quality attributes like security, up time, speed, or throughput. These are also heavily influenced by initial system design choices, which explains why these quality attributes are already taken into account as a matter of course in system design.

Let's consider an example from the world of building and construction (i.e., physical architecture) to make this concrete.

Example: Consider a village along the river. Over time, people settled also on the other side of the river, crossing the river with their own small boats to visit the other side. To boost the economy, and also to strengthen the ties between these two separate parts of the village, the city council wants to improve the connections between the two parts of the river. Over several meetings with experts and villagers, the city council settles on the requirements a new connection should satisfy and the constraints it should adhere to: the connection should allow villagers to go to the other side on foot, by bike, on a horse, and by car; allowing trucks to cross would be nice but is not mandatory; crossing time (by car) should be twenty minutes at most; and boats passing through the river should not be impeded.

Notice that in this case these functional requirements do not specify whether the connection should be realized by building a bridge or by setting up a ferry. On the other hand, possible design options will have been explored during the definition phase to ensure that the final specification can be met with a sensible design within the city council budget. In many cases, a particular solution strategy will already be chosen in this phase.

The *design* phase creates the design of the system that best matches the requirements and satisfies all constraints described in the functional requirements delivered by the definition phase. The design document describes the different system components, what each of these components do, how they relate to each other, and how the different components cooperate and exchange information. Typically, not all requirements can all be met at the same time, so certain trade-offs will have to be made (and documented) in the design. Designing systems typically proceeds in phases, wherein a coarse design is refined up to the point that the design is sufficiently detailed to be built.

Example: In our hypothetical village, a group of construction designers are given the functional requirements the connection between the two parts of the village should satisfy. They have dealt with this problem before and know such a connection can be realized by building a dam or a bridge, digging a tunnel, or setting up a ferry. A first pass over the requirements quickly rules out the option of using a dam: one of the requirements is that boats crossing the river should not be impeded by the connection. After a bit of study, and checking the available budget, digging a tunnel is also dismissed. Using a ferry, even though it's the least disruptive in terms of existing traffic on the river itself, is ruled out later because of the limited capacity and the fact that the crossing time would likely exceed the specified maximum of twenty minutes. This leaves the designers with the option to design a bridge. There are still many different types of bridges to choose from, so it takes a few more weeks before the designers deliver the construction drawing for a bridge that matches the requirements and satisfies the constraints.

During the *development* phase, the system design is turned into something that actually works: hardware is bought or constructed, devices are interconnected, software is written, and existing libraries and services are integrated. During this phase, individual components (or the overall system) are also tested. If necessary, the implementation or sometimes even the design is adjusted.

Example: The bridge in the construction drawing is built on a separate wharf on the left riverbank, close to where the bridge will be placed to join both parts of the village. The wharf decides where to buy the metal beams and bolts, welds the different parts together, and paints the bridge in the colors specified. Regular inspections ensure that the bridge is constructed according to its specifications and that all parts work as intended.

Once system development is complete, the *deployment* phase integrates the developed system into the actual real-world processes for which it was designed; the *operation* phase is concerned with the day-to-day usage and maintenance of the system; and the *decommissioning* phase ensures that the system is properly shut down and taken out of service.

Example: In our example, the implementation phase corresponds to preparing both quays for the placement of the bridge, closing the river to all marine traffic for a day, and lifting the bridge from the wharf and placing it in its final position. The operation phase consists of the citizens using the bridge to cross the river, as well as the police monitoring and guiding traffic on the bridge, and maintenance personnel regularly checking the bridge conditions, fixing issues when needed. The decommissioning phase starts with the decision to replace the bridge in the near future, and then concerns itself with the question of what to do with the old bridge (is it an icon that needs to be preserved, is the iron used worth something, etc.) and how to replace it.

The problem with privacy by design is that privacy as a software quality attribute is very different from other software quality attributes, like security or speed. The latter are more technical in nature, which makes them easier to specify and hence easier to implement. It's easier to specify security requirements (e.g., the information to be transmitted over networks should not be accessible to third parties) or speed requirements (e.g., the system should be able to process at least ten thousand transactions per second) and especially to verify that they are satisfied, compared to a privacy property, such as that the amount of personal data processed by the system must be minimal.

The reason is that privacy is a social normative construct, some of which are codified in law. The definition of *personal data* is ambiguous and complex (see chapter 1), and *processing* (a legal term in this case) means many more things than an engineer, a system designer with a technical background, may realize. For example, collecting, storing, sharing, or deleting data is also considered processing from a legal perspective. Also, the question whether the design actually processes the minimal amount of personal data to implement the desired functionality is a fuzzy one to answer. This means that it's hard for engineers to write specifications that properly address privacy concerns and hard for engineers to design and implement systems that satisfy these requirements. Legal concepts like privacy (or data protection) are too vague for engineers who need concrete goals, concrete requirements to get started.

The last few years, a considerable effort has been put into documenting, collecting, and systematizing privacy *design patterns*.[5] These help system designers to design systems in a more privacy-friendly way, especially as they embed and apply these softer legal norms in a particular context and describe the consequences (i.e., the solution) in a more concrete form that engineers are comfortable working with. But the privacy design patterns are only usable during the design phase of a system and not very helpful during the very early phases of system development—in particular, during the ideation and definition phases.

8.2 PRIVACY DESIGN STRATEGIES

To make privacy by design concrete and to support its application in the first phases of the system lifecycle as well, *privacy design strategies* were invented.[6]

A natural starting point to derive these privacy-preserving strategies is to look at when and how privacy is violated in a system, and then consider how these violations can be prevented. The challenge is to do this at a sufficiently high level of abstraction to not be bogged down in details while still being concrete enough to be useful. Stripped to the essence, we can view any system as an information storage (i.e., database) system. Current data protection legislation is pretty much written with that model of a system in mind.[7] In a database, information about people is stored in one or more tables. Each table (each with its own access conditions) stores certain sets of attributes about the people in the database. Sometimes, data is not stored at the level of individual persons but is instead aggregated based on certain relevant group properties (like postal codes). Within the legal framework, the collection of personal information should be proportional to the purpose for which it is collected, and this purpose should not be achievable through other, less invasive means.

In practice, this means that data collection should be *minimized*—for example, by not storing individual rows in a database table for each and every individual—and the number of attributes stored should correspond to the purpose. Data collected for one purpose should be stored *separately* from data stored for another purpose, and linking of these database tables should not be easy. When data about individuals are not necessary for the pertinent purpose, only *aggregate* data should be stored. Personal data should be properly protected, and strict access control procedures should *limit access* to authorized persons only. A data subject should be *informed* about the fact that data about her are being processed, and she should be able to request modifications and corrections where appropriate. In fact, the underlying principle of information self-determination dictates that she should be in *control*. Finally, the collection and processing of personal data should be done in accordance with a privacy policy, which should be actively *enforced*. The GDPR also stresses the fact that data controllers should be able to *demonstrate compliance* with data protection legislation.

We see that we can distinguish eight different privacy design strategies (see figure 8.2), divided between two different categories: data-oriented strategies and process-oriented strategies.

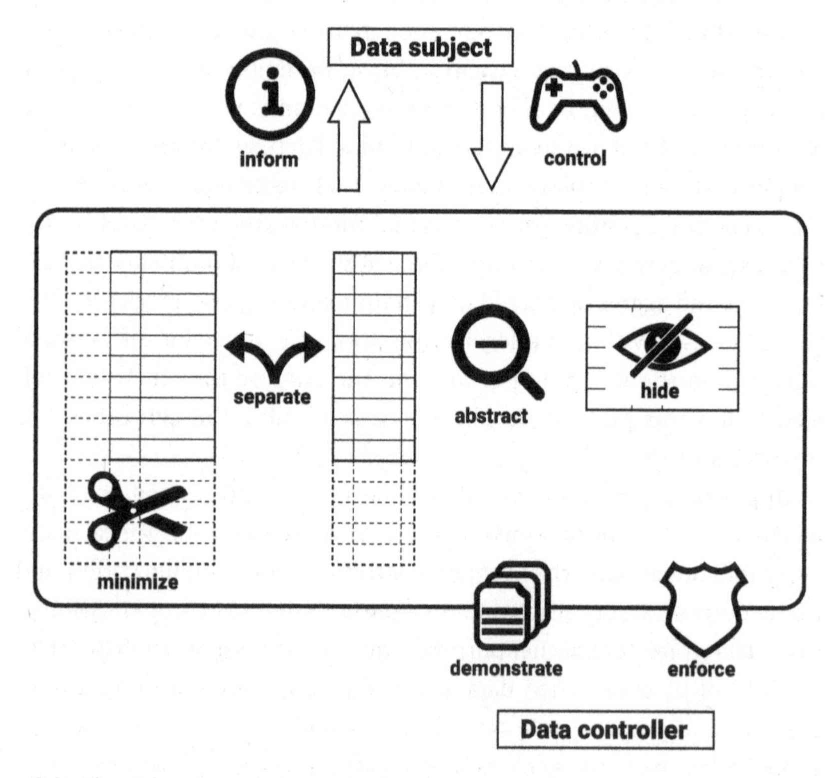

8.2 The eight privacy design strategies.

The four *data-oriented* strategies focus on the privacy-friendly processing of the data themselves. They are more technical in nature:

1. *Minimize*

   Limit the processing of personal data as much as possible.

2. *Separate*

   Separate the processing of personal data as much as possible.

3. *Abstract*

   Limit the detail with which personal data is processed as much as possible.

4. *Hide*

   Protect personal data or make it unlinkable or unobservable. Make sure it does not become public or known.

The four *process-oriented* strategies focus on the processes surrounding the responsible handling of personal data. They deal with the organizational aspects and the procedures that need to be in place:

5. *Inform*

   Inform data subjects about the processing of their personal data in a timely and adequate manner.

6. *Control*

   Provide data subjects adequate control over the processing of their personal data.

7. *Enforce*

   Commit to processing personal data in a privacy-friendly way, and adequately enforce this.

8. *Demonstrate*

   Demonstrate you are processing personal data in a privacy-friendly way.

In the following sections, we'll describe these privacy design strategies in more detail. For each strategy, we discuss why the strategy is relevant, what the strategy aims to accomplish, and how that can be achieved by giving concrete approaches and providing real-life examples. For each strategy we also provide a few more focused *tactics* that contribute to the overall strategy.[8]

We would like to stress that we use the term *personal data* in the definitions of the strategies in the (European) legal sense, as any piece of information that can be related either directly or indirectly to a natural person. Also, the term *processing* in the definitions must be interpreted in the (broad) legal sense of any activity that handles the data, including (but not limited to) its collection, use, alteration, deletion, or sharing.

Note that when describing a methodology for privacy by design, the focus is on protecting privacy in the best possible way. It is as though privacy is the only thing that matters. Of course, when applying privacy by design in practice, privacy concerns need to be weighed with other functional requirements and other software quality attributes of the system being designed. We will return to this issue later in this chapter.

8.2.1 DATA-ORIENTED STRATEGIES

Minimize The most obvious approach to protecting privacy is minimizing the amount of personal data you process. In the ideal case, you do not process any personal data at all, although in practice you almost always will to some extent.

Minimization is an important strategy because personal data that you do not store or process cannot be abused, misinterpreted, breached, subpoenaed, leaked, sold, and so on. In other words, this protects you against errors, malicious employees, incompetent third-party processors, overly inquisitive governments and law enforcement agencies, or greedy shareholders and investors. Also, minimization ensures that your users do not need to trust you to process their data responsibly. Instead of relying on rules or regulations, the system design itself prevents problems simply because the data is not there.

Considering minimization also forces you to think carefully about the fundamental values of your organization and the core business you are in. As the saying goes, "A cobbler should stick to his last." That is, if you are not in the primary business of profiling your customers for, say, advertising purposes, you should stay away from that. Minimization forces you to be specific about your purposes; don't be tempted to phrase them broadly.

Example: In 2014, ING, a large Dutch bank, decided to offer third parties the opportunity to reach its bank account holders with targeted advertising based on their transaction histories. This caused an uproar, and the bank quickly backtracked. ING customers considered this a huge breach of trust: financial transactions are quite sensitive—especially in the Netherlands, where people do not easily share their financial situations or even their salaries.

A few basic tactics can help when considering how to design a system in such a way that it collects as little information as possible.

First and foremost, either specifically *exclude* or specifically *select* the personal data you need. Be liberal with your grounds for exclusion and strict for your reasons to select. Both tactics work both when deciding whether to record personal data of certain *individuals*, as well as when deciding whether to record certain specific *attributes* about them.

Minimization is also achieved by regularly considering whether it's still necessary to process certain personal data. It's important to *delete* personal data as soon as it becomes irrelevant. One way to achieve this is to determine beforehand the period during which you need a particular data item and ensure it is automatically deleted as soon as this time expires. If the data item is part of a larger data record, update the field to a default value indicating it's unspecified. Be aware that changes in an organization, processes, or services may render certain data items irrelevant before their expiration time. So do not rely on this automatic process alone.

Completely *destroy* personal data as soon as they are no longer relevant. Ensure that the data cannot be recovered, even in unforeseen ways. Do not rely on logical removal strategies that only block the access to the data but leave (traces of) the data still accessible to skillful attackers. Remove data from backups as well and use secure ways to truly erase data from hard disks. One way is to use a process similar to that used by modern smartphones, which encrypt their data against a key and throw away the decryption key instead of actually erasing the data from secondary storage.

Excluding or selecting data is not only relevant the moment that you collect or receive data but also when you are (again) processing personal data collected earlier. Think carefully about the data you really need to achieve your goals. This often requires critical thinking about the design of your system. In many cases, a radically different, perhaps not so obvious design may enable you to achieve your goals while collecting much less personal data. We have seen many examples of this scattered throughout this book, like the restaurant reservation scheme in chapter 2.

Separate A much less obvious strategy to make systems more privacy friendly, but one with a profound impact, is to use the concept of separation. Instead of collecting and processing all personal data in one central location, the idea is to separate the processing either logically or physically. This prevents the unwanted combination of several pieces of personal data, each collected for a different purpose, into rich personal profiles. In the extreme case, separation may even guarantee that the service provider itself (i.e., the data controller) does not get access to the personal data at all.

This makes the separate strategy a strong alternative approach for those (many) cases in which it is hard to minimize the personal data you collect—for example, when designing a personalized service or when the primary functionality of the service simply processes a lot of personal data (like in health care or in the financial industry). In those cases, the separate strategy offers a different approach to still protect the data.

One approach is to logically *isolate* the collection and processing of personal data in different databases or applications. These databases or applications are either logically separated or actually run on different (yet still centrally located or controlled) hardware. This is actually quite a common approach—for instance, to separate the data contained in all the different databases maintained by the government, which when combined could deliver a very detailed profile of your personal life.

Another more fundamental approach is to *distribute* the collection and processing of personal data over different physical locations using databases and systems that are not under the control of a single entity. This implies the use of decentralized or even distributed system architectures instead of centralized ones. In practice, this means one should use the equipment (PC, laptop, smartphone) of the data subject himself as much as possible and use central components as little as possible. This idea is based on edge computing or P2P approaches and is discussed at length in chapter 6. Facial recognition can run locally on your own phone to recognize the people in the pictures you take and group your photos based on that information. A privacy-friendly version of such a social network would allow its users to store all updates and pictures locally on their own devices (e.g., their smartphones) and would share that information directly with their friends and acquaintances in a peer-to-peer fashion. In both cases, no data is stored or processed by a centralized component at all.

Again, separation requires you to think carefully about the data you really need to achieve your goals and where you need them.

Example: Historically, a passbook was used to record bank deposits or withdrawals, back in the days when people did not have bank accounts and wages were paid in cash. The passbook served as a local copy of all transactions, owned and controlled by the holder. Strictly speaking, only the passbook itself could have served as the authentic record, alleviating the bank of the need to maintain any information about the account and its holder. (In practice, banks also would have kept a record to prevent fraud.)

Abstract While the minimize strategy forces one to decide whether or not to process a particular piece of personal data, the abstract strategy addresses the more subtle question of the level of detail with which to process personal data. The less detailed a personal data item is—the more we "zoom out"—the lower the privacy risk is.

One way to achieve this is to *summarize* detailed attributes into more coarse-grained, general attributes. For example, one can record an age category instead of a birth date or a city of residence instead of a full address. In many cases (like special discounts for seniors or juniors or rules that require one to check whether someone is an adult), only the age matters, not the particular date of birth. In these cases, it suffices to record the attribute "over eighteen" or "senior citizen." Attribute-based credentials (see chapter 5) are based on this idea.

Another approach is to aggregate information about a *group* of people instead of processing personal information for each person in the group separately. Marketing data or other statistics are often compiled in this way, allowing one to obtain only the average statistic for all people that live within a specific postal code. The amount of protection this offers may be limited, however, and depends on the size and characteristics of the group (see the discussion on statistical disclosure control in chapter 3). If the group is homogeneous, then the value for the statistic will not vary much across group members. Then the mere fact that you are a member of this group reveals this statistic about you as well. If it is known that there is a strong correlation between certain music tastes and a propensity to commit fraud, then your taste in music will classify you as a potential fraudster (or not).[9] *Group privacy* is the research field devoted to studying these kinds of issues.[10]

Example: Smart meters are an example of a system that uses abstraction both over space as well as over *time*. For the stability of the electrical grid, detailed information on the energy use of a single household is not relevant. It suffices to monitor, in real time, the energy use of a whole street or block of houses. To determine an electricity bill, it isn't necessary to record energy use in real time. Instead, it's sufficient to send the accumulated energy use for, say, three months at a time to the energy supplier.

A final tactic is to *perturb* the data instead of processing the exact value of a personal data item. The idea is to use an approximation of that value or to adjust the value with some random noise. This idea can be used to make location-based systems more privacy friendly.

Location-based services use the location of the user in order to show relevant information (like a nearby restaurant or gas station, or the route to your hotel). Depending on the service, this location does not have to be exact, however. Consider the example of a restaurant recommendation app, popular with tourists. The naive approach would be to let the app send the exact location to the server of the recommendation service, which would then look up all relevant restaurants (and their ratings) within a few kilometers of that location. Instead of sending the actual location, the app can also report a coarse location. One way to do so is by rounding the actual location to the coordinates on a square kilometer grid. This reveals to the service provider only that the user is somewhere within this square kilometer. By increasing the size of the square—by coarsening the grid—privacy is increased.[11] The server responds with all the information relevant for anyone somewhere in this coarse location. If this results in a lot of information, the device itself can use the actual location to filter out only the really relevant data locally (in fact applying the separate strategy at the same time).

Hide Recall that the adequate protection of personal data is often a legal requirement (at least in the GDPR). In contrast to the minimize strategy, which forces one to decide whether or not to process certain personal data at all, the hide strategy focuses on the protection of this data once it's decided the data really is needed. It also addresses how to prevent inadvertently collecting metadata when ordinary data is being collected.

Hiding personal data can be achieved by protecting it (you know it's there but you can't access it), making it unlinkable (you know the data but not to which person it belongs), or making it unobservable (you are not even aware of the existence of the data).

There are several tactics one can deploy to achieve this.

Personal data can be protected by *restricting access* to it, setting up a strict *access control* policy that allows access only for those who really need it (the need to know principle). The policy should clearly describe who needs access to what and why. It should be described in such a way that it can easily and automatically be enforced. Apart from setting up an access control policy, you should also make it difficult to accidentally share or leak personal data. This can be as simple as setting up a firewall between different organizational units, properly protecting your web servers, or using a *data leakage prevention* system.

Apart from restricting access, one can *obfuscate* data to prevent its understandability or to prevent the underlying personal data from becoming known. An obvious approach (that we covered in chapter 3) is the use of encryption to secure data when it's transmitted over networks (data in transit) and when it's stored on hard disks or in databases (data at rest). Hashing (see chapter 1) can also be used to create a pseudonym or to create a verifiable tag that corresponds to the underlying personal data that was hashed without actually revealing it.

Instead of focusing on protecting the data itself, we can also try to sever (*dissociate*) the link between the data and the identity of the person to whom it belongs—for example, by removing directly identifying data from data records or by replacing full names or other identifiers with proper pseudonyms. Care should be taken to also remove implicit links like timestamps on events that, when retained, would allow one to determine afterward that certain events (e.g., incoming and outgoing payments) are related. Dissociation is thus a process that aims to pseudonymize or anonymize data sets. As discussed in chapter 3, completely anonymous data sets do not exist in practice: often one can use the retained data elements to deduce the identity of the person they pertain to. Therefore, do not rely on anonymization entirely.

A more thorough approach to achieve unlinkability (and unobservability) is to take a closer look at the metadata that is (often inadvertently) processed. A prime example is IP addresses that are used throughout the internet to route messages and are often stored in server logs. *Mixing* personal data (discussed at length in chapter 4) is a process that hides the source of an event or breaks the relationship between events in a more thorough way—for example, by hiding data in a cloud of other data.

8.2.2 PROCESS-ORIENTED STRATEGIES

Inform Transparency about what personal data are being processed, how they are processed, and for what purpose is an essential (though not sufficient) prerequisite for better privacy protection. It allows users to make informed decisions about using a system and agreeing to the processing of their personal data. Moreover, it allows society at large to verify whether organizations are processing our personal data responsibly. The inform strategy is closely related to the control strategy, to be discussed next. There are three tactics that one can use to implement the inform strategy: supply, explain, and notify.

Supplying information focuses on making sure that all the relevant information about the personal data you process is available. Make sure you have a privacy statement that provides all necessary information about *what* personal data are processed, *how* they are processed, and *why*. Clearly specify how long personal data are retained and how they are deleted. List all third parties with which you share these personal data, be clear about the conditions that cover each third-party data exchange, and specify how these conditions are enforced. Put a link to this *privacy statement* on your homepage, or in your app.[12] Clearly indicate how people with privacy questions can get in touch.

The privacy statement should contain all the nitty-gritty details pertaining to the way you process personal data, and as a result can be quite legalistic in nature. Therefore, you should also provide a more readable version that *explains* to the average user which personal data you process and why. Do this in a manner that is clear and easy to understand, even for a layperson. Target this information to different user groups: novices, experts, the authorities. Consider using a layered approach: first provide an overview, then provide links to more detailed information.

Example: *Privacy pictograms* can communicate the essence of a privacy policy at a glance.[13] For example, these icons can indicate the type of personal data processed, where they are processed, and whether they are shared with third parties (and if so, with whom).

Supplying information and providing an explanation are both passive approaches to the inform strategy. *Notifying* users (in real time) is a much more dynamic approach, in which you send a notification to a user the moment you process their personal data, share it with third parties, or become aware of a data leak. Notifications only work if they are short and informative and if their intrusiveness depends on their importance. Don't fall for the boy who cried wolf trap: do not notify too often or too intrusively. In particular, allow users to control for which events they wish to receive a notification.

Example: Apple's iOS shows a notification icon in the status bar whenever an application accesses the location services. This is an example of an *ambient notification*: the user is informed in a subtle, noninvasive way about the use of his personal data.

Informing users about the processing of their personal data (through a privacy statement) presupposes that there is a privacy policy in place (see the enforce strategy) on which the processing is based. Moreover, this information must be complete and up to date. This is harder than it first appears.

Control Providing control is a fundamental principle to protect privacy. The main goal of data protection in particular is not to totally prevent the processing and sharing of personal data, provided users have control and have a say in how their personal data is processed. Together with the inform strategy, control forces you to address consent, as well as data subject access rights, both cornerstones of the GDPR.

Asking users explicitly to *consent* to the processing of their personal data is the first tactic underlying the control strategy. You need to inform them beforehand about exactly which personal data will be processed, how they will be processed, and for which purpose (see also the inform strategy). Otherwise it is not considered informed consent and hence is invalid. Use an *opt-in* strategy (no processing without prior consent) instead of an *opt-out* strategy (processing takes place unless consent is withdrawn at a later stage): the default choice does *not* constitute consent. Don't use preselected checkboxes to subscribe people to newsletters, for example. Note that in many cases it should be possible to withdraw consent.

Consent is not always required to process personal data—for example, when you have a legitimate interest, you need the data to execute a contract (e.g., the postal address is required when ordering something online), or because there is a legal requirement to do so (e.g., banks verifying your identity).

When asking for consent, offer users a real *choice*: basic functionality should be accessible for people who do not consent to the processing of their personal data. Consider offering a (paid) alternative. Websites have to ask permission to place cookies.

Many of the "do you accept cookies" notifications do not comply: they do not offer a real choice as the website cannot be visited unless the cookie is accepted. A proper cookie statement offers a real choice to accept cookies and offers the option to choose which cookies to accept or not (e.g., those needed for anonymous website statistics or those used to connect with social networks).

Data subject access rights are addressed when offering users the means to *review* and *update* the personal data collected about them. A logical approach is to combine this with the inform approach that allows users to view the personal data collected.

You must also offer users a means to *retract* (or to ask for the deletion of) their personal information.

Example: A personal privacy dashboard clearly shows users which data are collected, how they are processed, for which purpose, and with whom they have been shared. Companies like Google have implemented such privacy dashboards.[14] Such dashboards are also used to allow users to change or delete personal information. Clearly, access to this dashboard must be tightly secured.

It isn't always possible or even required to allow users to correct their data or to delete their data when they ask you to. Sometimes, personal data are simply required to be retained. In medical records, it's undesirable to allow patients to edit entries with medical significance.

A radically different approach shifts the control of the personal data completely to the users themselves. Instead of organizations storing the personal data for all their customers, they ask their customers to each store those data themselves. The organizations later access that information through a standard interface under the control of the user. This is sometimes called *customer-managed relations*, as discussed at length in chapter 6.

Enforce Privacy should not only be guaranteed through technical means but also *enforced* through organizational means. It should be part of the organizational culture and be propagated by higher management. Otherwise, nobody will feel responsible. A clear *privacy policy* will provide scope and guidance. The enforce strategy is internally oriented, toward the organization itself. The strategy ensures that the externally communicated privacy statement (see the inform strategy) is also enforced internally through a privacy policy. Such a privacy policy must be created, then subsequently maintained and upheld.

Creating a privacy policy means that the organization should commit to privacy and assume responsibility for it. Assign resources to execute this policy. Determine for each process the goal and the (legal) ground: Is there a legitimate interest, or is consent required? Be clear about the business model.

Maintain the policy with all the necessary technical and organizational controls. Implement these controls. Assign responsibilities. Create an awareness campaign and train all personnel. Make sure third parties (processors) also comply with the policy.

Uphold the privacy policy. Circumstances change. Verify the privacy policy regularly and adjust its implementation whenever necessary. Establish prior criteria and evaluate your policy against them.

The privacy policy should be aligned with the overall business plan and mission statement of the organization. Make sure it is consistent with all other organizational policies.

Consideration should also be given to the system development processes within your organization. Adhere to the privacy by design philosophy and address privacy from the start. If you do not develop your own systems, then privacy by design thinking, and in particular the use of the privacy design strategies, also helps when setting the requirements for products or services to be procured.

Demonstrate This strategy addresses the new requirement in the GDPR that organizations need to demonstrate compliance with privacy regulations. The demonstrate strategy is externally oriented, toward the data protection authorities (possibly through the internal data protection officer).

The essence is to document extensively yet efficiently the ways in which the organization protects personal information and to do so in a surveyable and clarifying manner. Make sure that the documentation corresponds with reality and set up processes that ensure the documentation stays up to date. Record, audit, and report are the main tactics supporting the demonstrate strategy.

Record implies that, at the process/organizational level, you document all (important) steps taken and record all decisions made, including their motivation. At the technical level, record implies that you monitor and log all your systems (and respond to anomalies).

Audit regularly, not only the logs, but also the organizational processes in general and the way personal data is processed within the organization. Verify that what happens in practice corresponds to what the documentation says should happen.

Report the results of such audits to the Data Protection Authority (DPA) or keep them for later reference. Consult the DPA regularly, when possible.

The GDPR already envisions that certification schemes for privacy compliance (like TRUSTe or EuroPriSe) will become common; it may be helpful to be certified once these schemes are mature.[15] Alternatively, a benchmark with other organizations that operate within the same (business) sector could provide additional support for the privacy maturity of your organization.

Example: Performing a *data protection impact assessment* (DPIA), and especially recording the findings and properly documenting the decisions made based on it, is a good starting point. A DPIA has to be performed when personal data will be processed. Sometimes a limited DPIA suffices. When this indicates that significant privacy risks may arise, a full-fledged DPIA must be performed. A DPIA must be repeated every once in a while as circumstances may have changed.

Using formal methods and structured development environments when developing new systems is an advantage, as these create almost a proof of the fact that you have developed your system in a privacy-friendly way (depending on the specification, of course).

8.3 APPLYING THE PRIVACY DESIGN STRATEGIES

The primary purpose of the privacy design strategies is to guide the initial definition phase of a system development project, to ensure that privacy is adequately addressed in the functional design specification. The privacy design strategies impose certain (technical) goals that, when reached, improve the privacy of the overall system.

One could also view them as questions one can ask or talking points to raise during the software development process. How can I separate the processing of personal data? How can I properly inform my users about the processing of their personal data?

This can be done in a structured manner. Make sure all stakeholders involved in the project are represented, including the process owner and the technical expert. Also ensure that the end users (whose personal information will be processed) are represented as well. This guarantees that the process (and hence the analysis of the risks) takes not only the perspective of the data controller into account, but also that of the data subjects. Note that this clash of perspectives is one of the fundamental differences between security engineering and privacy by design and one of the reasons that the responsibility for addressing privacy protection within an organization should not be assigned to the same unit that is responsible for information security management. In other words, the chief information security officer (CISO) and the data protection officer (DPO) should be different people, each with their own independent staff.

Each of the strategies may be relevant in a particular context and help to reach a more privacy-friendly initial design. In other words: don't focus on just one strategy. It's not an either-or decision; they are all potentially useful. So apply them all, one by one, to make your system as privacy friendly as possible. Depending on the context, though, you may find certain strategies more applicable than others.

Consider all aspects related to the processing of personal data. That is, consider operating on, storing, retaining, collecting, sharing, changing, breaching, and deleting personal data. Investigate for each of the strategies (and associated tactics) whether they apply to each of these aspects. Don't limit your attention to ordinary personal data; also consider metadata (which may be collected inadvertently).

The fact that the privacy design strategies have been developed in the context of the classical waterfall development methodology does not mean that they cannot be applied in other, more modern approaches, like agile software development. Systems are defined and requirements specified in these approaches as well. However, these phases are embedded differently in these modern approaches. In fact, privacy design strategies may also be useful during the actual design and development phases to help select the best possible approach to solve a problem in a privacy-friendly manner. In that sense, they could be just as useful to agile software development squads. Another way to view this is to consider applying the design strategies to components of the overall system (instead of the system as a whole). In fact, one can apply the privacy design strategies iteratively: an initial design based on a first analysis using the privacy design strategies can be refined by applying the strategies again at a lower level of detail.

Finally, privacy design strategies are not only relevant when you develop systems yourself. They also can be used in procurement when determining the specifications for a product to be bought elsewhere or when drafting the system requirements for a system to be developed and built by an external contractor. Moreover, the strategies can be applied to (re)structure organizational processes as well. The privacy impact of a system is not only determined by the system itself. It's also determined by the way it's used within an organization.

9

BUSTED: PRIVACY ISN'T HARD IF YOU TRY

Nobody at the turn of this century, except perhaps a few die-hard civil rights activists, expected privacy to become such a dominant news item a decade later. But after the Snowden revelations, the Cambridge Analytica scandal, some serious data breaches at the Office of Personnel Management (the US federal human resource organization) and Ashley Madison (an extramarital dating service), and many other incidents, tech companies have finally come under growing scrutiny. Hardly a day goes by without yet another news story covering how this or that company tramples our privacy in such and such ways. As a result, legal protection of privacy has started to improve. Unfortunately, this has so far not really led to any significant changes in the way technology is designed and used. Apart from isolated efforts and fringe services offered by enthusiasts, the bulk of the services we use are still privacy invasive at their core. This book has hopefully convinced you that this is not a problem with technology itself, but with the way it's currently developed and used. And that privacy really isn't that hard if you try.

In a field as broad as privacy by design, it's unavoidable that there are many topics that are not covered in depth, if at all, in a book of this size. Important privacy-enhancing technologies like homomorphic encryption, private information retrieval, secure multiparty computation and secret sharing had to be omitted due to space constraints.[1] Also, the current heated debate over whether to grant law enforcement access to encrypted data and communications is important, but it warrants almost a separate chapter to really do justice to the complexity and nuances involved.[2] A whole new battleground has erupted over the question of the use of personal data in artificial intelligence and how such systems can be made fair, accountable, and transparent. We barely scratched the surface of that issue in chapter 6. A whole lot more could have been said about the limits of transparency alone, to name but one example.[3]

Privacy by design as a design philosophy goes beyond mere data protection compliance.[4] In essence, the idea is to provide the best possible level of privacy protection, based on currently available technology. According to Cavoukian's principles, privacy should not be achieved by sacrificing functionality.[5] However, this avoids talking about the elephant in the room: Does it make sense to talk about privacy by design when the main purpose of the system is to invade our privacy, whether by a government-run surveillance system or a commercial service with a business model based on selling personal data? In many cases the law simply prohibits certain forms of processing of personal data. But in other cases, organizations and business have to make tough decisions and adjust their original goals or change their initial plans to improve privacy. There is often a temptation to turn a blind eye or broaden the purpose, in order to allow for a little more data collection than is strictly necessary.

One particularly thorny issue (at least with the GDPR) is that one of the legitimate grounds for processing personal data is when there is a legal obligation to do so. As a result, countries are proposing laws that legally require organizations to collect, store, and share personal data that they would otherwise not be allowed to. Existing laws in fact already require organizations to collect and keep a lot of personal data. Dutch tax laws, for example, are very complex, meaning that the amount of taxes a Dutch citizen needs to pay may depend on very personal information. As a result, the Dutch tax authorities are sitting on a treasure trove of personal data. This is also the case for social security laws, for which very intimate personal information decides whether you are entitled to full social benefits.[6]

This shows that if we limit privacy by design thinking to just the creation of technical artifacts, we will never reap the full benefits. For that, we also need to apply privacy by design to the environments in which these systems are to be deployed, to the organizations and business processes in which they are used, and to the laws that shape what these systems are supposed to do or are allowed to do. Only then will we achieve proper privacy protection.

Many privacy-friendly approaches to designing services in a more privacy-friendly way exist, and this book has presented many examples. It's simply a matter of applying them. And we should start doing so, or demand that it is done by those in the position to do so. Like calls for safety or sustainability, such a demand is entirely reasonable given the state of the art of privacy by design.

A perfect privacy-friendly solution is not always possible, however. This should not deter us from trying to reach a reasonable compromise. Some good enough level of protection is preferred over no protection at all. For example, it already helps tremendously if the privacy protective measures we do apply make a privacy-invasive business case unprofitable, even if it leaves determined and highly resourced attackers undeterred. Let perfect not be the enemy of good. Instead, let us start by implementing *good enough* privacy-protecting measures now, have a continual discussion about what level of protection actually is good enough, advance the state of the art and its application in practice, and thus slowly raise the bar.

Significantly improving the privacy of the apps and services we use should be our first priority. But at some point, we need to dig deeper down into the technology stack and reconsider the designs for our computers and networks, both at the hardware and the operating system levels. These designs are half a century old by now and never fundamentally changed, while the world in which they are used has changed beyond recognition. We are stretching the boundaries of their use beyond the breaking point—not only in terms of privacy, by the way, but also in terms of security and reliability. It's time to start redoing the plumbing, instead of applying Band-Aids to temporarily stop some leakage while we frantically mop the floor against all odds.

GLOSSARY

ABC	Attribute-based credential
AES	Advanced Encryption Standard
AI	Artificial intelligence
AML	Anti-money laundering
ALPR	Automatic license plate recognition (also known as automatic number plate recognition, ANPR)
BBC	British Broadcasting Corporation
CEO	Chief executive officer
CD	Compact disc
CISO	Chief information security officer
CMR	Customer-managed relations
CJEU	Court of Justice of the European Union
CRM	Customer relationship management
CPU	Central processing unit
DES	Data Encryption Standard
DPA	Data Protection Authority
DPO	Data protection officer
EFF	Electronic Frontier Foundation
ER	Emergency room
EU	European Union
FIPPs	Fair information practice principles

FTC	Federal Trade Commission
GCHQ	Government Communications Headquarters
GDPR	General Data Protection Regulation
GPS	Global Positioning System
HIV	Human immunodeficiency virus
HTML	Hypertext markup language
IBM	International Business Machines
IdP	Identity provider
IoT	Internet of Things
IRMA	I Reveal My Attributes
ISP	Internet service provider
IP	Internet protocol
KYC	Know your customer
LGBTQ	Lesbian, gay, bisexual, transgender, and queer
LED	Light-emitting diode
MAC	Media access control
NFC	Near-field communication
NSA	US National Security Agency
OECD	Organisation for Economic Co-operation and Development
OS	Operating system
PC	Personal computer
PDS	Personal data store
PII	Personally identifiable information
PIN	Personal identification number
PKI	Public key infrastructure
PSD2	Payment Services Directive 2
QR	Quick response
RAM	Random-access memory
RP	Relying party
RSA	Rivest Shamir Adleman
SIM	Subscriber identity module
SMS	Short message service
SWAT	Special weapons and tactics
TIA	Total Information Awareness
TLS	Transport Layer Security

TV	Television
UK	United Kingdom
URL	Uniform Resource Locator
US	United States
USB	Universal Serial Bus
VPN	Virtual private network

NOTES

1 WE ARE NOT COLLECTING PERSONAL DATA

1. The camera was using a tool called automatic license plate recognition (ALPR)—also known as automatic number plate recognition (ANPR)—which is also used by traffic-enforcement cameras to automatically detect the license plate of a speeding car or a car that crosses a red traffic light.

2. O. S. Kerr, "The Mosaic Theory of the Fourth Amendment," *Michigan Law Review* 111, no. 3 (2012): 311–354.

3. Q-Park—one of the businesses managing such car parks—claims it only processes license plates locally and doesn't store them afterward (in the limited number of cases in which it uses license plate parking in the first place, according to a clarification provided by email in May 2019).

4. N. Purtova, "The Law of Everything: Broad Concept of Personal Data and Future of EU Data Protection Law," *Law, Innovation and Technology* 10, no. 1 (2018): 40–81.

5. Regulation (EU) 2016/679 of the European Parliament and of the Council of 27 April 2016, "On the Protection of Natural Persons with Regard to the Processing of Personal Data and on the Free Movement of Such Data, and Repealing Directive 95/46/EC (General Data Protection Regulation)," *Official Journal of the European Union L* 119 (May 4, 2016): 1–88; Regulation (EU) 2016/679 (GDPR), Article 4 (1). Emphasis added.

6. See Purtova, "The Law of Everything"; recital 26 of the GDPR; and the Breyer ruling of the European Court of Justice (judgement of October19, 2016, *Patrick Breyer v. Bundesrepublik Deutschland*, C-582/14 EU:C:2016:779), although that ruling was based on the earlier data-protection directive.

7. This is where the GDPR differs from earlier legislation, offering stronger protection than before. Recital 26 of the GDPR specifically mentions singling out individuals,

as opposed to the corresponding recital 26 of the previous Data Protection Directive; see Directive 95/46/EC of the European Parliament and of the Council of October 24, 1995, "On the Protection of Individuals with Regard to the Processing of Personal Data and on the Free Movement of Such Data," *Official Journal of the European Communities L* 281 (November 23, 1995): 31–50. But the Article 29 Working Party did consider such identifiers to fall under the scope of the definition of personal data under the old directive even back in 2007; see Article 29 Working Party, "Opinion 4/2007 on the Concept of Personal Data," June 20, 2007. See also Purtova, "The Law of Everything"; and F. J. Zuiderveen Borgesius, "Singling Out People without Knowing Their Names—Behavioural Targeting, Pseudonymous Data, and the New Data Protection Regulation," *Computer Law & Security Review* 32, no. 2 (2016): 256–271.

8. R. Leenes, "Do They Know Me?—Deconstructing Identifiability," *University of Ottawa Law & Technology Journal* 4, no. 1–2 (2008): 135–161.

9. These are recognizable identifiers and not lookup identifiers only if the account is not associated with a named individual.

10. Rb. Oost-Brabant, 26-11-2013, ECLI:NL:RBOBR:2013:6553.

11. Hof 's-Hertogenbosch, 19-08-2014, ECLI:NL:GHSHE:2014:2803.

12. According to M. Lafsky, "Attack of the Super Crunchers: Adventures in Data Mining," *Freakonomics* (blog), August 23, 2007, http://freakonomics.com/2007/08/23/attack-of-the-super-crunchers-ian-ayres-on-data-mining/. Visa denies this; see N. Ciarelli, "How Visa Predicts Divorce," *Daily Beast*, last updated July 14, 2017, https://www.thedailybeast.com/how-visa-predicts-divorce.

13. S. Boztas, "Look Away: Privacy Watchdog Warns Banks Not to Use Payments for Marketing," *DutchNews* (blog), July 3, 2019, https://www.dutchnews.nl/news/2019/07/privacy-watchdog-warns-banks-not-to-use-client-payment-details-for-marketing/; M. Gijzemijter, "Privacy Outrage Causes Bank to Ditch Plans for Targeted Ads Based on Customers' Spending Habits," *ZDNet*, March 18, 2014, https://www.zdnet.com/article/privacy-outrage-causes-bank-to-ditch-plans-for-targeted-ads-based-on-customers-spending-habits/.

14. G. Pogrund, "Home Office Tracks Debit Card Use to 'Spy' on Asylum Seekers," *The Times*, January 27, 2019.

15. Directive (EU) 2015/2366 of the European Parliament and of the Council of 25 November 2015, "On Payment Services in the Internal Market, Amending Directives 2002/65/EC, 2009/110/EC and 2013/36/EU and Regulation (EU) No 1093/2010, and Repealing Directive 2007/64/EC," *Official Journal of the European Union L* 337 (December 23, 2015): 35–126.

16. A Google subsidiary (Google Payment Ltd.) already has a license to issue electronic money and to provide payment services in the United Kingdom; see https://register.fca.org.uk/s/firm?id=001b000000m4IWpAAM, accessed July 15, 2019.

17. K. Poulsen, "PayPal Freezes WikiLeaks Account," *Wired*, April 12, 2010; A. Greenberg, "Visa, MasterCard Move to Choke WikiLeaks," *Forbes*, December 7, 2010.

18. T. S. Heydt-Benjamin, H.-J. Chae, B. Defend, and Kevin Fu, "Privacy for Public Transportation," in *Privacy Enhancing Technologies: 6th International Workshop, PET 2006*, ed. G. Danezis and P. Golle (New York: Springer, 2006), 1–19.

19. G. Coppola and D. Welch, "The Car of the Future Will Sell Your Data," *Bloomberg Businessweek*, February 20, 2018.

20. Kevin Bankston, Twitter, November 18, 2018, 11:48 a.m., https://twitter.com/kevinbankston/status/1064243930680778753?s=11.

21. M. L. Stone, *Big Data for Media* (Oxford: Reuters Institute for the Study of Journalism, November 2014).

22. J. Zaslow, "If TiVo Thinks You Are Gay, Here's How to Set It Straight," *Wall Street Journal*, November 26, 2002.

23. Regulation (EU) 2016/679 (GDPR), Article 5.1(b).

24. Regulation (EU) 2016/679 (GDPR), Recital 47, 70, Article 21.

25. *Digital Rights Ireland* (CJEU, Joined Cases C-293/12 and C-594/12, 8.04.2014).

26. Rb. Den Haag, 06-01-2020, ECLI:NL:RBDHA:2020:187.

27. "Santander Arrest," Hoge Raad, 09-09-2011, ECLI:NL:HR:2011:BQ8097.

28. S. Gürses, "Can You Engineer Privacy? The Challenges and Potential Approaches to Applying Privacy Research in Engineering Practice," *Communications of the ACM* 57, no. 8 (August 2014): 20–23; G. Danezis and S. Gürses, "A Critical Review of 10 Years of Privacy Technology," August 12, 2010, https://homes.esat.kuleuven.be/~sguerses/papers/DanezisGuersesSurveillancePets2010.pdf. The distinction between hard and soft privacy was drawn by George Danezis. See G. Danezis, "Distributed Ledgers: What Is So Interesting about Them?," *Conspicuous Chatter* (blog), September 27, 2018, https://conspicuouschatter.wordpress.com/2018/09/27/distributed-ledgers-what-is-so-interesting-about-them/.

29. B.-J. Koops, "The Concept of Function Creep," *Law, Innovation and Technology* 13, no. 1 (forthcoming). See also https://www.dictionary.com/browse/function-creep, accessed February 4, 2019.

30. Banksy is a famous example in this latter category, having started his career as a graffiti artist in the nineties in Bristol in the United Kingdom.

31. A. Pfitzmann and M. Hansen, *Anonymity, Unlinkability, Undetectability, Unobservability, Pseudonymity, and Identity Management—A Consolidated Proposal for Terminology*, version 0.34, August 10, 2010, http://dud.inf.tu-dresden.de/Anon_Terminology.shtml.

32. ENISA, *Pseudonymisation Techniques and Best Practices: Recommendations on Shaping Technology According to Data Protection and Privacy Provisions* (Attica, Greece: ENISA, November 2019).

33. In general, hash codes are not unique as the domain of inputs to the hash function is typically much larger than the range of available output hash codes. This means that in fact (infinitely) many possible inputs are mapped to a single output hash code. But as the range of hash functions is actually quite large (in practice,

hash functions have 256-bit outputs), the probability of a collision is negligible. We ignore these important details in the main text as they are not relevant for the exposition here.

34. People often confuse hashing and encryption. It is important to stress here that using a publicly known hash function—which, by definition, cannot be inverted by anyone—is really different from using a publicly known encryption function but keeping the cryptographic key secret. In a symmetric key setting, this key must be known and available to compute the equivalent of a hash code. But this allows the holder of that key to trivially decrypt and hence invert the code. Only in an asymmetric setting, wherein the public key is used for encryption to generate the hash code while the private key is destroyed right away, are the two methods roughly equivalent.

35. For example, SHA-3 FIPS180–4, *Secure Hash Standard,* NIST FIPS PUB 180-4 (Gaithersburg, MD: National Institute of Standards and Technology, US Department of Commerce, August 4, 2015).

36. It may even not be easy (although certainly possible) to come up with a plausible document that, when hashed, returns the same table of letter frequencies.

37. Actual hash codes are longer, typically between 128 and 256 bits—that is, sixteen to thirty-two bytes, which corresponds roughly to sequences of twenty-two to forty-four characters. For an illustration of the example given here, see https://xkcd.com/936/, accessed January 31, 2019.

38. This is not true for shorter passwords like *petname01!,* as we will see in a moment.

39. See www.surety.com; see also D. Oberhaus, "The World's Oldest Blockchain Has Been Hiding in the *New York Times* since 1995," *Motherboard/Vice,* August 27, 2018, https://www.vice.com/en_us/article/j5nzx4/what-was-the-first-blockchain.

40. There were 46,475,000 registered cars in Germany. See H. Bekker, "2018 Germany: Total Number of Registered Cars," *Car Sales Statistics* (blog), March 5, 2018, https://www.best-selling-cars.com/germany/2018-germany-total-number-registered-cars/. This may sound like a large number, but even a personal computer can execute millions of instructions per second these days. Depending on the particular hash function used, this means an ordinary PC can hash between one hundred thousand and one million license plates per second. Graphics processors can do this quite a lot faster.

41. The construction of dictionaries to break the protection offered by hashing can be made more difficult in two different ways. The first method is by applying a key-derivation function, which is essentially a hash function that is known to take a significant amount of time (say, a second) to compute its output. Constructing a dictionary with a million entries would then take an adversary seven days to compute. A dictionary for fifty million entries would take a year. The second method is called *salting,* which we will discuss later on in this chapter.

42. Even hashed passwords are at risk if the password used is too short or too easy to guess. This explains why even when password files contain only the hashes of passwords, hacks like the 2012 LinkedIn hack can allow criminals to recover the passwords of millions of accounts.

43. C. Percival and S. Josefsson, *The scrypt Password-Based Key Derivation Function*, RFC 7914 (RFC Editor, August 2016).

2 YOU HAVE ZERO PRIVACY ANYWAY—GET OVER IT

1. S. D. Warren and L. D. Brandeis, "The Right to Privacy: The Implicit Made Explicit," *Harvard Law Review* 4, no. 5 (December 15, 1890): 193–220.

2. D. Vincent, *Privacy: A Short History* (Cambridge: Polity, 2016); S. Keulen and R. Kroeze, "Privacy from a Historical Perspective," in *The Handbook of Privacy Studies*, ed. B. van der Sloot and A. de Groot (Amsterdam: Amsterdam University Press, 2018), 21–56.

3. P. Sprenger, "Sun on Privacy: 'Get Over It,'" *Wired*, January 26, 1999.

4. Economist, "The World's Most Valuable Resource," weekly edition, *Economist*, May 6, 2017, https://www.economist.com/weeklyedition/2017-05-06.

5. M. Weiser, "The Computer for the 21st Century," *Scientific American* 265, no. 3 (September 1991: 94–104.

6. B. Schneier, *Click Here to Kill Everybody* (New York: W. W. Norton & Company, 2018).

7. B. H. Bratton, *The Stack: On Software and Sovereignty* (Cambridge, MA: MIT Press, 2016).

8. B. W. Kernighan, *Understanding the Digital World: What You Need to Know about Computers, the Internet, Privacy, and Security* (Princeton, NJ: Princeton University Press, 2017).

9. The Stasi were the secret service of the German Democratic Republic (former East Germany).

10. See https://www.ftc.gov/news-events/press-releases/2013/12/android-flashlight-app-developer-settles-ftc-charges-it-deceived, accessed October 30, 2018.

11. See https://play.google.com/store/apps/details?id=com.flashlight.brightest.beacon.torch&hl=en, accessed July 16, 2019.

12. G. A. Fowler, "It's the Middle of the Night: Do You Know Who Your iPhone Is Talking To?," *Washington Post*, May 28, 2019.

13. IP addresses originally looked like this: 74.125.136.83 (i.e., four short numbers separated by three dots). This is the format of the original IPv4 addresses. As the number of devices that need an IP address currently exceeds the total number of available addresses, an update of the Internet Protocol (IPv6) provides a much larger address space.

14. We simplify matters considerably here.

15. As explained further ahead. Recall that all packets that traverse the internet to exchange data between your computer and the websites you visit also contain your own IP address as the sender.

16. Such a database is easily constructed, for example, with the help of the billions of smartphones that know their location using GPS, and that can help link these

locations to each and every IP address of each new network the smartphones connect to.

17. P. Eckersley, "How Unique Is Your Web Browser?," in *Privacy Enhancing Technologies, 10th International Symposium, PETS 2010*, ed. M. J. Atallah and N. J. Hopper (Berlin: Springer, 2010), 1–18.

18. E. Mills, "Device Identification in Online Banking Is Privacy Threat, Expert Says," *CNET*, April 24, 2009; P. Laperdrix, N. Bielova, B. Baudry, and G. Avoine, "Browser Fingerprinting: A Survey," arXiv:1905.01051 (2019), https://arxiv.org/abs/1905.01051.

19. On the one hand, cookies are more reliable for tracking than IP addresses as your IP address may change over time when you connect to the internet from different locations, whereas a cookie usually never changes after it is first set. On the other hand, cookies can be deleted (and many browsers do so by default).

20. J. Martin, T. Mayberry, C. Donahue, L. Foppe, L. Brown, C. Riggins, E. C. Rye, and D. Brown, "A Study of MAC Address Randomization in Mobile Devices and When it Fails," *Proceedings on Privacy Enhancing Technologies (PoPETs)* 2017, no. 4 (2017): 365–383.

21. This chapter only scratches the surface of this important topic. Luckily, many excellent books have been written about this—for example: P. E. Agre and M. Rotenberg, *Technology and Privacy: The New Landscape* (Cambridge, MA: MIT Press, 1998); D. J. Solove, *Understanding Privacy* (Cambridge, MA: Harvard University Press, 2008); W. Christl and S. Spiekermann, *Networks of Control: A Report on Corporate Surveillance, Digital Tracking, Big Data & Privacy* (Vienna: Facultas, 2016). Far fewer books discuss approaches to solve the problem instead, which is the main topic of this book. We refer to B. Schneier, *Data and Goliath: The Hidden Battles to Collect Your Data and Control Your World* (New York: W. W. Norton & Company, 2015); R. J. Cronk, *Strategic Privacy by Design* (Portsmouth, NH: IAPP, 2018); W. Herzog, *Privacy's Blueprint: The Battle to Control the Design of New Technologies* (Cambridge, MA: Harvard University Press, 2018).

22. We go by many different monikers that subtly change our rights and obligations towards the people using them. It matters whether you are considered a citizen versus a user. Interestingly, the only other "users" beyond those using computers are drug users. See https://english.stackexchange.com/questions/44138/why-are-customers-referred-to-as-users-in-software-and-drug-industry, accessed September 10, 2019.

23. S. Boztas, "Look Away: Privacy Watchdog Warns Banks Not to Use Payments for Marketing," *DutchNews.nl*, July 3, 2019, https://www.dutchnews.nl/news/2019/07/privacy-watchdog-warns-banks-not-to-use-client-payment-details-for-marketing/.

24. Wikipedia, "Global Internet Usage," last modified June 21, 2020, https://en.wikipedia.org/wiki/Global_Internet_usage.

25. J. Williams, *Stand out of Our Light: Freedom and Resistance in the Attention Economy* (Cambridge: Cambridge University Press, 2018); E. Pariser, *The Filter Bubble: What the Internet Is Hiding from You* (London: Viking /Penguin Books, 2011); V. F. Hendricks and M. Vestergaard, *Reality Lost: Markets of Attention, Misinformation and*

Manipulation (Cham: Springer, 2019). See J. Möller, N. Helberger, and M. Makhortykh, *Filter Bubbles in the Netherlands?* (Hilversum, Netherlands: Commissariaat voor de Media/UvA Institute for Information Law, 2019) for a critical note, arguing that at least in the Netherlands, few people are captured in a filter bubble as far as their online news consumption is concerned.

26. Here Technologies is a Netherlands-based mapping data company; see https://here.com. See also B. Ferris, "Do I Stay or Do I Go Now? Google Maps Has the Answer in One Tap," *Google* (blog), January 13, 2016, https://blog.google/products/maps/do-i-stay-or-do-i-go-now-google-maps/; D. Geere, "Algorithm Predicts Your Location in 24 Hours with 20-Metre Accuracy," *Wired*, August 14, 2012.

27. S. A. Thompson and C. Warzel, "Twelve Million Phones, One Dataset, Zero Privacy," *New York Times*, December 19, 2019.

28. Such sharing platforms bypass existing laws that regulate public transport or the hospitality business, creating unfair competition with taxis and hotels, while wrecking neighborhoods with the everlasting rumble of wheeled suitcases and soaring housing prices. But the focus in this book is on privacy, so we will for the most part ignore these additional ill effects of recent technological advances.

29. M. Veale (@mikarv), "When pushed with the GDPR, @spotify gives you a huge amount of telemetry data from their app (for me, 850mb of JSON files). Includes your A/B testing history, anything you've ever drag-dropped, connected, so on. This is how software works today," Twitter, June 28, 2018, 7:26 p.m., https://twitter.com/mikarv/status/1012386696934182912?lang=en.

30. C. Doctorow, "Microsoft Is About to Shut Off Its Ebook DRM Servers: 'The Books Will Stop Working,'" *Boing Boing*, June 28, 2019, https://boingboing.net/2019/06/28/jun-17-2004.html.

31. If you don't have access to a computer, or don't know how to operate one: tough luck. For a harrowing illustration of the possible consequences of such a point of view, watch *I, Daniel Blake*, directed by K. Loach, (BFI 2016).

32. See Schneier, *Data and Goliath* for many more.

33. R. Anderson, "Who Is the Opponent?," in *Security Engineering*, 3rd ed. (Hoboken, NJ: Wiley, 2020). See also the NSA Files, maintained by the *Guardian*, https://www.theguardian.com/us-news/the-nsa-files, accessed July 8, 2019.

34. G. Greenwald and E. MacAskill, "NSA Prism Program Taps in to User Data of Apple, Google and Others," *Guardian*, June 7, 2013.

35. J. Borger, "GCHQ and European Spy Agencies Worked Together on Mass Surveillance," *Guardian*, November 1, 2013.

36. B. Schneier, "How the NSA Attacks Tor/Firefox Users with QUANTUM and FOXACID," *Schneier on Security* (blog), October 7, 2013, https://www.schneier.com/blog/archives/2013/10/how_the_nsa_att.html.

37. E. Learned-Miller, G. B. Huang, A. RoyChowdhury, H. Li, and G. Hua, "Labeled Faces in the Wild: A Survey," in *Advances in Face Detection and Facial Image Analysis*, ed. M. Kawulok, M. E. Celebi, and B. Smolka (Cham: Springer, 2016), 189–248.

38. M. Galič, "Surveillance and Privacy in Smart Cities and Living Labs: Conceptualising Privacy *for* Public Space" (PhD thesis, Tilburg University, November 19, 2019).

39. S. Issenberg, "How Obama's Team Used Big Data to Rally Voters," *MIT Technology Review*, December 19, 2012.

40. According to Rayid Ghani, chief scientist of the 2012 Obama campaign. See R. Ghani, "Why What Cambridge Analytica Did Was Unacceptable," Medium, March 20, 2018, https://medium.com/@rayid/why-what-cambridge-analytica-did-was-unacceptable-eb5c313b55f8.

41. M. Mosk, T. Turner, and K. Faulders, "Russian Influence Operation Attempted to Suppress Black Vote: Indictment," *ABC News*, February 18, 2019. See also https://www.justice.gov/file/1035477/download, accessed July 10, 2019.

42. See the *Guardian*'s Cambridge Analytica files, https://www.theguardian.com/news/series/cambridge-analytica-files, accessed October 16, 2018. See also C. Cadwalladr and E. Graham-Harrison, "How Cambridge Analytica Turned Facebook 'Likes' into a Lucrative Political Tool," *Guardian*, March 17, 2018.

43. M. Kosinski, D. Stillwell, and T. Graepel, "Private Traits and Attributes Are Predictable from Digital Records of Human Behavior," *Proceedings of the National Academy of Sciences* 110, no. 15 (2013): 5802–5805.

44. C. Cadwalladr and E. Graham-Harrison, "Revealed: 50 Million Facebook Profiles Harvested for Cambridge Analytica in Major Data Breach," *Guardian*, March 17, 2018.

45. S. Kirchgaessner, "Cambridge Analytica Used Data from Facebook and Politico to Help Trump," *Guardian*, October 26, 2017.

46. C. Cadwalladr, "The Great British Brexit Robbery: How Our Democracy Was Hijacked," *Guardian*, May 7, 2017.

47. C. Cadwalladr, "Fresh Cambridge Analytica Leak 'Shows Global Manipulation Is Out of Control,'" *Guardian*, January 4, 2020.

48. The *Wall Street Journal* What They Know series, https://www.wsj.com/news/types/what-they-know, accessed December 28, 2019.

49. P. Kulp, "Ads Will Target Your Emotions and There's Nothing You Can Do about It," *Mashable*, May 2, 2017, https://mashable.com/2017/05/02/facebook-ad-targeting-by-mood/?europe=true; L. Matsakis, "Facebook's Targeted Ads Are More Complex Than It Lets On," *Wired*, April 25, 2018.

50. See, for example, Facebook for Business (https://www.facebook.com/business), Google Ad Manager (https://admanager.google.com/home/), or Google Marketing Platform (https://marketingplatform.google.com/about/).

51. F. Houweling (@freekh), "De VVD wil met deze advertentie mensen op Facebook bereiken die zijn geïnteresseerd in Geert Wilders," Twitter, January 26, 2018, 1:21 p.m., https://twitter.com/freekh/status/956864715128496128.

52. G. Venkatadri, E. Lucherini, and P. S. A. Mislove, "Investigating Sources of PII Used in Facebook's Targeted Advertising," *Proceedings on Privacy Enhancing Technologies* 2019, no. 1 (January 2019): 227–244.

53. R. H. Thaler and C. R. Sunstein, *Nudge: Improving Decisions about Health, Wealth, and Happiness*, revised and expanded edition (London: Penguin Books, 2009).

54. K. Petrasic, B. Saul, J. Greig, M. Bornfreund, and K. Lamberth, *Algorithms and Bias: What Lenders Need to Know*, Report (White & Case LLP, January 20, 2017); A. Johnson, "Big Data Recruiting: All You Need to Know to Get Started," *Harver* (blog), October 18, 2018, https://harver.com/blog/big-data-recruiting/.

55. Ovia, a free menstruation-tracking app, is "pitching a paid version of its app to insurers and large employers who want a heads-up on how many of their members or employees want to conceive." N. Kresge, I. Khrennikov, and D. Ramli, "Period-Tracking Apps Are Monetizing Women's Extremely Personal Data," *Bloomberg Businessweek*, January 24, 2019.

56. A. Woodie, "How Auto Insurers Detect and Use Your Driving 'Fingerprint,'" *datanami*, July 26, 2016, https://www.datanami.com/2016/07/26/auto-insurers-detect-use-driving-fingerprint/.

57. M. Allen, "Health Insurers Are Vacuuming Up Details about You—And It Could Raise Your Rates," *ProPublica*, July 17, 2018.

58. A. Hannak, G. Soeller, D. Lazer, A. Mislove and C. Wilson, "Measuring Price Discrimination and Steering on E-commerce Web Sites," in *IMC '14: Proceedings of the 2014 Internet Measurement Conference* (New York: ACM, 2014), 305–318.

59. J. Mikians, L. Gyarmati, V. Erramilli, and N. Laoutaris, "Detecting Price and Search Discrimination on the Internet," in *Proceedings of the 11th ACM Workshop on Hot Topics in Networks* (New York: ACM, 2012), 79–84.

60. J. Valentino-DeVries, J. Singer-Vine, and A. Soltani, "Websites Vary Prices, Deals Based on Users' Information," *Wall Street Journal*, December 24, 2012.

61. D. Mattioli, "On Orbitz, Mac Users Steered to Pricier Hotels," *Wall Street Journal*, August 23, 2012.

62. L. Beckett, "Everything We Know about What Data Brokers Know about You," *ProPublica*, June 13, 2014; D. C. Schmidt, *Google Data Collection* (Digital Content Next, August 2018); I. Bogost, "Welcome to the Age of Privacy Nihilism," *Atlantic*, August 23, 2018; J. Angwin, S. Mattu, and T. Parris Jr., "Facebook Doesn't Tell Users Everything It Really Knows about Them," *ProPublica*, December 27, 2016; Christl and Spiekermann, *Networks of Control*; W. Christl, Corporate Surveillance in Everyday Life (Cracked Labs, June 2017), https://crackedlabs.org/dl/CrackedLabs_Christl_CorporateSurveillance.pdf.

63. United States Senate, Committee on Commerce, Science, and Transportation, Office of Oversight and Investigations Majority Staff, *A Review of the Data Broker Industry: Collection, Use, and Sale of Consumer Data for Marketing Purposes*, staff report for Chairman Rockefeller, December 18, 2013, http://educationnewyork.com/files/rockefeller_databroker.pdf.

64. Federal Trade Commission, *Data Brokers: A Call for Transparency and Accountability* (Washington, DC: FTC, May 2014).

65. United States Senate, Committee on Commerce, Science, and Transportation, Office of Oversight and Investigations Majority Staff, *A Review of the Data Broker Industry: Collection, Use, and Sale of Consumer Data for Marketing Purposes*, staff report for Chairman Rockefeller, December 18, 2013, http://educationnewyork.com/files/rockefeller_databroker.pdf.

66. Warren and Brandeis already recognized back in 1890 the impact of business methods on our privacy. See Warren and Brandeis, "The Right to Privacy," 195–196.

67. Regulation (EU) 2016/679 (GDPR).

68. Judgment of May 13, 2014, *Google Spain*, C-131/12 EU:C:2014:317.

69. See https://www.scotusblog.com/case-files/cases/carpenter-v-united-states-2/, accessed July 10, 2019.

70. J. E. Cohen, "What Privacy Is For," *Harvard Law Review* 126 (May 20, 2013): 1904–1933.

71. D. Tokmetzis and M. Martijn, "Lees of luister: Alleen als we privacy zien als iets dat ons allen aangaat, kunnen we de techbedrijven temmen," *De Correspondent*, September 24, 2018.

72. UK Parliament Committee on Digital, Culture, Media and Sports, *Disinformation and "Fake News"*, interim report, July 29, 2018, https://publications.parliament.uk/pa/cm201719/cmselect/cmcumeds/363/36302.htm.

73. S. Zuboff, "You Are Now Remotely Controlled: Surveillance Capitalists Control the Science and the Scientists, the Secrets and the Truth," *New York Times*, January 24, 2020.

74. P. M. Regan, *Legislating Privacy: Technology, Social Values, and Public Policy* (Chapel Hill: University of North Carolina Press, 1995).

75. G. Orwell, *1984* (London: Secker & Warburg, 1949).

76. S. Zuboff, *The Age of Surveillance Capitalism: The Fight for a Human Future at the New Frontier of Power* (New York: PublicAffairs, 2019).

77. F. Kafka, *Der Process* (Berlin: Die Schmiede, 1925).

78. Other notable creative works that have addressed the issue of privacy in a compelling way are stories and books like E. M. Foster, "The Machine Stops," *Oxford and Cambridge Review*, November 1909; and A. Huxley, *Brave New World* (London: Chatto & Windus, 1932)—both of which appeared *before* the Second World War—as well as movies like S. Spielberg, *Minority Report* (20th Century Fox, 2002); and L. Wachowski and L. Wachowski, *The Matrix* (Warner Bros., 1999).

79. Solove, *Understanding Privacy*.

80. Warren and Brandeis, "The Right to Privacy."

81. A. Westin, *Privacy and Freedom* (New York: Atheneum, 1976).

82. E. Goffman, *The Presentation of Self in Everyday Life* (New York: Doubleday, 1959).

83. Agre and Rotenberg, *Technology and Privacy*.

84. H. Nissenbaum, "Privacy as Contextual Integrity," *Washington Law Review* 79, no. 1 (February 2004): 119–158; H. Nissenbaum, *Privacy in Context: Technology, Policy and the Integrity of Social Life* (Palo Alto, CA: Stanford University Press, 2010).

85. H. Nissenbaum (@HNissenbaum), "A right to privacy is a right to appropriate flow of information, neither secrecy nor control," Twitter, October 5, 2019, 8:19 p.m., https://twitter.com/hnissenbaum/status/1180548120272347136?s=11.

86. B.-J. Koops, B. Clayton Newell, T. Timan, I. Škorvánek, T. Chokrevski, and M. Galič, "A Typology of Privacy," *University of Pennsylvania Journal of International Law* 38 (2017): 483–575.

87. D. J. Solove, "A Brief History of Information Privacy Law," in *Proskauer on Privacy*, ed. R. P. Blaney, chapter 1 (New York: Practising Law Institute, 2006).

88. United Nations, "Universal Declaration of Human Rights," General Assembly Resolution 217 A(III), December 10, 1948; Council of Europe, "Convention for the Protection of Human Rights and Fundamental Freedoms," November 4, 1950.

89. Only within the European Union to be precise, though: European Union, "Charter of Fundamental Rights of the European Union," *Official Journal of the European Union C* 326 (October 26, 2012): 391–407.

90. Regulation (EU) 2016/679 (GDPR); Directive 95/46/EC (DPD), "On the Protection of Individuals with Regard to the Processing of Personal Data and on the Free Movement of Such Data." In other words, all the organizations that suddenly, at the very last moment, were struggling to comply with the GDPR were most probably in violation of its predecessor for ages.

91. C. J. Hoofnagle, B. van der Sloot, and F. Zuiderveen Borgesius, "The European Union General Data Protection Regulation: What It Is and What It Means," *Information & Communications Technology Law* 28, no. 1 (2019): 65–98.

92. The infamous "right to be forgotten."

93. M. Kiskis, "GDPR Is Eroding Our Privacy, Not Protecting It," *TNW*, August 5, 2018, https://thenextweb.com/contributors/2018/08/05/gdpr-privacy-eroding-bad/.

94. A. Cavoukian, *Privacy by Design: The 7 Foundational Principles*, report, revised version (Ontario: Information and Privacy Commissioner of Ontario, January 2011).

95. Taken from R. J. Cronk, *Strategic Privacy by Design*.

96. Normally, this is the case. However, in certain circumstances, even group size can be a proxy for identity. If, for example, in a particular restaurant, the only group of eleven ever to visit is always the Johnson family of eleven people, then clearly recording the group size is recording the fact that the Johnsons were visiting. This shows that even in seemingly obvious cases, data may in practice not be so anonymous after all. We return to the difficulty of truly anonymizing data in chapter 4.

97. Warren and Brandeis, "The Right to Privacy."

3 I'VE GOT NOTHING TO HIDE

1. We will turn to a different deconstruction of the security versus privacy paradox in chapter 7, where we will argue that security and privacy are not a zero-sum game and that both can very well be achieved at the same time.

2. D. J. Solove, "'I've Got Nothing to Hide' and Other Misunderstandings of Privacy," *San Diego Law Review*, no. 44 (2007): 745.

3. M. Martijn and R. Wijnberg, "Nee, je hebt wél iets te verbergen," *De Correspondent*, October 21, 2013.

4. M. P. Lynch, "Privacy and the Threat to the Self," *New York Times*, June 22, 2013.

5. M. Rasch, *Zwemmen in de oceaan: Berichten uit een postdigitale wereld* (Amsterdam: De Bezige Bij, 2017).

6. R. Tate, "Google CEO: Secrets Are for Filthy People," *Gawker*, April 12, 2009, https://gawker.com/5419271/google-ceo-secrets-are-for-filthy-people.

7. S. A. Bent, *Familiar Short Sayings of Great Men*, 6th ed., Bartleby.com, 2012 (Boston: Ticknor & Co., 1887).

8. J. Barbier, "Toen was pedofilie nog heel gewoon," *De Volkskrant*, April 11, 2014.

9. See also the discussion on the difference between privacy and data protection in chapter 2.

10. Kafka, *Der Process*.

11. J. Holvast, "Een centraal Jodenregistratiesysteem maakte het zo erg," *NRC*, May 5, 2015.

12. In fact, the US military used American Indians, native people who spoke languages that were literally unheard of outside of the United States, as a way to securely communicate by telephone in both world wars.

13. Alice and Bob are the dramatis personae in almost every paper or presentation on security and cryptography, introduced by Rivest, Shamir, and Adleman in their seminal paper that announced the invention of RSA. See R. L. Rivest, A. Shamir, and L. M. Adleman, "A Method for Obtaining Digital Signatures and Public-Key Cryptosystems," *Communications of the ACM* 21, no. 2 (1978): 120–126.

14. D. Kahn, *The Codebreakers* (New York: Macmillan, 1967).

15. Using the modern twenty-six letter Latin alphabet.

16. S. Singh, *The Code Book* (London: Fourth Estate, 1999). *The Code Book* in fact was one of my inspirations to start writing about technology for people without a technological background.

17. A. J. Menezes, P. C. van Oorschot, and S. A. Vanstone, *Handbook of Applied Cryptography* (Boca Raton, FL: CRC Press, 1996); J. Katz and Y. Lindell, *Introduction to Modern Cryptography*, 2nd ed. (Boca Raton, FL: CRC Press, 2015); N. P. Smart, *Cryptography Made Simple* (Berlin: Springer, 2016); D. Boneh and V. Shoup, *A Graduate Course in Applied Cryptography*, version 0.5 (January 2020), https://toc.cryptobook.us.

18. In general, the key can be shared with several people to create a secure broadcast channel, allowing each of the members to decrypt messages sent by any member. This would have allowed Caesar to send a single encrypted message that could be read by all of his generals.

19. FIPS 46, *Data Encryption Standard*, NBS FIPS PUB 46 (Washington, DC: National Bureau of Standards, US Department of Commerce, January 1977).

20. FIPS 197, *Advanced Encryption Standard*, NIST FIPS PUB 197 (Washington, DC: National Institute of Standards and Technology, US Department of Commerce, November 2001).

21. J. Austen, *Pride and Prejudice* (London: T. Egerton, 1813).

22. This is why many people use a VPN in the first place. As we discussed in the previous chapter, your IP address is a good proxy for your location—most certainly for the country you live in. This is used by Netflix to determine which content you have access to. In many countries, TV shows streamed on the internet are only accessible to inhabitants of the country. The BBC, for example, only allows access to people that live in the United Kingdom. If you use a VPN provider with servers in the United Kingdom, then if you visit the BBC website over this VPN, the BBC will think you live in the UK (it sees the IP address of the VPN provider) and will offer you access to the latest episode of *Blackadder*. Conveniently, many VPN providers offer you the option to select a particular country for the VPN server you wish to use at a particular point in time.

23. D. Johnson, "How Is NordVPN Unblocking Disney+? It Might Be through YOUR Own Computer. Even If You've Never Used Disney+ or NordVPN," Medium, November 28, 2019, https://medium.com/@derek./how-is-nordvpn-unblocking-disney-6c5104 5dbc30.

24. You may have heard of it by the name of its predecessor, Secure Sockets Layer (SSL).

25. Using the public key of the website, your browser could send encrypted messages to it, but the web server would not have a way to respond to them because it doesn't have your public key. Nor would you want the server to have your public key as you prefer to be anonymous. So instead the browser and the web server agree on a shared secret communication key instead, using the web server public key to guarantee authenticity. This shared communication key, called the *session key*, is used to encrypt the messages in both directions via a symmetric cipher.

26. For all practical purposes, that is. Website authentication is by no means foolproof.

27. See https://signal.org.

28. C. Meijer and B. van Gastel, "Self-Encrypting Deception: Weaknesses in the Encryption of Solid State Drives," in *2019 IEEE Symposium on Security and Privacy, SP 2019, San Francisco, CA, USA, May 19–23, 2019* (IEEE, 2019), 72–87.

29. In Apple's terminology, this is called the *class key* and is derived from the UID and the user's passcode. See Apple Inc., *Apple Platform Security* (2020), https://manuals.info .apple.com/MANUALS/1000/MA1902/en_US/apple-platform-security-guide.pdf.

30. If you use your fingerprint or face to unlock your device, the device key is not fully discarded but stored in a secure place within your device, from where it is released again when your fingerprint or face is successfully recognized.

31. Wikipedia, "iCloud Leaks of Celebrity Photos," last modified May 31, 2020, https://en.wikipedia.org/wiki/ICloud_leaks_of_celebrity_photos.

32. But do note that collecting personal data is possibly a privacy infringement or a data-protection infringement even if all the data collected is openly accessible already. The mere fact that all this data is collected and combined in one place may create privacy risks. And the specific ways in which Google makes this data accessible and determines which results are returned for a search query and in which order are also a concern. In fact, this latter aspect underlies the infamous "right to

be forgotten" verdict in the Google Spain case (Judgment of May 13, 2014, *Google Spain*, C-131/12 EU:C:2014:317).

33. M. Hiltzik, "A Gerrymandering Attempt that Went Hilariously Awry [UPDATED]," *Los Angeles Times*, August 31, 2015.

34. D. X. Song, D. A. Wagner, and A. Perrig, "Practical Techniques for Searches on Encrypted Data," in *2000 IEEE Symposium on Security and Privacy* (IEEE, 2000), 44–55.

35. B. Fuller, M. Varia, A. Yerukhimovich, E. Shen, A. Hamlin, V. Gadepally, R. Shay, J. D. Mitchell, and R. K. Cunningham, "SoK: Cryptographically Protected Database Search," in *2017 IEEE Symposium on Security and Privacy* (IEEE, 2017), 172–191.

36. E. R. Verheul, B. Jacobs, C. Meijer, M. Hildebrandt, and J. de Ruiter, *Polymorphic Encryption and Pseudonymisation for Personalised Healthcare*, IACR Cryptology ePrint Archive, report 2016/411 (2016), https://eprint.iacr.org/2016/411.

37. More complex data-sharing and analysis scenarios are certainly possible. In fact, a prototype implementing this technology is being piloted in the Personalized Parkinson Project (Parkinson op Maat). See, for example, https://pep.cs.ru.nl and https://www.parkinsonopmaat.nl/en/study. In this project, 650 patients are being monitored over a period of two years, and the data collected this way is shared, in pseudonymized form, with research institutes around the world.

38. I. Dinur and K. Nissim, "Revealing Information while Preserving Privacy," in *Proceedings of the Twenty-Second ACM SIGACT-SIGMOD-SIGART Symposium on Principles of Database Systems*, ed. F. Neven, C. Beeri, and T. Milo (New York: ACM, 2003), 202–210.

39. A. Hundepool, J. Domingo-Ferrer, L. Franconi, S. Giessing, E. Schulte Nordholt, K. Spicer, and P.-P. de Wolf, *Statistical Disclosure Control* (West Sussex, UK: Wiley, 2012).

40. A. Wood, M. Altman, A. Bembenek, M. Bun, M. Gaboardi, J. Honaker, K. Nissim, D. R. O'Brien, T. Steinke, and S. Vadhan, "Differential Privacy: A Primer for a Nontechnical Audience," *Vanderbilt Journal of Entertainment & Technology Law* 21, no. 1 (2018): 209–276.

41. L. Kissner (@LeaKissner), "OK, here goes: a true story about social scientists, gay men, and differential privacy. Not so long ago in the US it was exceedingly difficult to figure out what %age of the population was gay. Being gay was subject to censure and prosecution." Twitter, April 4, 2019, 7:07 a.m., https://twitter.com/leakissner/status/1113669471749599232?s=11.

42. C. Dwork, "Differential Privacy," in *Automata, Languages and Programming 2006, 33rd International Colloquium, ICALP 2006*, ed. M. Bugliesi et al. (Berlin: Springer, 2006), 1–12; C. Dwork and A. Roth, "The Algorithmic Foundations of Differential Privacy," *Foundations and Trends in Theoretical Computer Science* 9, nos. 3–4 (2014): 211–407.

43. Wood et al., "Differential Privacy"; Hundepool et al., *Statistical Disclosure Control*.

44. See also this video by minutephysics on YouTube: minutephysics, "Protecting Privacy with MATH (Collab with the Census," September 12, 2019, YouTube video, 12:31, https://www.youtube.com/watch?v=pT19VwBAqKA&feature=youtu.be.

45. For more references to information on differential privacy, see D. Desfontaines, "A Reading List on Differential Privacy," *Ted Is Writing Things* (blog), September 25, 2019, https://desfontain.es/privacy/differential-privacy-reading-list.html.

46. M. Fredrikson, E. Lantz, S. Jha, S. Lin, D. Page, and T. Ristenpart, "Privacy in Pharmacogenetics: An End-to-End Case Study of Personalized Warfarin Dosing," in *23rd USENIX Security Symposium* (USENIX Association, 2014), 17–32.

4 IT'S MERELY METADATA

1. J. Voorhees, "Antivirus Pioneer John McAfee Has Been Arrested," *Slate*, December 6, 2012, https://slate.com/news-and-politics/2012/12/john-mcafee-arrested-antivirus-pioneer-arrested-may-be-sent-back-to-belize-to-face-questions-about-murder.html.

2. World Economic Forum, *Personal Data: The Emergence of a New Asset Class* (Geneva: World Economic Forum, January 2011).

3. For example, the Time Machine functionality in Apple's MacOS.

4. I. Thomson, "How TV Ads Silently Ping Commands to Phones: Sneaky SilverPush Code Reverse-Engineered," *Register*, November 20, 2015, https://www.theregister.com/2015/11/20/silverpush_soundwave_ad_tracker/.

5. N. Hoffelder, "Adobe Is Spying on Users, Collecting Data on Their eBook Libraries," *Digital Reader*, October 6, 2014, https://the-digital-reader.com/2014/10/06/adobe-spying-users-collecting-data-ebook-libraries/.

6. Kindle Direct Publishing Help Center (Amazon), "Royalties in Kindle Unlimited and Kindle Owners' Lending Library," August 13, 2019, https://kdp.amazon.com/en_US/help/topic/G201541130.

7. See https://support.office.com/en-us/article/remove-hidden-data-and-personal-information-by-inspecting-documents-presentations-or-workbooks-356b7b5d-77af-44fe-a07f-9aa4d085966f, last updated January 8, 2019.

8. S. Das and A. D. I. Kramer, "Self-Censorship on Facebook," in *Proceedings of the 7th International Conference on Weblogs and Social Media (ICWSM)*, ed. E. Kiciman et al. (Palo Alto, CA: AAAI Press, 2013); C. Johnston, "Facebook Is Tracking What You Don't Do on Facebook," *Ars Technica*, December 16, 2013.

9. Wikipedia, "Mouse Tracking," last modified, April 17, 2020, https://en.wikipedia.org/wiki/Mouse_tracking.

10. To be precise, every network interface on your computer that allows you to connect your computer to a network (whether by WiFi, Bluetooth, or Ethernet) has a separate MAC address. MAC addresses have a structure that allows the manufacturer of a device to be determined given its MAC address. Because MAC addresses are only relevant for a direct connection with the local area network, the websites you visit (which typically are not directly connected to your device) do not get to see your MAC address.

11. See https://en.wikipedia.org/wiki/Bluetooth, accessed July 10, 2019; and https://en.wikipedia.org/wiki/Wi-Fi, accessed July 10, 2019.

12. Location data, battery status information, and application (un)install information were used as evidence in a Dutch murder case: H. Modderkolk, "Hoe Google-data in een moordzaak leidden naar de echtgenote," *De Volkskrant*, August 8, 2019.

13. R. Coulthart, "Metadata Access Is Putting Whistleblowers, Journalists and Democracy at Risk," *Sydney Morning Herald*, May 4, 2015; M. Meaker, "Europe Is Using Smartphone Data as a Weapon to Deport Refugees," *Wired*, July 2, 2018.

14. D. Cole, "'We Kill People Based on Metadata,'" *New York Review of Books*, May 10, 2014.

15. WhatsApp's privacy policy allows it to use this data for friend suggestions, but Facebook denies it is actually using this data: A. Tait, "Why Does Facebook Recommend Friends I've Never Even Met?," *Wired*, May 29, 2019.

16. K. Hill, "Facebook Recommended That This Psychiatrist's Patients Friend Each Other," *Splinter*, August 29, 2016.

17. Facebook first confirmed that location data was one of the factors to suggest new friends, but later claimed location data was not used for that purpose: E. Hunt, "How Does Facebook Suggest Potential Friends? Not Location Data—Not Now," *Guardian*, June 29, 2016.

18. K. Hill, "Facebook Is Using Your Phone's Location to Suggest New Friends—which Could Be a Privacy Disaster," *Splinter*, June 28, 2016, https://splinternews.com/facebook-recommended-that-this-psychiatrists-patients-f-1793861472.

19. M. Latzer, M. Büchi, and N. Festic, *Internetverbreitung und digitale Bruchlinien in der Schweiz 2019*, Themenbericht (Switzerland: World Internet Project, 2019).

20. W. H. Porter, *Proverbs, Arranged in Alphabetical Order* (Boston: James Munroe and Company, 1845), 10. The following poem (Carmen 70) by Gaius Valerius Catullus also illustrates eloquently the relative value of what people say: "Nulli se dicit mulier mea nubere malle quam mihi, non si se Iuppiter ipse petat. dicit: sed mulier cupido quod dicit amanti, in vento et rapida scribere oportet aqua." See http://rudy.negenborn.net/catullus/text2/l70.htm, accessed November 4, 2019.

21. Cole, "'We Kill People Based on Metadata.'"

22. P. Leskin, "Your iPhone Keeps a Detailed List of Every Location You Frequent—Here's How to Delete Your History and Shut the Feature Off for Good," *Business Insider*, April 2, 2019.

23. Martin et al., "A Study of MAC Address Randomization in Mobile Devices and When it Fails."

24. This does still allow such services to measure the number of people at one particular location, and even allows them to measure the movement of these people over brief moments of time during which the MAC address stays constant.

25. P. Samarati and L. Sweeney, "Protecting Privacy when Disclosing Information: k-Anonymity and Its Enforcement through Generalization and Suppression" (Technical Report SRI-CSL-98-04, Computer Science Laboratory, SRI International, 1998); L. Sweeney, "k-Anonymity: A Model for Protecting Privacy," *International Journal of Uncertainty, Fuzziness and Knowledge-Based Systems* 10, no. 5 (2002): 557–570.

26. A. Machanavajjhala, D. Kifer, J. Gehrke, and M. Venkitasubramaniam, "*L*-Diversity: Privacy beyond *k*-Anonymity," *ACM Transactions on Knowledge Discovery from Data* 1, no. 1 (2007): 3.

27. M. R. Koot, "Measuring and Predicting Anonymity" (PhD thesis, University of Amsterdam, June 27, 2012); A. Hern, "'Anonymised' Data Can Never Be Totally Anonymous, Says Study," *Guardian*, July 23, 2019; Article 29 Working Party, "Opinion 5/2014 on Anonymisation Techniques," April 10, 2014.

28. Pfitzmann and Hansen, *Anonymity, Unlinkability, Undetectability, Unobservability, Pseudonymity, and Identity Management.*

29. Typically (but not always) considered only from the perspective of an external adversary. The recipient of a message may know the person that sent the message already or may be able to tell from the contents.

30. M. Edman and B. Yener, "On Anonymity in an Electronic Society: A Survey of Anonymous Communication Systems," *ACM Computing Surveys* 42, no. 1 (2009): 5:1–5:35; G. Danezis and C. Diaz, "A Survey of Anonymous Communication Channels", Microsoft Research Technical Report (MSR-TR-2008-35) (January 2008).

31. Wikipedia, "Penet Remailer," last modified May 16, 2020, https://en.wikipedia.org/wiki/Penet_remailer; Danezis and Diaz, "A Survey of Anonymous Communication Channels."

32. Such free email services also allow you to register an arbitrary email address and do not really check your identity when registering for such an address. They do log your IP address when you register or access your email later, though, so these free email services have a similar centralized record that allows them—and others, like law enforcement—to recover your identity. (See chapter 2 for more on how IP addresses can be traced back to natural persons.)

33. An outgoing email of a particular length sent at a particular time probably corresponds to an incoming email of about the same length received just a fraction of a second earlier. Even if the content of the email is encrypted, the header of the email, which contains the recipient's real or anonymous email address, is not. The header cannot be encrypted because email servers always need access to this info to determine what to do with the message. See also Edman and Yener, "On Anonymity in an Electronic Society"; Danezis and Diaz, "A Survey of Anonymous Communication Channels."

34. G. Danezis, R. Dingledine, and N. Mathewson, "Mixminion: Design of a Type III Anonymous Remailer Protocol," in *2003 IEEE Symposium on Security and Privacy* (IEEE Computer Society, 2003), 2–15.

35. D. Chaum, "Untraceable Electronic Mail, Return Addresses, and Digital Pseudonyms," *Communications of the ACM* 24, no. 2 (1981): 84–88.

36. This is one difference between mix networks and onion routers, to be discussed next.

37. Leaving the analogy for a moment, when messages are actually sent over the internet, a mix node learns not only the IP address of the next mix node on the

path, but also the IP address of the previous mix node on the path—that is, the one that sent the message.

38. Danezis and Diaz, "A Survey of Anonymous Communication Channels."

39. R. Dingledine, N. Mathewson, and P. F. Syverson, "Tor: The Second-Generation Onion Router," in *13th USENIX Security Symposium*, ed. M. Blaze (USENIX Association, 2004), 303–320.

40. See https://www.torproject.org.

41. P. Syverson, "Onion Routing," 2005, https://www.onion-router.net.

42. Although they could detect this information by looking carefully at the IP address of the connection.

43. J. Ball, B. Schneier, and G. Greenwald, "NSA and GCHQ Target Tor Network that Protects Anonymity of Web Users.", *Guardian*, October 4, 2013. See also https://edwardsnowden.com/docs/doc/tor-stinks-presentation.pdf.

44. Tor Community, "Types of Relays on the Tor Network," https://community.torproject.org/relay/types-of-relays/.

45. Unless the web server enforces secure browsing—that is, uses HTTPS in the link—itself.

46. J. P. Barlow, "A Declaration of the Independence of Cyberspace," February 8, 1996, https://www.eff.org/cyberspace-independence.

47. P. Winter, A. Edmundson, L. M. Roberts, A. Dutkowska-Zuk, M. Chetty, and N. Feamster, "How Do Tor Users Interact with Onion Services?," in *27th USENIX Security Symposium*, ed. W. Enck and A. P. Felt (USENIX Association, 2018), 411–428.

48. Moreover, the addresses used in this example follow a previous version of the Tor onion service specification. A newer version with longer addresses has been proposed.

5 WE ALWAYS NEED TO KNOW WHO YOU ARE

1. C. P. Pfleeger and S. L. Pfleeger, *Security in Computing*, 4th ed. (Upper Saddle River, NJ: Prentice-Hall, 2007).

2. See chapter 8 for a discussion on how to properly (i.e., securely) use passwords.

3. Such a document can be an arbitrary piece of data, like a digital bank note or a Word document, for example. As we will discuss later, digital signatures are also used to sign certificates and credentials to prove their authenticity.

4. Public keys in and of themselves are just pieces of random-looking data that do not contain any identifying information. By looking at a public key, you cannot see who it belongs to. You either need to keep track of who gave it to you, or you need a trusted source that reliably tells you who it belongs to.

5. M. Bauer, M. Meints, and M. Hansen, *D3.1: Structured Overview on Prototypes and Concepts of Identity Management Systems* (FIDIS, 2005).

6. The identity provider may in fact forward additional information to the relying party.

7. Through a mechanism called OAuth; see https://oauth.net.

8. See https://www.bankid.com and https://www.digid.nl.

9. G. Alpár, J.-H. Hoepman, and J. Siljee, "The Identity Crisis: Security, Privacy and Usability Issues in Identity Management," *Journal of Information System Security* 9, no. 1 (2013): 23–53.

10. Assuming for the moment (unrealistically) that users at least use different, hard-to-guess passwords for each of their accounts.

11. A large majority of people actually are affected by essentially this risk without really being aware of it. Most of us have a single email address that we use either as the account name for all our accounts or as the recovery email address for when we forget our passwords. A hacker with access to this email account can invoke a password recovery process and thus gain access to all our online accounts.

12. C. M. Ellison, "The Nature of a Usable PKI," *Computer Networks* 31 (1999): 823–830.

13. K. Cameron, "The Laws of Identity" (May 11, 2005), https://www.identityblog.com/stories/2005/05/13/TheLawsOfIdentity.pdf.

14. Instead of writing that a certain attribute type has a certain attribute value, we will more colloquially use the term *attribute* to refer to the type and use the term *value* to refer the value.

15. We restrict our discussion here to identity management for natural persons, but pretty much everything easily translates to non-natural persons or arbitrary objects or entities that can be assigned attributes in some context.

16. Traditionally, a certificate that ties a claim to a specified individual (usually specified through its public key) would have been used for this. Certificates are much simpler to construct than credentials. They lack the basic privacy protective features of credentials, however. This is why we do not explicitly discuss them in the main text of this chapter.

17. In fact, it does not contain the actual user key, but a derived value that ensures that in order to use the credential, the user key must be known. Conceptually, we could say it contains the hash of the user key.

18. W. Lueks, G. Alpár, J.-H. Hoepman, and P. Vullers, "Fast Revocation of Attribute-Based Credentials for Both Users and Verifiers," *Computers & Security* 67 (2017): 308–323.

19. This is called the *all or nothing* defense against credential pooling.

20. Biometry like fingerprints or retina scans could in theory be used for this, but in practice biometry has many limitations (like poor revocation and poor error rates for a decent security level).

21. Traditionally, such systems have been called *anonymous credentials* in the literature. Recently, the terminology has changed to stress the fact that even though the underlying technology guarantees full anonymity, this anonymity is easily thwarted once you disclose a single identifying attribute, like your name or social security number.

22. In many, but not all, cases, the user has to be fully identified in order to determine the appropriate attribute values. This step of the issuing process is therefore not privacy preserving at all. In some cases, however, showing some more or less anonymous attribute contained in another credential may be enough to issue a new credential. For example, we could imagine that a special "is allowed to buy alcoholic beverages" credential can be obtained in the US whenever a person seeking it can prove to be over twenty-one years old.

23. D. Chaum, "Security without Identification: Transaction Systems to Make Big Brother Obsolete," *Communications of the ACM* 28, no. 10 (1985): 1030–1044.

24. See https://www.microsoft.com/en-us/research/project/u-prove/. See also S. Brands, *Rethinking Public Key Infrastructures and Digital Certificates: Building in Privacy* (Cambridge, MA: MIT Press, 2000).

25. See https://www.zurich.ibm.com/identity_mixer/; IBM Research Zürich Team, *Specification of the Identity Mixer Cryptographic Library* (Zürich: IBM Research, February 2012); J. Camenisch and A. Lysyanskaya, "An Efficient System for Non-transferable Anonymous Credentials with Optional Anonymity Revocation," in *Advances in Cryptology—EUROCRYPT 2001*, International Conference on the Theory and Application of Cryptographic Techniques, ed. B. Pfitzmann (Berlin: Springer, 2001), 93–118.

26. See https://privacybydesign.foundation.

27. See https://github.com/privacybydesign.

28. See, for example, https://agechecked.com.

29. J.-J. Quisquater, M. Quisquater, M. Quisquater, L. C. Guillou, M. A. Guillou, G. Guillou, A. Guillou, G. Guillou, S. Guillou, and T. A. Berson, "How to Explain Zero-Knowledge Protocols to Your Children," in *Advances in Cryptology—CRYPTO '89*, 9th Annual International Cryptology Conference, ed. G. Brassard (Berlin: Springer, 1989), 628–631.

30. This rules out a classical challenge-response protocol based on signatures, typically used in authentication schemes to prove possession of a private key corresponding to a known public key. In such a protocol, the verifier sends a random challenge to the prover, asking the prover to sign the challenge with her private key. The verifier can verify the correctness of the response using the public key. But the same response can also be shown to anybody else to convince them the prover must have known the private key.

31. If Victor and Walter are really good friends, then Walter may trust Victor enough to be sure he won't try to deceive him. But in that case, he might as well stop wasting his time watching the full video and simply trust Victor when he tells him Peggy knows the secret.

32. Goffman, *The Presentation of Self in Everyday Life.*

33. B. van den Berg, "The Situated Self: Identity in a World of Ambient Intelligence" (PhD diss., Erasmus University Rotterdam, 2009).

34. I. Kerr, C. Lucock, and V. Steeves, *Lessons from the Identity Trail: Anonymity, Privacy and Identity in a Networked Society* (Oxford: Oxford University Press, March 18, 2009).

35. M. Koning, P. Korenhof, G. Alpár, and J.-H. Hoepman, "The ABCs of ABCs: An Analysis of Attribute-Based Credentials in the Light of Data Protection, Privacy and Identity," in *Internet, Law & Politics: A Decade of Transformations: Proceedings of the 10th International Conference on Internet, Law & Politics*, ed. J. Balcells (Barcelona: UOC-Huygens Editorial, 2014), 357–374.

36. B. Latour, *Reassembling the Social: An Introduction to Actor-Network-Theory* (Oxford: Oxford University Press, 2005).

37. Via Google Pay for Android or Apple Wallet for iOS. The discussion assumes that these wallets indeed only store their information locally.

38. Because of the strong unlinkability properties of attribute-based credentials, a voter could present their eligibility attribute many times to vote many times without anybody noticing. Attribute-based credentials can actually prevent this by forcing the voter to also show a fixed and voting-specific pseudonym that nevertheless is unknown to the issuer and hence cannot be linked back to the identity of the voter.

39. This is very similar to the *trust on first use* (TOFU) principle for public key authentication, as is used, for instance, by the Secure Shell (SSH) protocol. See D. Wendlandt, D. G. Andersen, and A. Perrig, "Perspectives: Improving SSH-style Host Authentication with Multi-path Probing," in *Proceedings of the 2008 USENIX Annual Technical Conference (USENIX '08)*, ed. R. Isaacs and Y. Zhou (USENIX Association, 2008), 321–334.

40. M. S. Merkow, "Secure Electronic Transactions (SET)," in *The Internet Encyclopedia*, vol. 3, ed. H. Bidgoli (Hoboken, NJ: Wiley, 2004), 247–260.

41. J.-H. Hoepman, "Privately (and Unlinkably) Exchanging Messages Using a Public Bulletin Board," in *ACM Workshop on Privacy in the Electronic Society 2015*, ed. I. Ray, N. Hopper, and R. Jansen (New York: ACM, 2016), 85–94.

6 YOUR DATA IS SAFE WITH US

1. S. Schuemie, "Google Start Privacy Tour in Leiden," *Sleutelstad*, March 22, 2017, https://sleutelstad.nl/2017/03/22/google-start-privacy-tour-leiden/.

2. Part of this section is based on material I wrote earlier; see J.-H. Hoepman, "De wereld volgens Google," *XOT* (blog), May 29, 2017, https://blog.xot.nl/2017/05/29/de-wereld-volgens-google/.

3. The original website, https://privacy.google.nl/, now redirects to https://safety.google, as further evidence that Google sees privacy as a safety issue.

4. NOS Nieuws, "Charme-offensief Facebook: grote privacy-advertentie in Nederlandse kranten," April 17, 2018, https://nos.nl/artikel/2227728-charme-offensief-facebook-grote-privacy-advertentie-in-nederlandse-kranten.html.

5. J. Powell, "Your Privacy Is Our Business," *New York Times*, April 27, 2019.

6. J.-H. Hoepman, "Lessons to Be Learned from the Polar Incident," *XOT* (blog), July 9, 2018, https://blog.xot.nl/2018/07/09/lessons-to-be-learned-from-the-polar-incident/.

7. D. Tokmetzis, M. Martijn, R. Bol, and F. Postma, "Here's How We Found the Names and Addresses of Soldiers and Secret Agents Using a Simple Fitness App," *De Correspondent*, July 8, 2018.

8. J. Hsu, "The Strava Heat Map and the End of Secrets," *Wired*, January 29, 2018.

9. Privacy International, "No Body's Business but Mine: How Menstruation Apps Are Sharing Your Data," September 9, 2019, PI, https://privacyinternational.org/long-read/3196/no-bodys-business-mine-how-menstruations-apps-are-sharing-your-data.

10. M. Green, "How Safe Is Apple's Safe Browsing?," *A Few Thoughts on Cryptographic Engineering* (blog), October 13, 2019, https://blog.cryptographyengineering.com/2019/10/13/dear-apple-safe-browsing-might-not-be-that-safe/.

11. The privacy protection of this scheme is good but not perfect, as it does leak information over time that a malicious provider of such a safe browsing system could exploit. See T. Gerbet, A. Kumar, and C. Lauradoux, "A Privacy Analysis of Google and Yandex Safe Browsing," in *46th Annual IEEE/IFIP International Conference on Dependable Systems and Networks, DSN 2016* (IEEE Computer Society, 2016), 347–358.

12. A. Hern, "Apple Contractors 'Regularly Hear Confidential Details' on Siri Recordings," *Guardian*, July 26, 2019.

13. See https://www.tensorflow.org.

14. We will not discuss these further in the text, but good books on the subject include the following: F. Pasquale, *The Black Box Society: The Secret Algorithms That Control Money and Information* (Cambridge, MA: Harvard University Press, 2016); C. O'Neill, *Weapons of Math Destruction: How Big Data Increases Inequality and Threatens Democracy* (New York: Crown, 2016). There are also dedicated conferences to the topic, like the ACM Conference on Fairness, Accountability, and Transparency (ACM FAT).

15. For example, Mydex (https://www.mydex.org) or Qiy (https://www.qiyfoundation.org).

16. J.-H. Hoepman, "Digitale kluis is doos van Pandora," *XOT* (blog), April 4, 2001, https://blog.xot.nl/2001/04/04/digitale-kluis-is-doos-van-pandora/.

17. See https://solid.inrupt.com.

18. See Tim Berners-Lee, "One Small Step for the Web . . . ," Medium, September 29, 2018, https://medium.com/@timberners_lee/one-small-step-for-the-web-87f92217d085.

19. A. Robertson, "Twitter Is Funding Research into a Decentralized Version of Its Platform," *Verge*, December 11, 2019, https://www.theverge.com/2019/12/11/21010856/twitter-jack-dorsey-bluesky-decentralized-social-network-research-moderation.

20. This section is partially based on previous work. See J.-H. Hoepman, "Hansel and Gretel and the Virus: Privacy Conscious Contact Tracing," *XOT* (blog), March 25, 2020, https://blog.xot.nl/2020/03/25/hansel-and-gretel-and-the-virus-privacy-conscious-contact-tracing/; J.-H. Hoepman, "Google Apple Contact Tracing (GACT): a wolf in sheep's clothes," *XOT* (blog), April 19, 2020, https://blog.xot.nl/2020/04/19/google-apple-contact-tracing-gact-a-wolf-in-sheeps-clothes/.

21. P. Mozur, R. Zhong, and A. Krolik, "In Coronavirus Fight, China Gives Citizens a Color Code, with Red Flags," *New York Times*, March 1, 2020.

22. L. Ferretti, C. Wymant, M. Kendall, L. Zhao, A. Nurtay, L. Abeler-Dörner, M. Parker, D. Bonsall, and C. Fraser, "Quantifying SARS-CoV-2 Transmission Suggests Epidemic Control with Digital Contact Tracing," *Science*, March 31, 2020.

23. J. Bay, "Automated Contact Tracing Is Not a Coronavirus Panacea," Medium, April 11, 2020, https://blog.gds-gov.tech/automated-contact-tracing-is-not-a-coronavirus-panacea-57fb3ce61d98.

24. C. Troncoso et al., *Decentralized Privacy-Preserving Proximity Tracing*, whitepaper (DP-3T Consortium, May 25, 2020). See also https://www.google.com/covid19/exposurenotifications/ and https://www.apple.com/covid19/contacttracing/.

25. S. Vaudenay, *Analysis of DP3T*, Cryptology ePrint Archive, report 2020/399, April 8, 2020, https://eprint.iacr.org/2020/399.

26. See the Facebook Investor Relations Quarterly earnings page: https://investor.fb.com/financials/default.aspx.

27. See the Alphabet Investor Relations Earnings page: https://abc.xyz/investor/.

28. See "The Federal Budget in 2017: An Infographic," available at https://www.cbo.gov/publication/53624.

29. Central Intelligence Agency, "The World Factbook," November 17, 2019, https://www.cia.gov/library/publications/the-world-factbook/fields/224.html.

30. J. Frederik and M. Martijn, "The New Dot Com Bubble Is Here: It's Called Online Advertising," *De Correspondent*, November 6, 2019.

31. S. Guha, B. Cheng, and P. Francis, "Privad: Practical Privacy in Online Advertising," in *Proceedings of the 8th USENIX Symposium on Networked Systems Design and Implementation, NSDI 2011*, ed. D. G. Andersen and S. Ratnasamy (USENIX Association, 2011); V. Toubiana et al., "Adnostic: Privacy Preserving Targeted Advertising," in *Proceedings of the Network and Distributed System Security Symposium, NDSS 2010* (Internet Society, 2010).

32. Zuboff, *The Age of Surveillance Capitalism*.

33. M. Veale, "A Critical Take on the Policy Recommendations of the EU High-Level Expert Group on Artificial Intelligence," *European Journal of Risk Regulation*, January 23, 2020, 1–10.

34. E. Morozov, "Capitalism's New Clothes," *Baffler*, February 4, 2019.

35. J.-H. Hoepman, "Stop the Apple and Google Contact Tracing Platform (or Be Ready to Ditch Your Smartphone)," *XOT* (blog), April 11, 2020, https://blog.xot.nl/2020/04/11/stop-the-apple-and-google-contact-tracing-platform-or-be-ready-to-ditch-your-smartphone/.

36. T. Sharon, "When Google and Apple Get Privacy Right, Is There Still Something Wrong?," Medium, April 15, 2020, https://medium.com/@TamarSharon/when-google-and-apple-get-privacy-right-is-there-still-something-wrong-a7be4166c295; M. Veale, "Privacy Is Not the Problem with the Apple-Google Contact-Tracing Toolkit," *Guardian*, July 1, 2020.

37. See Oliver Widder, http://geek-and-poke.com.

7 PRIVACY AND SECURITY ARE A ZERO-SUM GAME

1. Parts of this chapter are based on earlier materials: J.-H. Hoepman, "Revocable Privacy," *XOT* (blog), November 21, 2008, https://blog.xot.nl/2008/11/21/revocable-privacy/.

2. M. Smith and M. Green, "A Discussion of Surveillance Backdoors: Effectiveness, Collateral Damage and Ethics," February 5, 2016, http://mattsmith.de/pdfs/SurveillanceAndCollateralDamage.pdf.

3. This is not the case for Bitcoin; see S. Nakamoto, "Bitcoin: A Peer-to-Peer Electronic Cash System" (October 31, 2008), https://bitcoin.org/bitcoin.pdf. Bitcoin (and most of the other cryptocurrencies) records all transactions between merely pseudonymous accounts on a public distributed ledger. These pseudonymous accounts are easily linked to their actual owners using a few basic heuristics. See S. Meiklejohn et al., "A Fistful of Bitcoins: Characterizing Payments among Men with no Names," in *Proceedings of the 2013 Internet Measurement Conference IMC 2013*, ed. K. Papagiannaki, P. Krishna Gummadi, and C. Partridge (New York: ACM, 2013), 127–140; S. Goldfeder et al., "When the Cookie Meets the Blockchain: Privacy Risks of Web Payments via Cryptocurrencies," arXiv:1708.04748 (2017), https://arxiv.org/abs/1708.04748.

4. At least for handling transactions. Obtaining cash and depositing cash still involves a bank or some kind of intermediary.

5. For a colorful description of David's background and work, see S. Levy, *Crypto: How the Code Rebels Beat the Government: Saving Privacy in the Digital Age* (New York: Viking Press, 2001).

6. D. Chaum, "Blind Signatures for Untraceable Payments," in *Advances in Cryptology—CRYPTO*, ed. D. Chaum, R. L. Rivest, and A. T. Sherman (New York: Plenum Press, 1982), 199–203.

7. Chaum, "Security without Identification."

8. D. Chaum, A. Fiat, and M. Naor, "Untraceable Electronic Cash," in *Advances in Cryptology—CRYPTO '88*, 8th Annual International Cryptology Conference, ed. S. Goldwasser (Berlin: Springer, 1988), 319–327.

9. J.-H. Hoepman, "Distributed Double Spending Prevention," in *15th Int. Workshop on Security Protocols 2007*, ed. B. Christianson et al. (Berlin: Springer, 2010), 152–165.

10. Wikipedia, "DigiCash," last modified December 30, 2019, https://en.wikipedia.org/wiki/DigiCash.

11. J.-H. Hoepman, "Revocable Privacy," *ENISA Quarterly Review* 5, no. 2 (June 2009): 16–17; W. Lueks, M. Everts, and J.-H. Hoepman, "Revocable Privacy: Principles, Use Cases, and Technologies," in *Annual Privacy Forum (APF 2015)* (Berlin: Springer, 2016), 124–143.

12. Like the corresponding legal concept of *traceable anonymity*, coined by Daniel Solove. See D. J. Solove, "The Virtues of Anonymity," *New York Times*, March 11, 2016.

13. L. Lessig, *Code and Other Laws of Cyberspace* (New York: Basic Books, 1999).

14. Lueks, Everts, and Hoepman, "Revocable Privacy: Principles, Use Cases, and Technologies."

15. A. Shamir, "How to Share a Secret," *Communications of the ACM* 22, no. 11 (1979): 612–613.

16. Chaum's work was highly influential, and Stadler explored the concept further in his PhD thesis back in 1996: M. Stadler, "Cryptographic Protocols for Revocable Privacy" (PhD thesis, Swiss Federal Institute of Technology, Zürich, 1996). More recent examples of revocable privacy approaches include limiting the amount a person can spend at a single merchant while remaining anonymous or revoking anonymity of users that do not pay their bill at a merchant. See J. Camenisch, S. Hohenberger, and A. Lysyanskaya, "Balancing Accountability and Privacy Using E-Cash (Extended Abstract)," in *Security and Cryptography for Networks 2006*, 5th International Conference, ed. R. D. Prisco and M. Yung (Berlin: Springer, 2006); J. Camenisch, T. Groß, and T. S. Heydt-Benjamin, "Rethinking Accountable Privacy Supporting Services: Extended Abstract," in *Proceedings of the 4th Workshop on Digital Identity Management*, ed. E. Bertino and K. Takahashi (New York: ACM, 2008), 1–8.

17. D. Galindo and J.-H. Hoepman, "Non-interactive Distributed Encryption: A New Primitive for Revocable Privacy," in *ACM Workshop on Privacy in the Electronic Society 2011*, ed. Y. Chen and J. Vaidya (New York: ACM, 2011), 81–92; W. Lueks, J.-H. Hoepman, and K. Kursawe, "Forward-Secure Distributed Encryption," in *Privacy Enhancing Technologies—14th International Symposium, PETS*, ed. E. D. Cristofaro and S. J. Murdoch (Amsterdam: Springer, 2014), 123–142.

18. See https://www.wikipedia.org.

19. It blocks editing of pages over Tor in general, for example. See Wikipedia, "Wikipedia: Advice to Users Using Tor," last modified May 21, 2019, https://en.wikipedia.org/wiki/Wikipedia:Advice_to_users_using_Tor. It allows the creation of pseudonymous accounts, but it does log the IP addresses through which such accounts are accessed: Wikipedia, "Wikipedia: Wikipedia Is Anonymous," last modified April 17, 2019, https://en.wikipedia.org/wiki/Wikipedia:Wikipedia_is_anonymous. The title of that page is really a misnomer; Wikipedia is pseudonymous at best.

20. W. Lueks, M. Everts, and J.-H. Hoepman, "Vote to Link: Recovering from Misbehaving Anonymous Users," in *ACM Workshop on Privacy in the Electronic Society 2016*, ed. E. R. Weippl, S. Katzenbeisser, and S. D. C. di Vimercati (New York: ACM, 2016), 111–122.

8 PRIVACY IS HARD

1. The following sections are based on earlier material: J.-H. Hoepman, "Privacy Design Strategies," in *IFIP TC11 International Information Security Conference 2014*, ed. N. Cuppens-Boulahia et al. (Berlin: Springer, 2014. A preliminary version was presented at the Amsterdam Privacy Conference (APC 2012) and the Privacy Law Scholars Conference (PLSC 2013); M. Colesky, J.-H. Hoepman, and C. Hillen, "A Critical Analysis of Privacy Design Strategies," in *2016 International Workshop on Privacy Engineering—IWPE'16* (IEEE Computer Society, 2016), 33–40; J.-H. Hoepman,

Privacy Design Strategies: The Little Blue Book (May 2018), https://www.cs.ru.nl/~jhh/publications/pds-booklet.pdf.

2. Cavoukian, *Privacy by Design.*

3. Federal Trade Commission, *Privacy Online: Fair Information Practices in the Electronic Marketplace: A Report to Congress* (Washington, DC: FTC, May 2000); Organisation of Economic Co-Operation and Development, *OECD Guidelines on the Protection of Privacy and Transborder Flows of Personal Data* (OECD, 1980).

4. In all fairness, many systems are developed in a rather ad hoc manner wherein there is no clear separation among these different phases. Moreover, certain phases may be skipped altogether or actually be performed in a seemingly random order. This is the case in *agile* development approaches in particular, in which the system is built incrementally.

5. See https://privacypatterns.org and https://privacypatterns.cs.ru.nl.

6. Hoepman, "Privacy Design Strategies"; Colesky, Hoepman, and Hillen, "A Critical Analysis of Privacy Design Strategies"; Hoepman, *Privacy Design Strategies: The Little Blue Book.*

7. Regulation (EU) 2016/679 (GDPR).

8. A more thorough discussion can be found in Hoepman, *Privacy Design Strategies: The Little Blue Book.*

9. B. Kramer, "Waarom de Belastingdienst jouw Spotify-playlist wil hebben," *Vice*, April 3, 2017, https://www.vice.com/nl/article/qk9ae3/waarom-de-belastingdienst-jouw-spotify-playlist-wil-hebben.

10. L. Taylor, L. Floridi, and B. van der Sloot, eds., *Group Privacy: New Challenges of Data Technologies* (Cham: Springer, 2017).

11. M. Gruteser and D. Grunwald, "Anonymous Usage of Location-Based Services through Spatial and Temporal Cloaking," in *Proceedings of the First International Conference on Mobile Systems, Applications, and Services (MobiSys 2003)* (USENIX, 2003).

12. We distinguish between the (external) *privacy statement* and the (internal) *privacy policy* (see the enforce strategy).

13. J.-H. Hoepman, "Using Icons to Summarise Privacy Policies: An Analysis and a Proposal," *XOT* (blog), September 21, 2016, https://blog.xot.nl/2016/09/21/using-icons-to-summarise-privacy-polices-an-analysis-and-a-proposal/.

14. See https://myaccount.google.com/.

15. See https://www.trustarc.com/privacy-certification-standards/ and https://www.european-privacy-seal.eu/EPS-en/Home.

9 BUSTED: PRIVACY ISN'T HARD IF YOU TRY

1. B. Hayes, "Alice and Bob in Cipherspace," *American Scientist* 100, no. 5 (September–October 2012): 362; B. Chor, O. Goldreich, E. Kushilevitz, and M. Sudan, "Private Information Retrieval," *Journal of the ACM* 45, no. 6 (1998): 965–981; R. Cramer, I.

B. Damgård, and J. B. Nielsen, *Secure Multiparty Computation and Secret Sharing* (Cambridge: Cambridge University Press, 2015).

2. See J.-H. Hoepman, "The Second Crypto War Is Not about Crypto," *XOT* (blog), December 8, 2015, https://blog.xot.nl/2015/12/08/the-second-crypto-war-is-not-about-crypto/; J.-H. Hoepman, "Laughing about the Laws of Mathematics Does Not Win the Crypto War," *XOT* (blog), July 17, 2017, https://blog.xot.nl/2017/07/17/laughing-about-the-laws-of-mathematics-does-not-win-the-crypto-war/.

3. J.-H. Hoepman, "Transparency Is the Perfect Cover-up (if the Sun Does Not Shine)," in *Being Profiled: Cogitas Ergo Sum: 10 Years of Profiling the European Citizen*, ed. E. Bayamlioğlu et al. (Amsterdam: Amsterdam University Press, 2018), 46–51.

4. L. Mitrou, "The General Data Protection Regulation: A Law for the Digital Age?," in *EU Internet Law: Regulation and Enforcement*, ed. T.-E. Synodinou et al. (Cham: Springer, 2017).

5. Cavoukian, *Privacy by Design*.

6. In the Netherlands, this includes information about the number of days in a week you stay/sleep with your partner who otherwise lives somewhere else. Above a certain threshold, this partner is expected to support you financially.

INDEX